ABSOLUTE KEY TO OC

THE TAROT
OF THE BOHEMIANS.

THE MOST ANCIENT BOOK IN THE WORLD.

For the exclusive use of Initiates.

By PAPUS.

TRANSLATED BY A. P. MORTON.

"All intellectual light, like all physical light, comes from the East, and I come with it, also from the East."—NARAD, *the Bohemian.*

Copyright © 2018 Read Books Ltd.
This book is copyright and may not be
reproduced or copied in any way without
the express permission of the publisher in writing

British Library Cataloguing-in-Publication Data
A catalogue record for this book is available from
the British Library

TO

The Occult Science

AND

TO ALL ITS DISCIPLES.

ABSOLUTE KEY TO OCCULT SCIENCE.

Frontispiece.

PREFACE.

The Tarot pack of cards, transmitted by the Gypsies from generation to generation, is the primitive book of ancient initiation. This has been clearly demonstrated by Guillaume Postel, Court de Gébelin, Etteila, Eliphas Levi, and J. A. Vaillant.

The key to its construction and application has not yet been revealed, so far as I know. I therefore wished to fill up this deficiency by supplying Initiates, *i.e.* those who are acquainted with the elements of occult science, with an accurate guide, which would assist them in the pursuit of their studies.

The uninitiated reader will find in it the explanation of the lofty philosophy and science of ancient Egypt; whilst ladies are enabled to practise the use of the divining Tarot, by methods which we have rendered easy in Chapter XX.

The book has been so arranged that each part forms

PREFACE.

a complete whole, which can, if necessary, be studied separately.

I have used every effort to be as clear as possible; the public that has warmly welcomed my other books will, I hope, forgive the imperfections inherent to a work of this kind.

PAPUS.

CONTENTS.

PART I.

THE "GENERAL KEY TO THE TAROT," GIVING THE ABSOLUTE KEY TO OCCULT SCIENCE.

                                                                  PAGE

CHAP. I.—INTRODUCTION TO THE STUDY OF THE TAROT: Approaching End of Materialism—Synthesis—The Occult Science—The Secret Societies—The Cultus—The People, Transmitter of Esoterism—The Gypsies—The Sacred Word of Freemasonry—Our Work 3

II.—THE SACRED WORD YOD-HE-VAU-HE: The Kabbalah and the Sacred Word—The Yod—The He—The Vau—The 2nd He—Synthesis of the Sacred Word 17

III.—THE ESOTERISM OF NUMBERS: The Theosophic Numbers and Operations—Signification of the Numbers 26

IV.—ANALOGY BETWEEN THE SACRED WORD AND NUMBERS: The Kabbalistic Word and the Series of Numbers—Explanation of the *Tetractys* of Pythagoras—Figuration of the General Law 32

CONTENTS.

CHAP.	PAGE
V.—THE KEY TO THE MINOR ARCANA: Formation of the Tarot—Study of a Colour—The Four Figures—The Ten Numbers—Affinity between the Figures and the Numbers—Study of the Four Colours—A Comprehensive Glance over the Minor Arcana	35
VI.—THE KEY TO THE MAJOR ARCANA: The Major Arcana—1st Ternary—2nd Ternary—1st Septenary—2nd Septenary—The Three Septenaries and the Ternary of Transition ...	51
VII.—CONNECTION BETWEEN THE MAJOR AND MINOR ARCANA: Domination of the 1st Septenary—Affinities of the 2nd Septenary in the Tarot, Card by Card—Ditto of the 3rd Septenary—General Affinities—Affinities of *Yod, He, Vau,* and of the 2nd *He*	61
General Figure giving the Key to the Tarot ...	68

PART II.

SYMBOLISM IN THE TAROT.
APPLICATION OF THE GENERAL KEY TO THE SYMBOLISM.

VIII.—INTRODUCTION TO THE STUDY OF SYMBOLISM: The Symbols—The Primitive Terms—Key of Symbolism—Definition of the Sense of one of the Symbols—General Law of Symbolism	71
IX.—HISTORY OF THE SYMBOLISM OF THE TAROT. INQUIRY INTO ITS ORIGIN: The Tarot is an Egyptian Book—Its Transformations—Mantegna's Pack—Venetian Tarot—Florentine Tarot—Bolognese Tarot—Hindu Tarot—	

CONTENTS.

Chinese Tarot—Modern Tarots—Etteila—Marseilles—Besançon—Watillaux—Oswald Wirth—Italian and German Tarots—Constitution of the Symbolism of the Tarot—The 16 Primitive Hieroglyphic Signs—The 22 Hebrew Letters 81

X.—THE SYMBOLICAL TAROT. THE 1ST SEPTENARY. ARCANA 1 TO 7. THEOGONY: Scheme of Work—Key to the 1st Septenary—The 1st Card of the Tarot the Origin of all the others—The Three Principles of the Absolute—The Trinity—Figure of the 1st Card and its Affinities 96
 2nd Card—The High Priestess (Beth) ... 112
 3rd Card—The Empress (Gimel) ... 115
 4th Card—The Emperor (Daleth) ... 119
 5th Card—The Pope (He) 123
 6th Card—The Lovers (Vau) 127
 Summary—Constitution of God 132

XI.—2ND SEPTENARY. ANDROGONY: Key to the 2nd Septenary 133
 7th Card—The Chariot (Zain) 135
 8th Card—Justice (Cheth) 138
 9th Card—The Hermit (Teth) 142
 10th Card—The Wheel of Fortune (Yod) 145
 11th Card—Strength (Kaph) 148
 12th Card—The Hanged Man (Lamed) ... 151
 Summary—Constitution of Man 155

XII.—3RD SEPTENARY. COSMOGONY: Key to the 3rd Septenary 156
 13th Card—Death (Mem) 158
 14th Card—Temperance (Nun) 161
 15th Card—The Devil (Samech) ... 164

CONTENTS.

CHAP.		PAGE
	16th Card—The Lightning-struck Tower (Zain) ...	168
	17th Card—The Star (Phe) ...	171
	18th Card—The Moon (Tzaddi) ...	174
	Summary—Constitution of the Universe ...	177
XIII.—General Transition ...		178
	19th Card—The Sun (Qoph) ...	179
	20th Card—The Judgment (Resh) ...	182
	21st Card—The Foolish Man (Shin) ...	185
	22nd Card—The Universe (Tau) ...	188
	Summary ...	192
XIV.—General Summary of the Symbolical Tarot: Involution and Evolution ...		193
	Theogony: The Absolute according to Wronski, Lacuria, and the Tarot—Theogony of Divers Religions identical with that of the Tarot—Summary ...	194
	Androgony: Figure with Summary ...	210
	Cosmogony: Figure with Summary ...	214
	Figure containing the Symbolism of all the Major Arcana, enabling the Signification of each Card to be easily defined ...	220—221

PART III.

APPLICATIONS OF THE TAROT.

XV.—General Key to the Applications of the Tarot: The Principle and the Forms—The 21st Card of the Tarot is a Figure-Principle—The Tarot—The Year—The Month—The Day—The Human Life 225

CONTENTS.

CHAP.		PAGE

XVI.—THE ASTRONOMIC TAROT: Egyptian Astronomy—The Four Seasons—The Twelve Months—The Thirty-six Decani—The Planets—Absolute Analogy with the Tarot—Figure containing the Application of the Tarot to Astronomy—Key to the Astrological Works of Christian—Oswald Wirth's Astronomical Tarot 233

XVII.—THE INITIATIVE TAROT: Ch. Barlet's Essay on this Subject—Involution and Evolution—The Hours of Apollonius of Tyana—The Phases of Initiation represented by the Tarot ... 253
Barlet's Work upon the COSMOGONIC TAROT ... 253

XVIII.—THE KABBALISTIC TAROT: Deductions by Etteila upon the *Book of Thoth*—Example of the Application of the Tarot to the Kabbalah, the Hierogram of Adam by Stanislas de Guaita 291

XIX.—THE AUTHORS WHO HAVE INTERESTED THEMSELVES IN THE TAROT: Raymond Lulle—Cardan—Postel—The Rosicrucians—Court de Gébelin—Etteila—Claude de Saint-Martin—J. A. Vaillant—Christian—Eliphas Levi—St. de Guaita—Joséphin Péladan—*The Platonist*—Theosophical Publications—F. Ch. Barlet—O. Wirth—Poirel—Ely Star—H. P. Blavatsky—Ch. de Sivry—Mathers 297

XX.—THE DIVINING TAROT IN SEVEN LESSONS. *Introduction:* To our Lady Readers—Astronomy and Astrology—Intuition—Fortune-telling by the Tarot in Seven Lessons ... 301
1st *Lesson*—Simplification of the Rules of Fortune-telling by the Tarot 305
2nd *Lesson*—Minor Arcana—Signification

CONTENTS.

CHAP.		PAGE
	—A good Memory unnecessary for their retention—Key to the Divining Tarot	307
	3rd *Lesson*—Major Arcana—Signification from a Divining Point of View	316
	4th *Lesson*—Basis of the Application of this Knowledge—Arrangement of the Cards	318
	5th *Lesson*—Reading the Tarot—Rapid Process—Elaborate Process	322
	6th *Lesson*—Etteila's original and unpublished Method of reading the Tarot (from one of his rarest works). 1st Deal—2nd Deal—3rd Deal—4th Deal	327
	7th *Lesson*—Conclusion—Bibliography	333
XXI.	APPLICATION OF THE TAROT TO GAMES: The Royal Game of the Human Life according to the Egyptians—The Unity of Games in the Tarot	335
XXII.	CONCLUSION OF THE WORK	343
	INDEX	349
	TABLE OF THE AUTHORS AND PRINCIPAL WORKS QUOTED	353

INTRODUCTION

TO

THE STUDY OF THE TAROT.

THE TAROT.

CHAPTER I.

INTRODUCTION TO THE STUDY OF THE TAROT.

Approaching End of Materialism—Synthesis—The Occult Science—The Secret Societies—The Cultus—*The People*, Organ of the Transmission of Esoterism—The Gypsies—The Sacred Word of Freemasonry—Our Work.

"Therefore you must open the book and carefully weigh the statements made in it. Then you will know that the drug within is of very different value from the promise of the box, that is to say, that the subjects treated in it are not so frivolous as the title may imply."—RABELAIS.

WE are on the eve of a complete transformation of our scientific methods. Materialism has given us all that we can expect from it, and inquirers, disappointed as a rule, hope for great things from the future, whilst they are unwilling to spend more time in pursuing the path adopted in modern times. Analysis has been carried, in every branch of knowledge, as far as possible, and has only deepened the moats which divide the sciences.

Synthesis becomes necessary; but how can we realize it?

If we would condescend to waive for one moment our belief in the indefinite progress and fatal superiority of later generations over the ancients, we should at once perceive that the colossal civilizations of antiquity possessed Science, Universities, and Schools.

India and Egypt are still strewn with valuable remains, which reveal to archæologists the existence of this ancient science.

We are now in a position to affirm that the dominant character of this teaching was synthesis, which condenses in a few very simple laws the whole of the acquired knowledge.

But the use of synthesis had been almost entirely lost, through several causes, which it is important to enumerate.

Amongst the ancients, knowledge was only transmitted to men whose worth had been proved by a series of tests. This transmittal took place in the temples, under the name of *mysteries*, and the adept assumed the title of *priest* or *Initiate*.[1] This science was therefore secret or occult, and thus originated the name of *occult science*, given by our contemporaries to the ancient synthesis.

Another reason for the limited diffusion of the higher branches of knowledge, was the length and difficulty of the journeys involved before the most important centres of initiation could be reached.

However, when the Initiates found that a time was approaching when these doctrines might be lost to humanity, they made strenuous efforts to save the law of synthesis from oblivion. Three great methods were used for this purpose—

1. Secret societies, a direct continuation of the *mysteries;*
2. The cultus, a symbolic translation of the higher doctrines, for the use of the people;

[1] See Jamblichus, Porphyry, and Apuleius.

3. Lastly, the people itself became the unconscious depository of the doctrine.

Let us now see what use each of these groups made of the treasure confided to it.

THE SECRET SOCIETIES.

The school of Alexandria was the principal source from which the secret societies of the West arose.

The majority of the Initiates had taken refuge in the East, and quite recently (in 1884) the West discovered the existence in India, and above all in Thibet, of an occult fraternity, which possessed, practically, the ancient synthesis in its integrity. The Theosophite Society was founded with the object of uniting Western initiation with Oriental initiation.

But we are less interested in the existence of this doctrine in the East, than in the history of the development of the initiative societies in the West.

The Gnostic sects, the Arabs, Alchemists, Templars, Rosicrucians, and lastly the Freemasons, form the Western chain in the transmission of occult science.

A rapid glance over the doctrines of these associations is sufficient to prove that the present form of Freemasonry has almost entirely lost the meanings of the traditional symbols, which constitute the trust which it ought to have transmitted through the ages.

The elaborate ceremonials of the ritual appear ridiculous to the vulgar common sense of a lawyer or grocer, the actual modern representatives of the profound doctrines of antiquity.

We must, however, make some exceptions in favour of great thinkers, like Ragon and a few others.

In short, Freemasonry has lost the doctrine confided to it, and cannot by itself provide us with the synthetic law for which we are seeking.

THE CULTUS.

The secret societies were to transmit in their symbolism the scientific side of primitive initiation, the religious sects were to develop the philosophical and metaphysical aspects of the doctrine.

Every priest of an ancient creed was one of the *Initiates*, that is to say, he knew perfectly well that only one religion existed, and that the cultus merely served to translate this religion to the different nations according to their particular temperaments. This fact led to one important result, namely, that a priest, no matter which of the gods he served, was received with honour in the temples of all the other gods, and was allowed to offer sacrifice to them. Yet this circumstance must not be supposed to imply any idea of *polytheism*. The Jewish High Priest in Jerusalem received one of the Initiates, Alexander the Great, into the Temple, and led him into the Holy of Holies, to offer sacrifice.

Our religious disputes for the supremacy of one creed over another would have caused much amusement to one of the ancient Initiate priests; they were unable to suppose that intelligent men could ignore the unity of all creeds in one fundamental religion.

Sectarianism, chiefly sustained by two creeds, equally

blinded by their errors, the Christian and the Mussulman, was the cause of the total loss of the secret doctrine, which gave the key to Synthetic Unity.

Still greater labour is required to re-discover Synthesis in our Western religions, than to find it in Freemasonry.

The Jews alone possessed, no longer the spirit, but the letter of their oral or Kabbalistic traditions. The Bible, written in Hebrew, is marvellous from this point of view, for it contains all the occult traditions, although its true sense has never yet been revealed. Fabre d'Olivet commenced this prodigious work, but the ignorant descendants of the Inquisition at Rome have placed these studies on the list of those prohibited.[1] Posterity will judge them.

Yet every cultus has its tradition, its book, its Bible, which teach those who know how to read them the unity of all creeds, in spite of the difference existing in the ritual of various countries.

The *Sepher Bereschit* of Moses is the Jewish Bible, the *Apocalypse* and the *Esoteric Gospels* form the Christian Bible, the *Legend of Hiram* is the Bible of Freemasonry, the *Odyssey* the Bible of the so-called polytheism of Greece, the *Æneid* that of Rome, and lastly the *Hindu Vedas* and the *Mussulman Koran* are well known to all students of ancient theology.

To any one possessing the key, all these Bibles reveal the same doctrine; but this key, which can open Esoterism, is lost by the sectarians of our Western creeds. It is therefore useless to seek for it any longer amongst them.

[1] See Fabre d'Olivet, *La Langue Hébraïque Restituée.*

THE PEOPLE.

The Sages were under no illusions respecting the possible future of the tradition, which they confided to the intelligence and virtue of future generations.

Moses had chosen a people to hand down through succeeding ages the book which contained all the science of Egypt; but before Moses, the Hindu Initiates had selected a nation to hand down to the generations of the future the primitive doctrines of the great civilizations of the Atlantides.

The people have never disappointed the expectations of those who trusted it. Understanding none of the truths which it possessed, it carefully abstained from altering them in any way, and treated the least attack made upon them as sacrilege.

Thus the Jews have transmitted intact to us the letters which form the Sepher of Moses. But Moses had not solved the problem so authoritatively as the Thibetans.

It was a great thing to give the people a book which it could adore respectfully, and always guard intact; but to give it a book which would enable it to live, was yet better.

The people intrusted with the transmission of occult doctrines from the earliest ages was the Bohemian or Gypsy race.

THE GYPSIES.

The Gypsies possess a Bible, which has proved their means of gaining a livelihood, for it enables them to tell

INTRODUCTION.

fortunes; at the same time it has been a perpetual source of amusement, for it enables them to gamble.

Yes; the game of cards called the Tarot, which the Gypsies possess, is the Bible of Bibles. It is the book of Thoth Hermes Trismegistus, the book of Adam, the book of the primitive Revelation of ancient civilizations.

Thus whilst the Freemason, an intelligent and virtuous man, has lost the tradition; whilst the priest, also intelligent and virtuous, has lost his esoterism; the Gypsy, although both ignorant and vicious, has given us the key which enables us to explain all the symbolism of the ages.

We must admire the wisdom of the Initiates, who utilized vice and made it produce more beneficial results than virtue.

The Gypsy pack of cards is a wonderful book according to Court de Gébelin[1] and Vaillant.[2] This pack, under the name of TAROT,[3] THORA,[4] ROTA,[5] has formed the basis of the synthetic teachings of all the ancient nations successively.[6]

In it, where a man of the people only sees a means of amusement, the thinker will find the key to an obscure tradition. Raymond Lulle has based his *Ars Magna* upon the Tarot; Jerome Cardan has written a treatise upon subtility from the keys of the Tarot;[7] Guillaume Postel has found in it the key to the ancient mysteries; whilst Louis-Claude de Saint-Martin, the unknown

---

[1] Court de Gébelin.—*Le Monde Primitif.*
[2] Vaillant.—*Les Rômes, Histoire des Bohémiens.*
[3] Eliphas Levi.—*Rituel de la Haute Magie.*
[4] Vaillant.—*Op. cit.*
[5] Guillaume Postel.—*Clavis.*
[6] Vaillant.—*Loc. cit.*
[7] Eliphas Levi.—*Op. cit.*

philosopher, finds written in it the mysterious links which unite God, the Universe, and Man!

Through the Tarot we are now able to discover and develop the synthetic law, concealed in all these symbolisms.

The hour is approaching when the missing word will be refound. Masters, Rosicrucian and Kadosh, you who form the sacred triangle of Masonic initiation, do you remember!

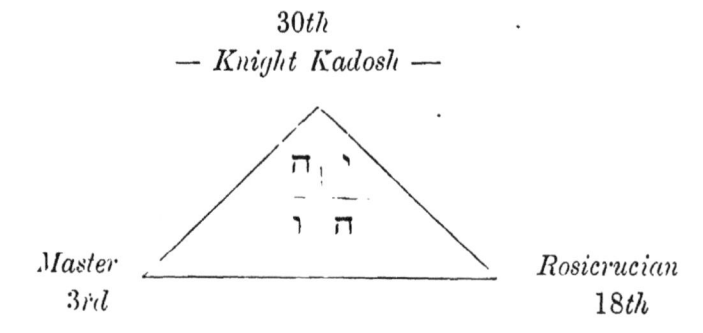

```
                    30th
                — Knight Kadosh —
                        י ה
                        ו ה
   Master                              Rosicrucian
    3rd                                   18th
```

Remember, MASTER, that illustrious man, killed through the most cowardly of conspiracies; remember *Hiram*, whose resurrection, promised by the Branch of Acacia, thou art looking for in faith!

Remember, ROSICRUCIAN, the *mysterious word* which thou hast sought for so long, of which the meaning still escapes thee!

Remember, KADOSH, the *magnificent symbol* which radiated from the centre of the luminous triangle, when the real meaning of the letter G was revealed to thee!

HIRAM—INRI—YOD-HE-VAU-HE! indicate the same mystery under different aspects.

He who understands one of these words possesses the key which opens the *tomb of Hiram*, the symbol of the synthetic science of the Ancients; he can open the tomb and fearlessly grasp the *heart* of the revered Master, the symbol of esoteric teaching.

The whole Tarot is based upon this word, ROTA, arranged as a wheel.

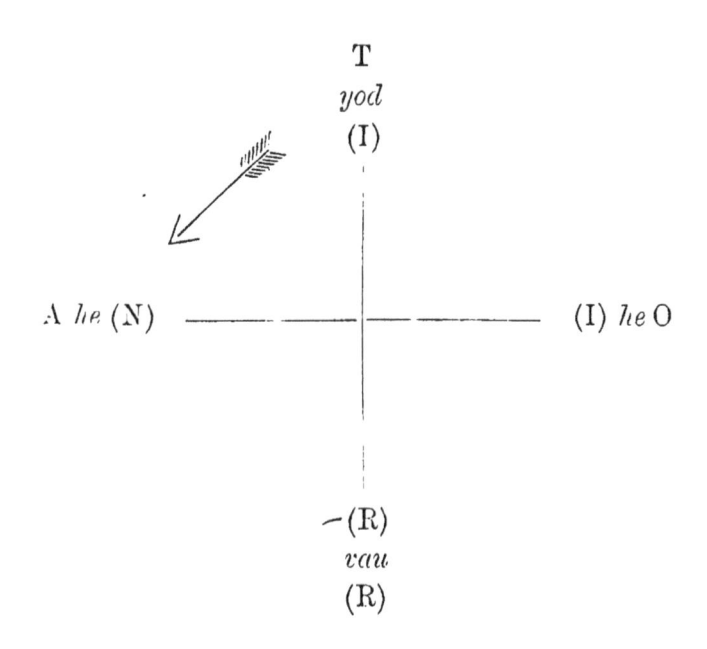

```
                    T
                   yod
                   (I)

  A he (N) ─────────┼───────── (I) he O

                   ─(R)
                   vau
                   (R)
```

INRI! is the word which indicates the Unity of your origin, Freemasons and Catholics!

Igne Natura Renovatur Integra.

Iesus Nazareus Rex Iudeorum are the opposite poles, scientific and religious, physical and metaphysical, of the same doctrine.

YOD-HE-VAU-HE (יהוה) is the word which indicates to you both, Freemasons and Kabbalists, the Unity of your origin. TAROT, THORA, ROTA are the words which point out to you all, Easterns and Westerns, the Unity of your requirements and of your aspirations in the eternal

Adam-Eve, the source of all our knowledge and of all our creeds.

All honour, therefore, to the Gypsy Nomad, to whom we are indebted for the preservation of this marvellous instrument, the synthetic summary of the whole teaching of antiquity.

OUR WORK.

We will commence by a preliminary study of the elements of the Kabbalah and of numbers.

Supplied with these data, we will explain the construction of the Tarot in all its details, studying separately each of the pieces which compose our machine, then studying the action of these pieces upon each other. Upon this point we shall be as explicit as possible. We will then touch upon some applications of the machine, but upon a few only, leaving to the genuine inquirer the work of discovering others. We must confine our personal work to giving a key, based upon a synthetic formula; we can only supply the implement of labour, in order that those who wish for knowledge may use it as they like; and we feel assured that they will understand the utility of our efforts and of their own.

Lastly, we will do our best to explain the elements of divination by the Tarot as practised by the Gypsies.

But those who think that occult science should not be revealed must not be too angry with us. Experience has taught us that everything may be fearlessly said, those only who should understand can understand; the others will accuse our work of being obscure and incomprehensible.

We have warned them by placing at the head of our work—

For the exclusive use of Initiates.

It is one characteristic of the study of true occult science, that it may be freely explained to all men. Like the parables, so dear to the ancients, it appears to many only the expression of the flight of a bold imagination: we need, therefore, never be afraid of speaking too openly, the Word will only reach those who should be touched by it.

To you all, philosophers of Unity, enemies of scientific, social, and religious sectarianism, I now address myself, to you I dedicate this result of several years' study. May I thus aid in the erection of the temple which you are about to raise to the honour of the UNKNOWN GOD, from whom all the others emanate throughout Eternity!

PART I.

GENERAL KEY TO THE TAROT,
GIVING THE ABSOLUTE KEY TO OCCULT SCIENCE.

CHAPTER II.

יהוה.

THE SACRED WORD YOD-HE-VAU-HE.

The Kabbalah and the Sacred Word—The Yod—The He—The Vau—The second He—Synthesis of the Sacred Word.

ACCORDING to the ancient oral tradition of the Hebrews, or *Kabbalah*,[1] a sacred word exists, which gives to the mortal who can discover the correct way of pronouncing it, the key to all the sciences, divine and human. This word, which the Israelites never uttered, and which the High Priest pronounced once a year, amidst the shouts of the laity, is found at the head of every initiative ritual, it radiates from the centre of the flaming triangle at the

[1] "It appears, according to the most famous rabbis, that Moses himself, foreseeing the fate which awaited his book, and the false interpretations which would be given to it in the course of time, resorted to an oral law, which he delivered verbally to reliable men, whose fidelity he had tested, and whom he charged to transmit it to others in the secret of the sanctuary, who in their turn, transmitting it from age to age, secured its preservation even for the most distant posterity. This oral law, which modern Jews still flatter themselves that they possess, is called the Kabbalah, from a Hebrew word which signifies that which is received, that which comes from elsewhere, that which passes from hand to hand."—FABRE D'OLIVET, *La Langue Hébraïque Restituée*, p. 29.

33rd degree of the Freemasonry of Scotland, it is displayed above the gateways of our old cathedrals, is formed of four Hebrew letters, and reads thus, *Yod-he-vau-he,* יהוה.

It is used in the *Sepher Bereschit,* or Genesis of Moses, to designate the divinity, and its grammatical construction recalls even by its formation [1] the attributes which men have always delighted to ascribe to God. Now we shall see that the powers attributed to this word are real up to a certain point, for with its aid the symbolical gate of the arch, which contains the explanation of the whole doctrine of ancient science, is easily opened. It is therefore necessary to enter into some detail respecting it.

The word is formed of four letters, *Yod* (י), *he* (ה), *vau* (ו), *he* (ה). This last letter *he* is repeated twice.

A number is attributed to each letter of the Hebrew alphabet. We must look at those which relate to the letters we are now considering.

$$\begin{aligned} \text{י} \quad \text{Yod} &= 10 \\ \text{ה} \quad \text{he} &= 5 \\ \text{ו} \quad \text{vau} &= 6 \end{aligned}$$

[1] "This name presents first the sign which indicates life, repeated twice, and thus forming the essentially living root EE (הה). This root is never used as a noun, and is the only one which enjoys this prerogative. It is from its formation not only a verb, but a unique verb, from which all the others are merely derivations; in short, the verb הוה (ÉVÉ), to be, being. Here, as we can see, and as I have carefully explained in my grammar, the sign of intelligible light ו (VÔ) is placed in the midst of the root of life. Moses, when using this unique verb to form the proper name of the Being of Beings, added to it the sign of potential manifestation and of eternity, י (I); he thus obtained יהוה (IEVE), in which the facultative Being is placed between a past tense without origin, and a future without limit. This admirable word thus exactly signifies the Being who is, who was, and who will be."—FABRE D'OLIVET, *La Langue Hébraïque Restituée.*

The total numerical value of the word יהוה is therefore

10 + 5 + 6 + 5 = 26.

Let us now study each letter separately.

THE YOD.

The *Yod*, shaped like a comma or a dot, represents the *principle* or *origin* of all things.

The other letters of the Hebrew alphabet are all produced by different combinations of the letter *Yod*.[1] The synthetic study of nature had led the ancients to conclude that *one law only* existed, and ruled all natural productions. This law, the basis of analogy, placed the Unity-principle at the origin of all things, and regarded them as the *reflections* at various degrees of this Unity-principle. Thus the *Yod*, which alone forms all the other letters, and therefore all the words and all the phrases of the alphabet, was justly used as the image and representation of this *Unity-principle*, of which the profane had no knowledge.

Thus the law which presided over the creation of the Hebrew language is the same law that presided over the creation of the Universe, and to know the one is to know the other, unreservedly. The *Sepher Yetzirah*,[2] one of the most ancient books of the Kabbalah, proves this fact.

Before proceeding any further, let us illustrate the definition which we have just given of the Yod by an example. The first letter of the Hebrew alphabet, the Aleph (א), is composed of four yods placed opposite to each other; the other letters are all formed on the same basis.[3]

---
[1] See the *Kabbala Denudata*.
[2] Translated into English by Dr. Wynn Westcott.
[3] See the *Kabbala Denudata*.

The numerical value of the yod leads to other considerations. The Unity-principle, according to the doctrine of the Kabbalists, is also the Unity-end of beings and of things, so that eternity, from this point of view, is only an eternal present. The ancients used a dot in the centre of a circle as the symbol of this idea, the representation of the Unity-principle (*the dot*) in the centre of eternity (*the circle*, a line without beginning or end).[1]

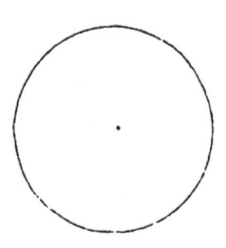

According to these demonstrations, the *Unity* is regarded as the *whole*, of which all created beings are only the *constituent parts;* just as the Unity-man is formed of an agglomeration of molecules, which compose his being.

The Kabbalah, therefore, places at the origin of all things the absolute assertion of the being by itself of the Ego-Unity, which is represented by the *yod* symbolically, and by the number 10. This number 10, representing the All-principle 1, with the Zero-nothing 0, well supplies the requisite conditions.[2]

[1] See Kircher, *Œdipus Ægyptiacus;*
 „ Lenain, *La Science Kabbalistique;*
 „ J. Dée, *Monas Hieroglyphica.*
[2] See Saint-Martin, *Des rapports qui existent entre Dieu, l'Homme et l'Univers.*
 „ Lacuria, *Harmonies de l'Être exprimées par les nombres.*

THE HE.[1]

But the Ego cannot be realized except through its opposition to the Non-Ego. The assertion of the Ego is scarcely established, when we must instantly realize a reaction of the Ego, Absolute, upon itself, from which the conception of its existence will be drawn, by a kind of division of the Unity. This is the origin of *duality*, of opposition, of the *Binary*, the image of femininity, even as the Unity is the image of the masculine. Ten, divided by itself, in opposition to itself, then equals $\frac{10}{2} = 5$, five, the exact number of the letter *He*, the second letter of the great sacred name.

The He therefore represents the passive in relation to the Yod, which symbolizes the active; the Non-Ego in relation to the Ego, the *woman* relatively to the *man*; the *substance* relatively to the *essence*; *life* in its relation to the *soul*, &c., &c.

THE VAU.[2]

But the opposition of the Ego and the Non-Ego immediately gives rise to another factor; this is the *Affinity* existing between this Ego and this Non-Ego.

Now the *Vau*, the sixth letter of the Hebrew alphabet, produced by 10 (yod) + 5 (he) = 15 = 6 (or 1 + 5), signifies *link* or *analogy*. It is the link which, uniting

---

[1] See Eliphas Levi, *Dogme et Rituel de la Haute Magie*; *la Clef des Grands Mystères*;—Lacuria, *op. cit.*

[2] See Fabre d'Olivet, *La Langue Hébraïque Restituee.*

antagonisms in the whole of nature, constitutes the third word of this mysterious Trinity.

Ego—Non-Ego.

Affinity of the Ego with the Non-Ego.

THE 2ND HE.

Nothing can exist beyond this Trinity, considered as a law.

The Trinity is the synthetic and absolute formula to which all the sciences converge; and this formula, forgotten with regard to its scientific value, has been transmitted to us integrally, by all the religions of the world, the unconscious depositaries of the SCIENCE WISDOM of primitive civilizations.[1]

Thus the great sacred name is formed of three letters only. The fourth term of the name is formed by the repetition of the second letter, the *He*.

This repetition indicates the passage of the Trinitarian law into a new application; that is, to speak correctly, a transition from the metaphysical to the physical world, or generally, of any world whatever to the world that immediately follows it.[2]

The knowledge of the property of the second He is the

---

[1] See Louis Lucas, *Le Roman alchimique*.

"*Præter hæc tria numera non est alia magnitudo, quod tria sunt omnia, et ter undecunque, ut pythagorici dicunt; omne et omnia tribus determinata sunt.*"—ARISTOTLE. (Quoted by Ostrowski, page 24 of his *Mathèse*.)

[2] Ostrowski has seen this clearly. "The passage of 3 in 4 corresponds to that of the Trimurti in Maïa, and as the latter opens the second ternary of the pregenesetic decade, so the figure 4 opens that of the second ternary of our genesetic decimal."—*Mathèse*, p. 25.

THE SACRED WORD YOD-HE-VAU-HE.

key to the whole divine name, in every application of which it is susceptible. We shall presently see *the proof of this statement.*

SUMMARY UPON THE WORD YOD-HE-VAU-HE.

Now that we have separately studied each of the letters that compose the sacred name, we will apply the law of synthesis to them, and sum up the results obtained.

The word *Yod-he-vau-he* is formed of four letters, signifying:

The Yod   The active principle pre-eminent.
               The Ego = 10.

The He   The passive principle pre-eminent.
               The Non-Ego = 5.

The Vau   The Median letter, the *link*, which unites the active to the passive.
               The Affinity between the Ego and the Non-Ego = 6.

These three letters express the Trinitarian law of the Absolute.

The 2nd He   The second He marks the passage from one world to another. The Transition.

This second *He* represents the complete Being, comprising in one Absolute Unity the three letters which compose it: Ego, Non-Ego, Affinity.

It indicates the passage from the noumenal to the phenomenal or reciprocal; it serves as means of ascension from one scale to another.

REPRESENTATION OF THE SACRED WORD.

The word *Yod-he-vau-he* can be represented in various ways, which are all useful.

The circle can be drawn in this way—

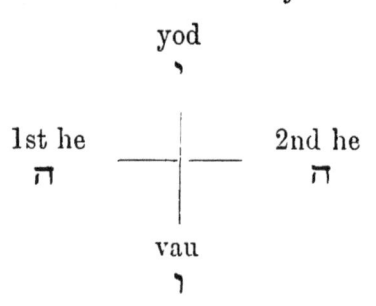

```
                yod
                 י
                 |
1st he  ————+———— 2nd he
  ה              |       ה
                 |
                vau
                 ו
```

But since the second *He*, the sign of transition, becomes the active entity in the following scale, *i. e.* since this *He* only represents a *yod* in germ,[1] the sacred word can be represented, with the *second he under the first yod*, thus—

        yod   1*st he*   *vau*
   2*nd he*

Lastly, a third method of representing the word consists in enveloping the Trinity, *Yod-he-vau*, with the tonalisating letter, or second He, thus—

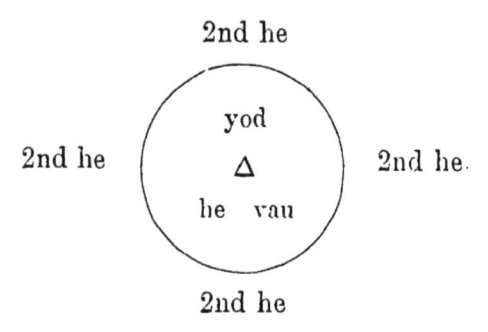

```
              2nd he
              ┌───┐
              yod
  2nd he      △        2nd he
              he  vau
              └───┘
              2nd he
```

[1] The second He, upon which we are intentionally dwelling at some length, may be compared to *a grain of wheat* relatively to the

THE SACRED WORD YOD-HE-VAU-HE.

Now we will leave these data, to which we must return later on, and speak of the occult or Pythagorean conception of numbers.

---

ear. The ear, the Trinity, manifest or *yod-he-vau*, exerts all its activity in the production of the grain of wheat, or second *He*. But this grain of wheat is only the *transition* between the ear which gave it birth, and the ear to which it will itself give birth in the following generation. It is the transition between one generation and another which it contains in germ; this is why the second *He* is a *Yod* in germ.

CHAPTER III.

THE ESOTERISM OF NUMBERS.

The Theosophic Numbers and Operations — Signification of the Numbers.

THE NUMBERS.

THE ancients had a conception of numbers which is almost lost in modern times.

The idea of the Unity in all its manifestations led to numbers being considered as the expression of absolute laws. This led to the veneration expressed for the 3 or for the 4 throughout antiquity, which is so incomprehensible to our mathematicians.

It is however evident that if the ancients had not known how to work any other problems than those we now use, nothing could have led them to the ideas we find current in the Hindu, Egyptian, and Greek Universities.[1]

What then are these operations, that our savants do not know?

[1] See Fabre d'Olivet, *La Langue Hébraïque Restituée* et Saint-Yves d'Alveydre, *Mission des Juifs*.

They are of two kinds: theosophic reduction and theosophic addition.

These operations are theosophic because they cause *the essential laws* of nature to penetrate throughout the world; they cannot be included in the science of phenomena, for they tower above it, soaring into the heights of pure intellectuality.

They therefore formed the basis of the secret and oral instruction confided to a few chosen men, under the name of *Esoterism*.

1. *Theosophic Reduction*.

Theosophic reduction consists in reducing all the numbers formed of two or several figures to the number of a single figure, and this is done by adding together the figures which compose the number, until only one remains.

EXAMPLE:

$$10 = 1 + 0 = 1$$
$$11 = 1 + 1 = 2$$
$$12 = 1 + 2 = 3$$
$$126 = 1 + 2 + 6 = 9$$
$$2488 = 2 + 4 + 8 + 8 = 22 = 2 + 2 = 4$$

This operation corresponds to that which is now called the *proof by* 9.

2. *Theosophic Addition*.

Theosophic addition consists in ascertaining the theosophic value of a number, by adding together arithmetically all the figures from the unity to itself inclusively.

Thus the figure 4, in theosophic addition, equals all

the figures from 1 to 4 inclusively added together, that is to say, $1+2+3+4=10$.

The figure 7 equals—

$$1+2+3+4+5+6+7=28=2+8=10.$$

Theosophic reduction and addition are the two operations which it is indispensable to know, if we would understand the secrets of antiquity.[1]

Let us now apply these rules to all the numbers, that we may discover the law which directs their progression.

Theosophic reduction shows us, first of all, that all numbers, whatever they may be, are reducible in themselves to the nine first, since they are all brought down to numbers *of a single figure.*

But this consideration is not sufficient, and *theosophic addition* will now furnish us with new light.

Through it we find that 1, 4, 7, 10 are equal to 1.

for : $1 = 1$
$4 = 1+2+3+4 = 10 = 1$
$7 = 1+2+3+4+5+6+7 = 28 = 10 = 1$
$10 = 1$

So that all the three numbers ultimately return to the figure 1, thus—

    1. 2. 3   4. 5. 6
    4 = 10 = 1   7 = 28 = 10 = 1

---

[1] See for more details *Traité Élémentaire de Science Occulte*, by Papus, chap. ii.

THE ESOTERISM OF NUMBERS.

Or one could write—

1. 2. 3
(1)
4. 5. 6
(1), etc.

The results of this consideration are: (1) That all the numbers in their evolution, reproduce the 4 first;
(2) That the last of these 4 first, the figure 4, represents the unity at a different octave.

The sequence of the numbers may therefore be written in this way—

1. 2. 3
4. 5. 6
7. 8. 9
10. 11. 12
13. 14. 15
16. 17. 18
19..........

We may notice that 4, 7, 10, 13, 16, 19, etc., are only *different conceptions* of the unity, and this may be proved by the application of theosophic addition and reduction thus—

1 = 1
4 = 1 + 2 + 3 + 4 = 10 = 1
7 = 1 + 2 + 3 + 4 + 5 + 6 + 7 = 28 = 10 = 1
10 = 1
13 = 4 = 10 = 1
16 = 7 = 28 = 10 = 1
19 = 10 = 1, etc., etc.

We see that in every three numbers the series reverts to the unity abruptly, whilst it returns to it progressively in the two intermediate numbers.

Let us now repeat that the knowledge of the laws of numbers and the study of them, made as we have here indicated, will give the key to all occult science.

We must now sum up all the preceding statements in the following conclusion: that all numbers may be reduced, in a final analysis, to the series of the 4 first, thus arranged—

$$1.\ 2.\ 3$$
$$4$$

THE SIGNIFICATION OF NUMBERS.

But our knowledge of the numerical science of the ancients does not end here. It also attributed a meaning to each number.

Since we have reduced the series of all the numbers to the 4 first, it will suffice for us to know the meaning attributed to these 4 first.

The Unity represents the creative principle of all numbers, since the others all emanate from it; it is the active principle pre-eminent.

But the Unity alone cannot produce anything except by opposing itself to itself thus $\frac{1}{1}$ From this proceeds duality, the principle of opposition represented by two, the passive principle pre-eminent.

From the union of the Unity and Duality proceeds the third principle, which unites the two opposites in one common neutrality, $1 + 2 = 3$. Three is the neuter principle pre-eminent.

But these three principles all reduce themselves into

THE ESOTERISM OF NUMBERS.

the fourth, which merely represents a new acceptation of the Unity as an active principle.[1]

The law of these principles is therefore as follows—

Unity or return to unity.	Opposition antagonism.	Action of opposition upon the unity.
Active 1	Passive 2	Neuter 3
Active 4	Etc.	

```
                Active
                  1
                  |
   Passive  _____|_____  Passive-Active
      2           |             4
                  |
               Neuter
                  3
```

[1] See for further enlightenment the *Traité Élémentaire de Science Occulte*, p. 49 and following.

CHAPTER IV.

ANALOGY BETWEEN THE SACRED WORD AND NUMBERS.

The Kabbalistic Word and the Series of Numbers—Explanation of the *Tetractys* of Pythagoras—Figuration of the General Law.

NUMBERS AND THE KABBALISTIC WORD.

THIS sequence of numbers 1, 2, 3, and 4, representing the active, the passive, the neuter, and a second active principle, corresponds in all points with the series of the letters of the sacred name, so that the latter may be thus written—

$$\text{Yod} - \text{He} - \text{Vau}$$
$$\text{2nd He} = \text{Yod, etc.,}$$

which demonstrates analogically that—

    1 represents Yod
    2   —   He
    3   —   Vau
    4   —   The 2nd He

We can prove the truth of these analogies by the identity of the action of the *number* 4, which becomes a unity ($4 = 10 = 1$), and of the *second He*, which represents the Yod of the following sequence.

THE SACRED WORD AND NUMBERS.

In comparing the two identical series we obtain the following figures—

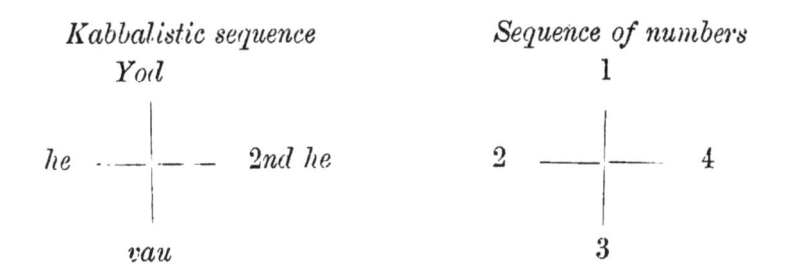

Kabbalistic sequence

```
        Yod
         |
he  ——---|--— 2nd he
         |
        vau
```

Sequence of numbers

```
         1
         |
    2 ---|--- 4
         |
         3
```

Identity of the two sequences

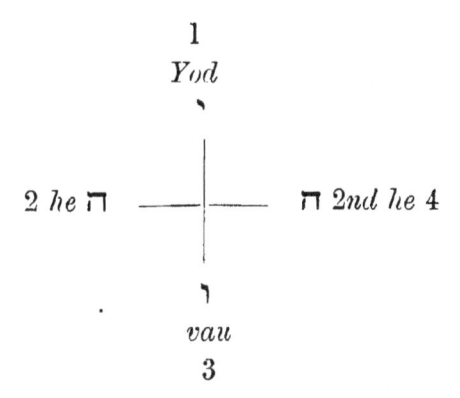

```
            1
           Yod
            ﭏ
            |
   2 he ה ——|—— ה 2nd he 4
            |
            ו
           vau
            3
```

We can now understand why Pythagoras, initiated in Egypt into the mysteries of the sacred word *Yod-he-vau-he*, replaced this word in his esoteric teachings by the sequence of the 4 first numbers or tetractys.

This sequence of the numbers is, in all points, identical with the sequence of the letters of the sacred name, and the tetractys of Pythagoras, 1, 2, 3, 4, equals and absolutely represents the word *Yod-he-vau-he*.

The sequence of the numbers, or the sequence of the letters, therefore, resolves itself definitely into the following data—

1 Term positive and generator.
   The *Yod* or the 1.
1 Term negative or generant.
   The *He* or the 2.
1 Term neuter or generated proceeding from the two preceding.
   The *Vau* or the 3.
1 Term of transition individualizing itself in the following sequence.
   The 2nd *He* or the 4.

Provided with these preliminary data, which are absolutely indispensable, let us now take our pack of cards, or *Tarot*, and see if we cannot find the universal law in it—

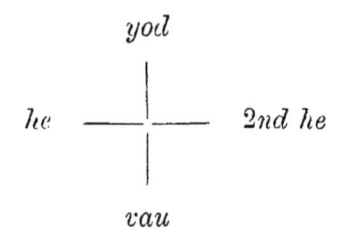

```
                yod
                 |
       he   ————|———— 2nd he
                 |
                vau
```

symbolized through antiquity by the Cross.

CHAPTER V.

THE KEY TO THE MINOR ARCANA.

Formation of the Tarot—Study of a Colour—The Four Figures—The Ten Numbers—Affinity between the Figures and the Numbers—Study of the Four Colours—General Study of the Minor Arcana.

THE KEY TO THE MINOR ARCANA.

THE Tarot is composed of 78 cards, divided as follows—

    56 cards called the *minor* arcana.
    22 cards called the *major* arcana.

The 56 minor arcana are formed of 4 series of 14 cards each.

The 22 major arcana are formed of 21 numbered cards, and of one un-numbered.

In order to study the Tarot with success, we must then arrange the following packets—

    4 packets of 14 cards each.
            14 + 14 + 14 + 14   =   56
    1 packet of 21 cards............... =   21
    1 packet of 1 card................ =   1
                  Total........   78

We shall presently return to the origin of this marvellous conception of the human mind, but for the present we must confine ourselves to the dissection of the machine, and to displaying its mysterious arrangement.

Starting from a fixed and immovable principle, the constitution of the sacred tetragrammaton, *Yod-he-vau-he*, the Tarot develops the most divers combinations, without one departure from its basis. We shall now unveil this wonderful construction, which confirms in its application the universal law of analogies.

The explanations which follow may appear dry to some persons; but they must remember that we are now giving them an almost infallible key to the ancient or occult science; and they will understand that they must open the door of the sacred arch for themselves.

STUDY OF A COLOUR.

Let us now take one of the packets of fourteen cards and analyze its construction.

This packet, taken as a whole, corresponds to one of the *colours* of our pack of cards. The 4 packets respectively represent the *wands* or *sceptres*, corresponding to our clubs; the *cups* or *goblets*, corresponding to our hearts; the *swords*, corresponding to our spades; and *money* or *Pentacles*, corresponding to our diamonds.

We shall now study one of these packets, for instance that of *Sceptres*.

The packet consists of 4 figures: the king, queen, knight, and knave, and of ten cards which simply bear numbers.

The ace, two, three, four, five, six, seven, eight, nine, and ten.

KING OF SCEPTRES
QUEEN OF SCEPTRES
KNAVE OF SCEPTRES
KNIGHT OF SCEPTRES

THE FOUR FIGURES.

We must first consider the four figures—
The king represents the active, the man, or male.
The queen represents the passive, the woman, or female.
The knight represents the neuter, the adolescent.
Lastly, the knave represents the 4th term of this sequence, which may be figured in this way—

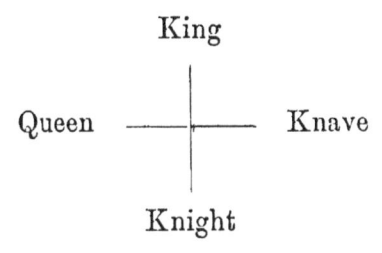

```
              King
               |
   Queen ——————+—————— Knave
               |
             Knight
```

This sequence is only an application of the general law *Yod-he-vau-he*, which we already know, and the analogy is easily established—

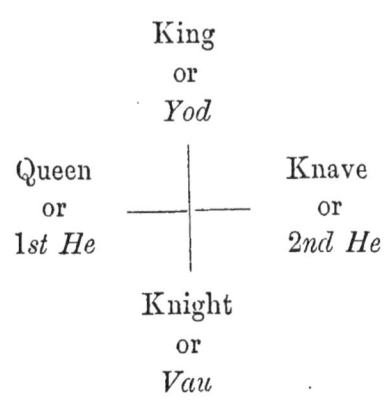

```
              King
               or
              Yod

   Queen       |        Knave
    or    —————+—————    or
   1st He      |        2nd He

             Knight
               or
              Vau
```

The knave therefore corresponds with the *second He*, i. e. it is only a term of transition; but transition between what?
Between the four figures and the ten numbers following.

THE TEN NUMBERS.

Let us now study these numbers. We are acquainted with *the Law* of numbers, or law of the sequences, which we have already stated in these terms—

$$1 - 2.\ 3$$
$$4 - 5.\ 6$$
$$7 - \text{etc.}$$

The ten cards cannot escape from this law, and we can at once arrange them in series.

The first series will be formed of the ace, or 1, representing the *active*, of the 2 personating the *passive*, of the 3 for the *neuter*, and lastly of the 4, which represents the transition from one series to another.

1, 2, 3, 4 therefore correspond also with the *Yod-he-vau-he*, and are thus formulated—

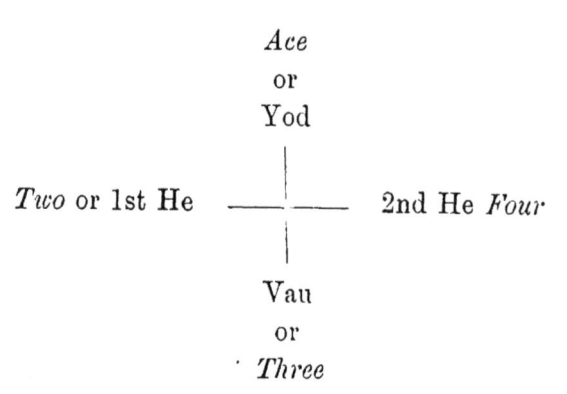

```
                    Ace
                    or
                    Yod
                     |
  Two or 1st He  ————|————  2nd He Four
                     |
                    Vau
                    or
                   Three
```

The other series follow the same rule exactly, the *second He* of the preceding series becoming the *Yod* of the following series: thus 4, the fourth term of the first series, becomes the first term of the second series; 7, the fourth term of the second, becomes the first term of the third, as follows—

THE KEY TO THE MINOR ARCANA.

THE SERIES OF NUMBERS.

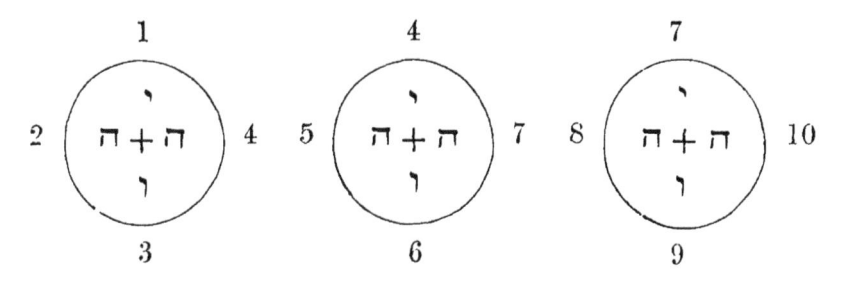

$$2 \begin{pmatrix} 1 \\ \text{ה} + \text{ה} \\ \text{ו} \\ 3 \end{pmatrix} 4 \quad 5 \begin{pmatrix} 4 \\ \text{ה} + \text{ה} \\ \text{ו} \\ 6 \end{pmatrix} 7 \quad 8 \begin{pmatrix} 7 \\ \text{ה} + \text{ה} \\ \text{ו} \\ 9 \end{pmatrix} 10$$

We see that the same law, *Yod-he-vau-he*, can be applied to these series. Since this law is also applicable to the four figures, we can make a comparison based on the following proposition—

Two terms (the numbers and the figures) equal to a same third (the law *Yod-he-vau-he*) are equal between themselves.

THE SEQUENCE IN ONE COLOUR.

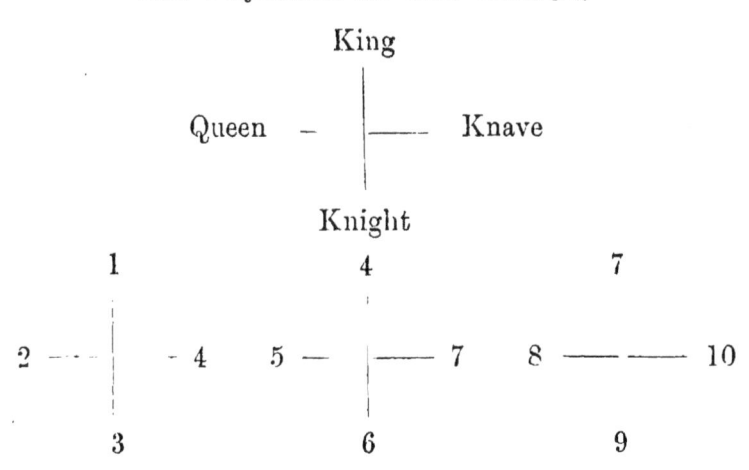

```
                King
                 |
   Queen —     ——— Knave
                 |
                Knight
```

$$2 --- \begin{vmatrix} 1 \\ \\ 3 \end{vmatrix} -4 \quad 5 - \begin{vmatrix} 4 \\ \\ 6 \end{vmatrix} - 7 \quad 8 ——— 10 \atop 9$$

If we now group all the numbers of the sequence according to the letter of the tetragrammaton, to which they are analogous, we shall find—

```
Representing Yod              1 — 4 — 7
Representing the 1st He       2 — 5 — 8
Representing the Vau          3 — 6 — 9
Representing the 2nd He         10
```

```
                   (1. 4. 7)
                     Yod
                      |
(2. 5. 8)  1st He  ——+——  2nd He  (10)
                      |
                     Vau
                   (3. 6. 9)
```

The figure 10 therefore acts for the *numbers*, as the knave acts for the figures, that is to say, it serves as a *transition*. Between what?

Between one colour and another.

AFFINITY BETWEEN THE FIGURES AND THE NUMBERS.

We have already studied both the figures and the numbers separately, let us now see what connection exists between the figures and the numbers.

If we group the similar terms according to the identical *Law* which rules them, we shall find them as follows—

```
The King is the    Yod  of  1. 4. 7
The Queen —        He   of  2. 5. 8
The Knight —       Vau  of  3. 6. 9
The Knave — 2nd He      of  10
```

The sequence of the figures is reproduced *three times* in the series of numbers, that is to say, that each series of numbers represents a conception of the figures in each of the three Kabbalistic worlds.

The series 1, 2, 3, 4 represents the emanation of the sequence king, queen, knight, knave in the divine world.

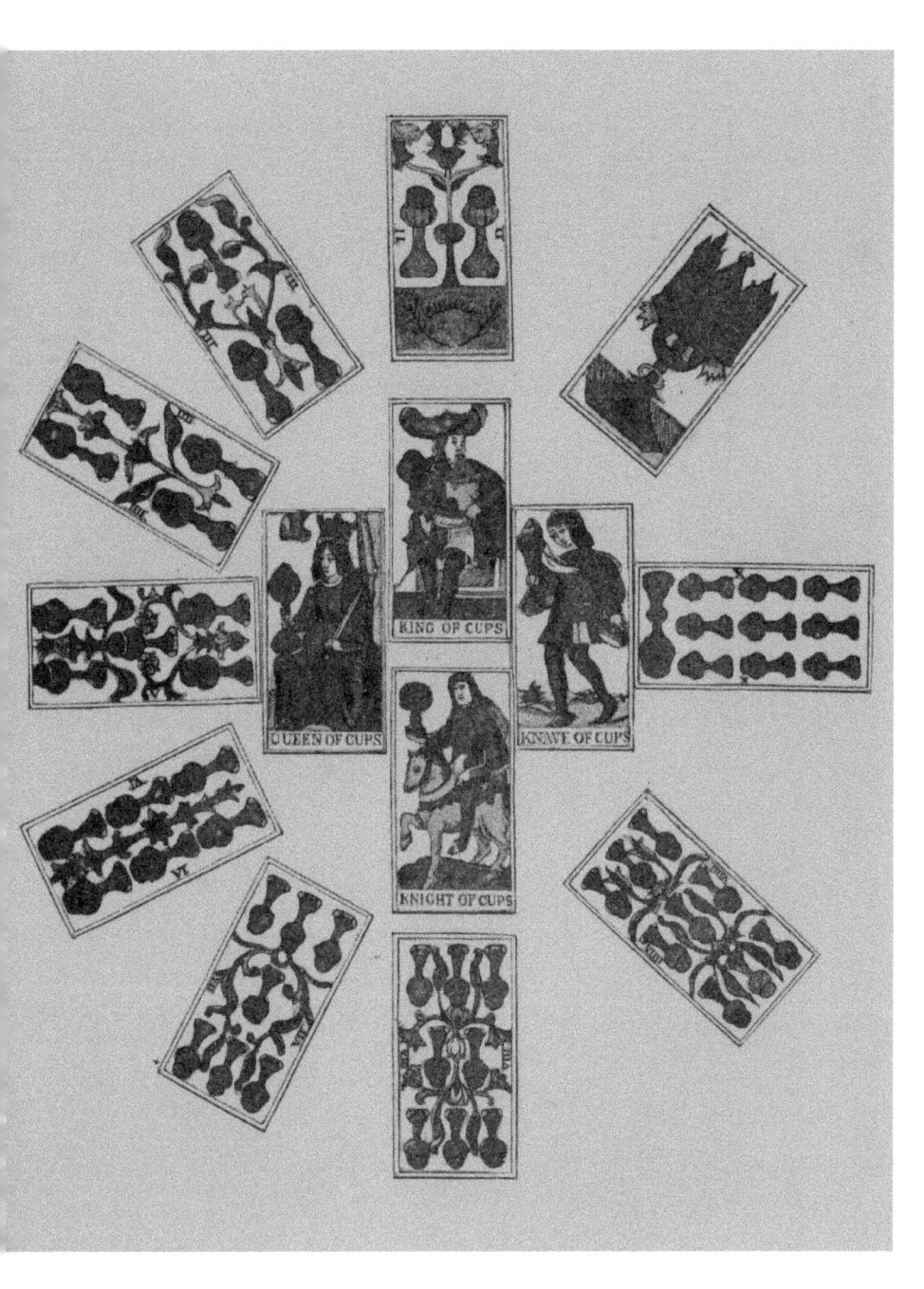
KING OF CUPS
QUEEN OF CUPS
KNAVE OF CUPS
KNIGHT OF CUPS

THE KEY TO THE MINOR ARCANA.

The series 4, 5, 6, 7 represents this evolution in the
man world.
The series 7, 8, 9, 10 represents this evolution in the
aterial world.
Each colour is a complete whole, formed after the
anner of beings.

Of a material body:
>   (Knight — 7.8.9)

Of a vital force:
>   (Queen — 4.5.6)

Of an intellect:
>   (King — 1.2.3)

Of reproductive organs:
>   (Knave — 10)

Each of these parts can subdivide itself into three others,
the numbers indicate.[1]

Let us, however, return to our deduction, and by
mming up the results obtained, we shall find—

Representations of the *Yod*:
>   The King
>   The 1 or Ace
>   The 4
>   The 7

Representations of the *He*:
>   The Queen
>   The 2
>   The 5
>   The 8

---

[1] We wished to make this application of the Tarot in order to
ow Initiates what results might be expected from the laws
plained by studying it.

Representations of the *Vau:*
>   The Knight
>   The 3
>   The 6
>   The 9

Representations of the *2nd He:*
>   The Knave
>   The 10

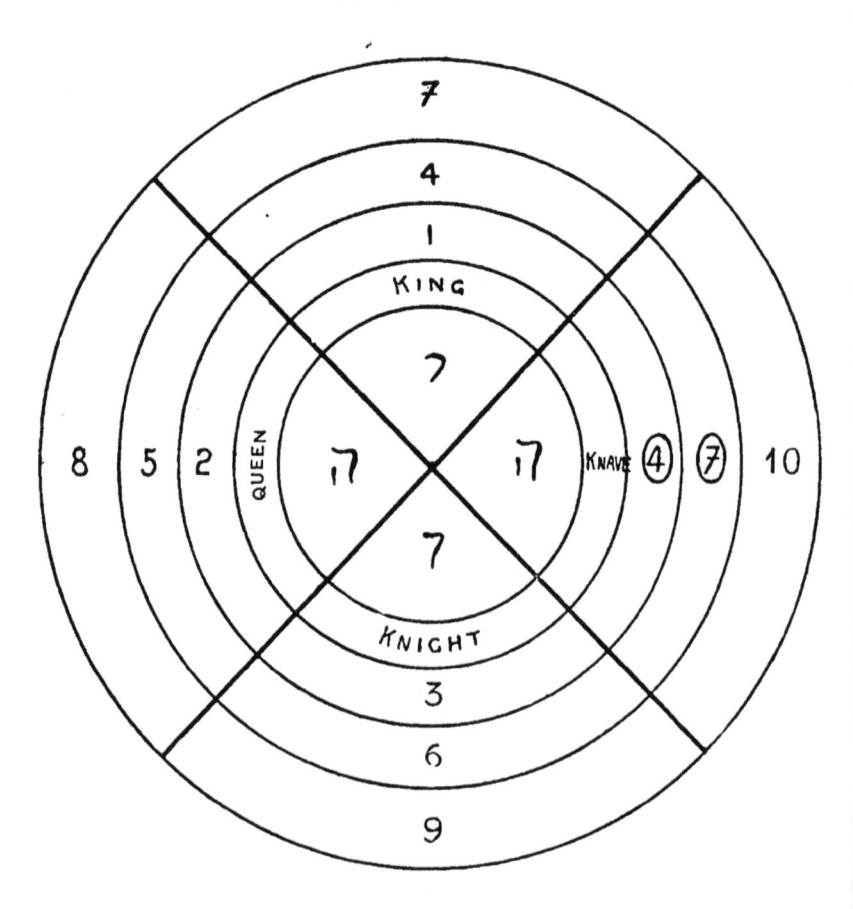

FIGURATION OF ONE COLOUR.

THE KEY TO THE MINOR ARCANA. 43

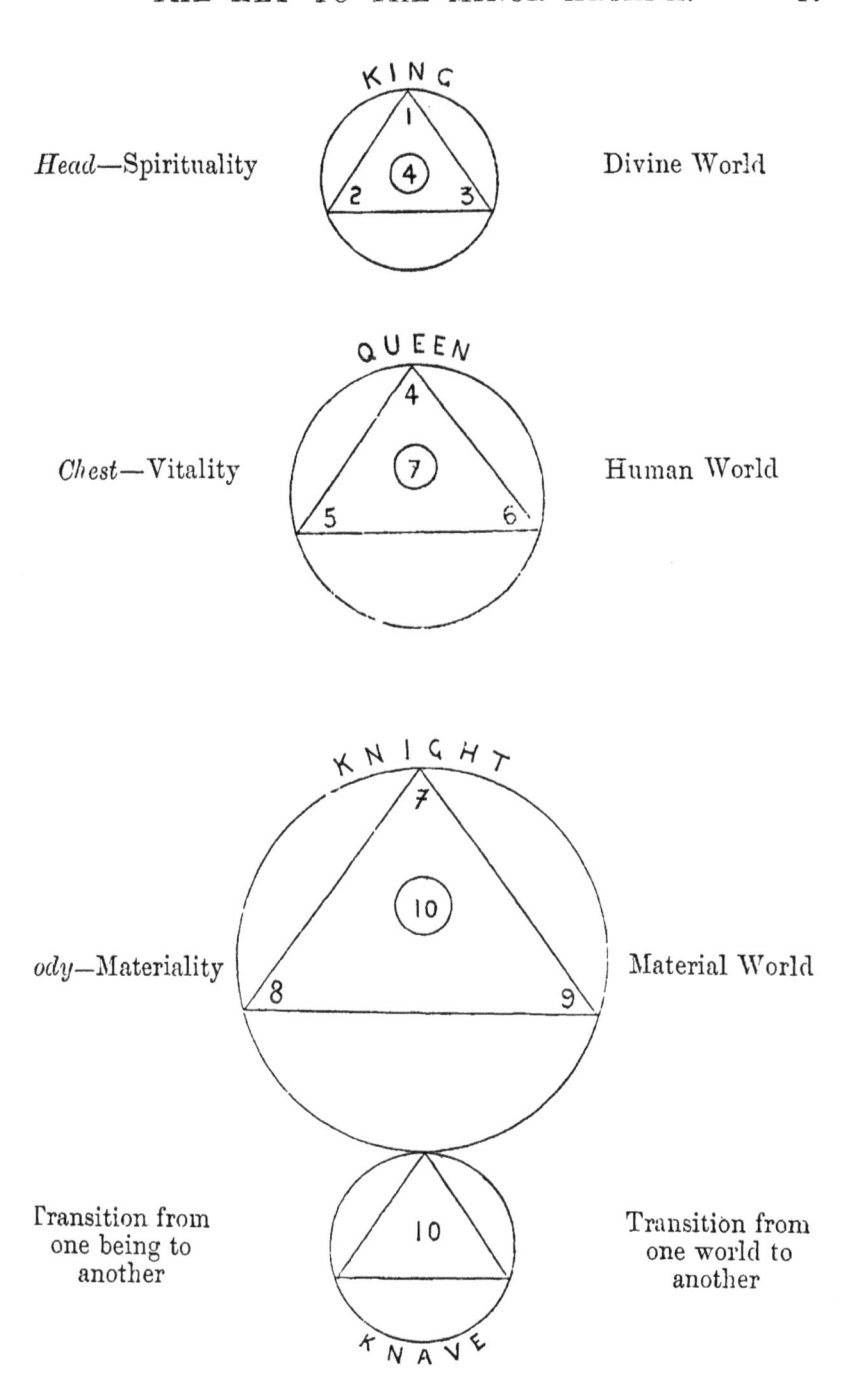

Head—Spirituality   KING (1, 2, 3, 4)   Divine World

Chest—Vitality   QUEEN (4, 5, 6, 7)   Human World

Body—Materiality   KNIGHT (7, 8, 9, 10)   Material World

Transition from one being to another   KNAVE (10)   Transition from one world to another

STUDY OF THE FOUR COLOURS.

Supplied with these data, let us continue our study and apply the same principle to the other cards.

The laws which we have defined for the constitution of one colour, apply in the same way to the other three colours.

But when we consider the four colours of the Tarot, new deductions will be called forth. We must remember that these four colours are: the Sceptre, the Cup, the Sword, and the Money or Pentacles.

The Sceptre represents the Male or the Active.
The Cup is the image of the Passive or Feminine.
The Sword represents the union of the two by its crucial form.
Lastly, the Pentacles represent the second He.

The authors who have philosophically studied the Tarot are all unanimous in asserting the analogy that exists between the tetragrammaton and the four colours. Guillaume Postel,[1] and above all Eliphas Levi,[2] have developed these studies with great results, and they show us the four letters of the tetragrammaton applied in the symbolism of every cultus.

We must pause one moment to notice the analogy between these letters and the symbols of the Christian religion.

The Yod or Sceptre of the Tarot is represented by the episcopal crosier.

The 1st He or Cup is represented by the Chalice.

The Vau or Sword by the Cross, bearing the same form.

The 2nd He or Pentacles by the Host, the transition from the natural to the Supernatural world.

[1] *Clavis abscunditarum rerum.*
[2] Eliphas Levi, *Dogme et Rituel de la Haute Magie.*

KING OF SWORDS
QUEEN OF SWORDS
KNAVE OF SWORDS
KNIGHT OF SWORDS

THE KEY TO THE MINOR ARCANA.

The series which we have studied in one colour is defined equally strictly in the four colours regarded as a whole, thus—

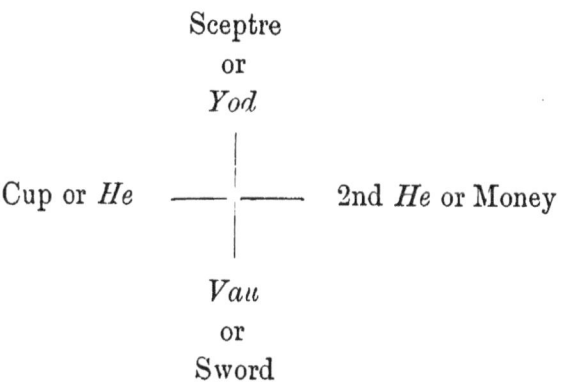

```
                    Sceptre
                      or
                     Yod
                      |
                      |
Cup or He  ———————————|——————————  2nd He or Money
                      |
                      |
                     Vau
                      or
                     Sword
```

A COMPREHENSIVE GLANCE OVER THE MINOR ARCANA.

If we look back a little, we can easily judge the road we have traversed.

The four colours considered *in globo* have shown us the application of the law *Yod-he-vau-he*.

But the same law is reproduced in each of the colours taken separately.

The four figures represent *Yod-he-vau-he*;

The four series of numbers also.

Let us then arrange all the cards according to their affinities, and we shall obtain the following results—

$$\left.\begin{array}{l}\text{The 4 Kings}\\ \text{The 4 Aces}\\ \text{The 4 Fours}\\ \text{The 4 Sevens}\end{array}\right\} = Yod$$

$$\left.\begin{array}{l}\text{The 4 Queens}\\ \text{The 4 Twos}\\ \text{The 4 Fives}\\ \text{The 4 Eights}\end{array}\right\} = He$$

The 4 Cavaliers
The 4 Threes
The 4 Sixes
The 4 Nines
} = *Vau*

The 4 Knaves
The 4 Tens
} = *He*

If we wished to represent this arrangement by a synthetic diagram, we should place the sacred name in *the centre* of a circle divided into four parts, which respectively correspond with each of the letters *Yod-he-vau-he*. In each of the quarters, the cards that are analogous to the letters of the tetragrammaton will radiate from the centre. See the diagram on page opposite.

The figures have the same connection with the colours as the numbers have with the figures.

The sequence of the figures is reproduced in the three worlds by the numbers; the same thing takes place in the sequence of colours: Sceptre, Cup, Sword, Pentacles are reproduced in the figures.

The Sceptre is the *Yod* of the 4 Kings.
The Cup is the *He* of the 4 Queens.
The Sword is the *Vau* of the 4 Knights.
The Pentacles is the *He* of the 4 Knaves.

And just as each colour has a complete whole, formed of a body, of a soul, and of a mind or vital force, so the four colours form a complete whole thus composed :—

The material body of the minor arcana :

The 4 Knights
The 4 Sevens
The 4 Eights
The 4 Nines

THE KEY TO THE MINOR ARCANA.

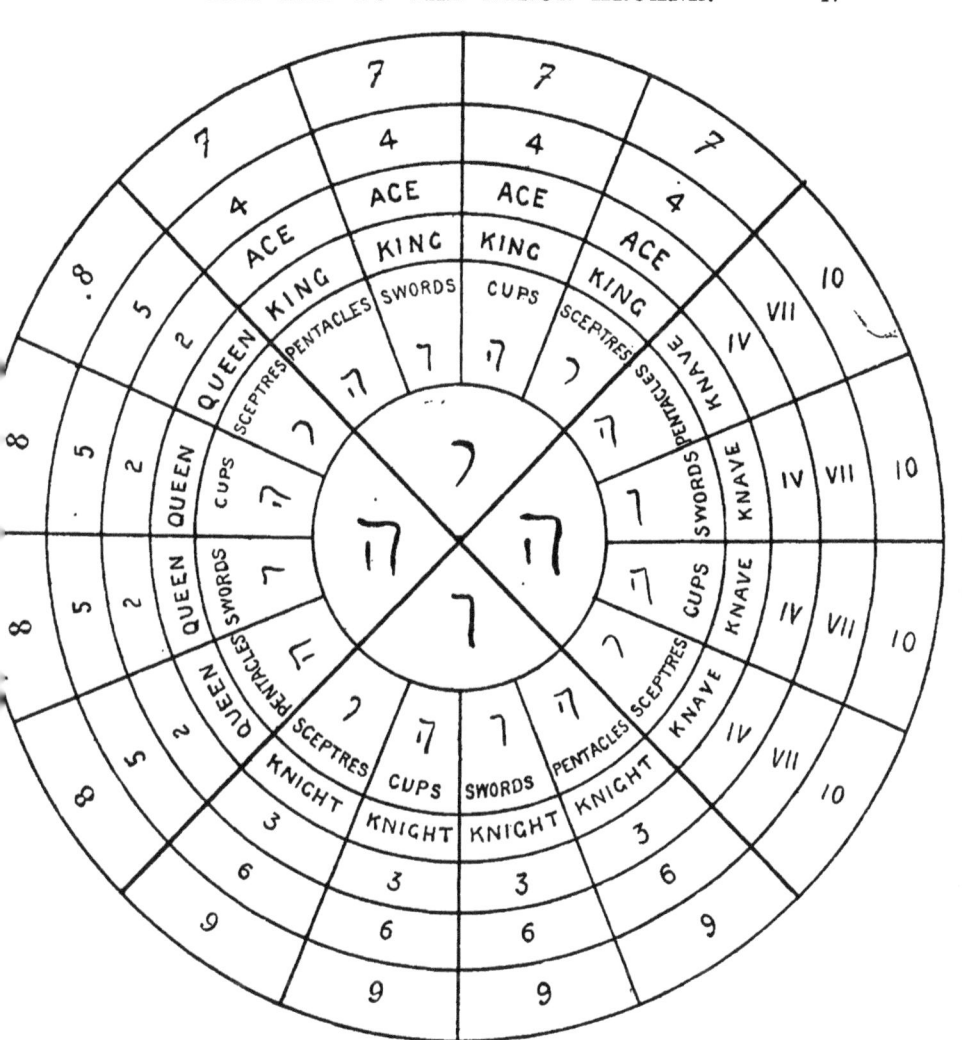

GENERAL FIGURE OF THE MINOR ARCANA.—*Disposition of Series.*

The vital body of the minor arcana:
>   The 4 Queens
>   The 4 Fours
>   The 4 Fives
>   The 4 Sixes

SCEPTRES

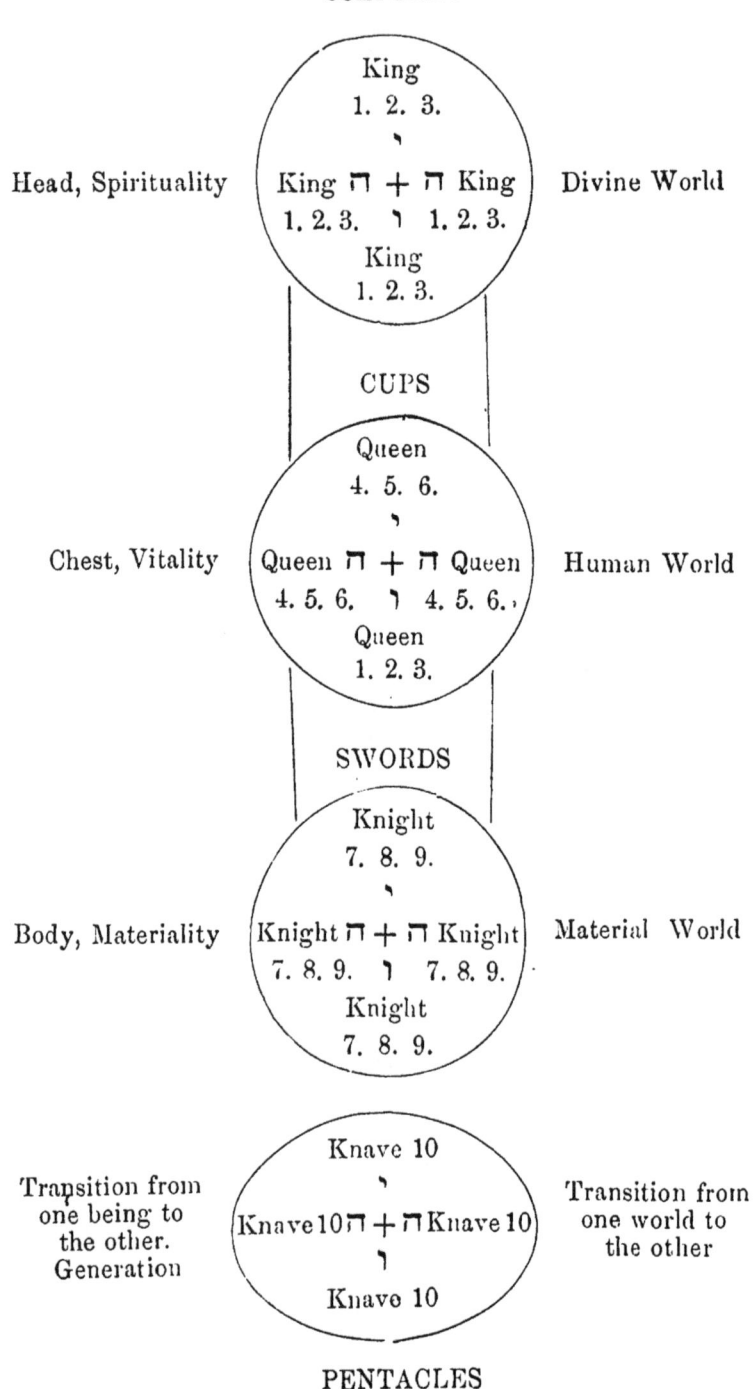

Head, Spirituality

King
1. 2. 3.
י
King ה + ה King
1. 2. 3. ו 1. 2. 3.
King
1. 2. 3.

Divine World

CUPS

Chest, Vitality

Queen
4. 5. 6.
י
Queen ה + ה Queen
4. 5. 6. ו 4. 5. 6.
Queen
1. 2. 3.

Human World

SWORDS

Body, Materiality

Knight
7. 8. 9.
י
Knight ה + ה Knight
7. 8. 9. ו 7. 8. 9.
Knight
7. 8. 9.

Material World

Transition from one being to the other. Generation

Knave 10
י
Knave 10 ה + ה Knave 10
ו
Knave 10

Transition from one world to the other

PENTACLES

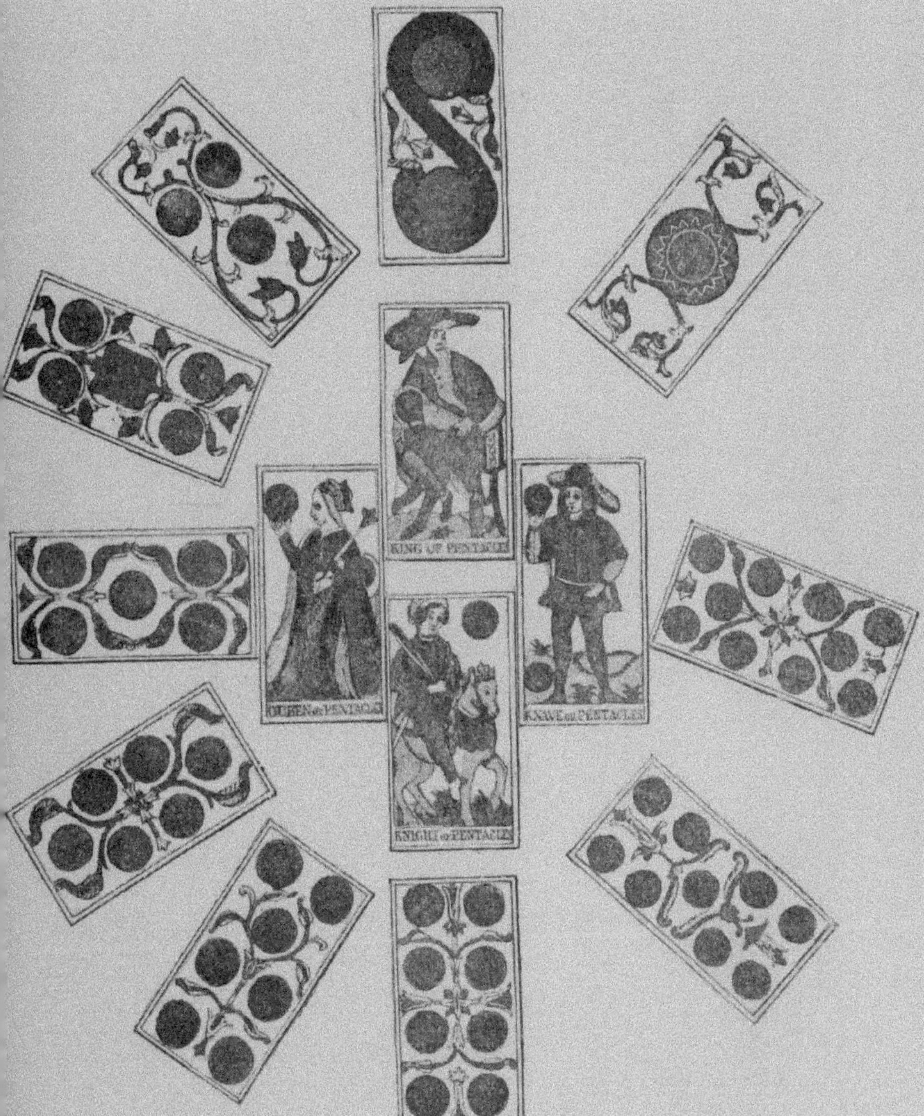
KING OF PENTACLES
KNAVE of PENTACLES
KNIGHT of PENTACLES

The intellectual body:
> The 4 Kings
> The 4 Aces
> The 4 Twos
> The 4 Threes

Reproductive organs:
> The 4 Knaves
> The 4 Tens

We can only point out the very instructive affinities shown in these figures; they can be carried to a great length.

We give these indications in order to demonstrate the management of *analogy*, the method of the occult science, to which we have so frequently alluded in our preceding works.

We need only compare this last diagram, which represents the four colours, with the first, which depicted one only, to see at once that the law upon which these two diagrams are constructed is the same, only that the applications of it are varied.

It is the same law by which the cells that form the human being group themselves to constitute *organs*, the organs group themselves to form *members*, and the grouping of the latter produces the *individual*.[1]

We have drawn the following conclusion from all that we have already stated—

The *Pentacles*, responding to the second *He*, indicates a transition.

Between what?

Between the *minor and major arcana*.

[1] See the *Traité Élémentaire de Science Occulte*, chap. iii.

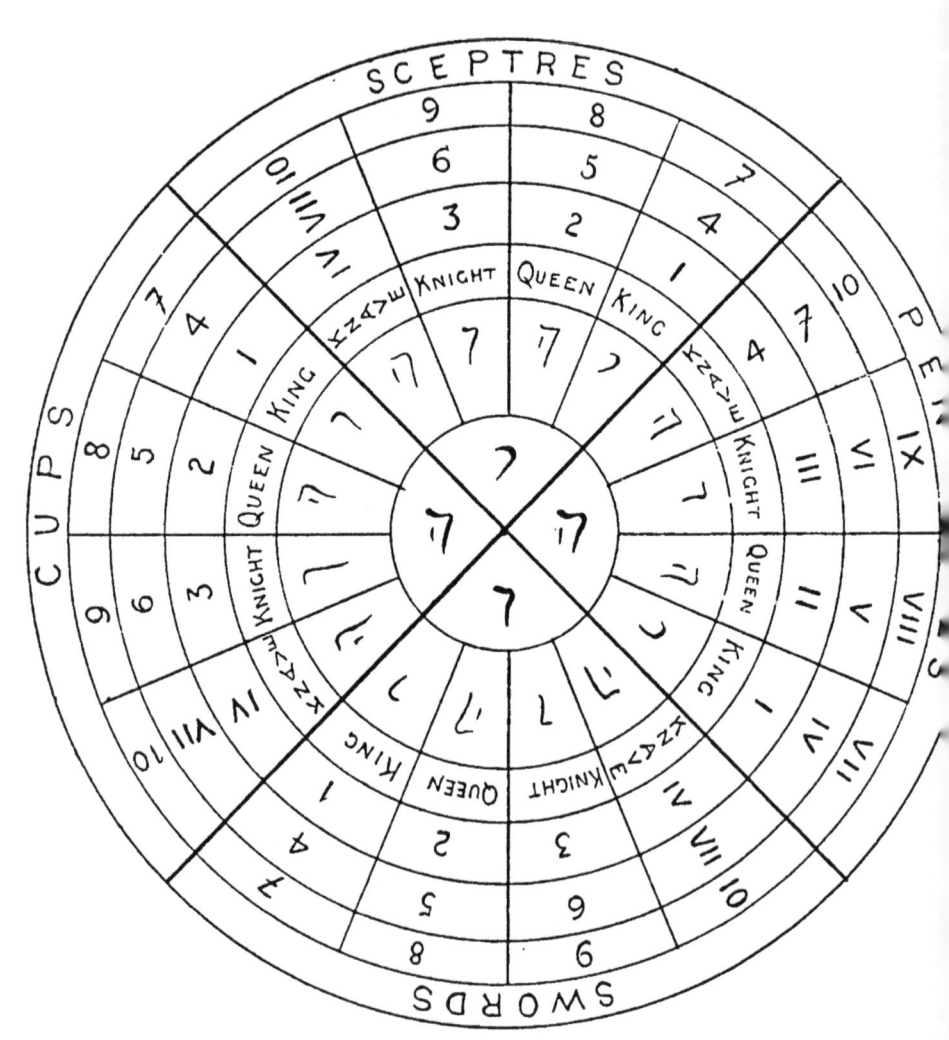

GENERAL KEY TO MINOR ARCANA.

CHAPTER VI.

THE KEY TO THE MAJOR ARCANA.

The Major Arcana—1st Ternary—2nd Ternary—1st Septenary—2nd Septenary—The Three Septenaries and the Ternary of Transition.

THE MAJOR ARCANA.

THE fundamental difference which exists between the minor and major arcana, is that in the latter the figures and numbers are united, whilst in the former they are distinct.

There are 22 major arcana, but one of them bears a 0, so that, in reality, there are only 21 great or major arcana.

Most of the authors who have studied the Tarot have devoted all their attention to these 22 cards, without noticing the others, which, however, contain the real key to the system.

But we will leave these digressions and commence the application of the law *Yod-he-vau-he* to this portion of the Tarot.

A little reflection will suggest to us that there should be *some sequences* in the major arcana as well as in the minor arcana. But how are we to define the limits of these series?

Each card of the minor arcana bears a symbol which easily connects it with the whole scheme (Sceptre, Cup, Sword, or Pentacles); it is different in this case. Each card bears a *different symbol*. Therefore it is not *symbolism* that can guide us here, at all events for the moment.

Besides the symbol, each card expresses an idea. This idea is already a better guide, for it is easier to classify than the symbol; but this guide does not yet offer all the security that we could desire, for it may be read differently by various persons. Again, the idea proceeds from the action of the symbol upon the other term expressed by the card, *the number*.

The number is certainly the most reliable element, the easiest to follow in its evolutions; it is, therefore, the number that will guide us; and through it we shall discover the two other terms.

Let us now recall our explanation of the numbers, and we shall easily define the series of the major arcana.

However, from the commencement we must make one great reservation. The series which we are about to enumerate are the *most usual*, but they are not the *only ones*.

This said, we will now study the four first major arcana.

The numbers 1, 2, 3, 4 at once indicate the classification to be adopted and the nature of the terms.

    1 corresponds to *Yod*, and is active.
    2   —   to *He*   —   passive.
    3   —   to *Vau*   —   neuter.
    4   —   to the 2nd *He*, and indicates transition.

This 4th arcanum corresponds to the Knave and to the 10 of the minor arcana, and becomes *Yod* in the next or following series.

THE KEY TO THE MAJOR ARCANA. 53

If we wish to make a figure of the first ternary 1, 2, 3, we should do it in this way—

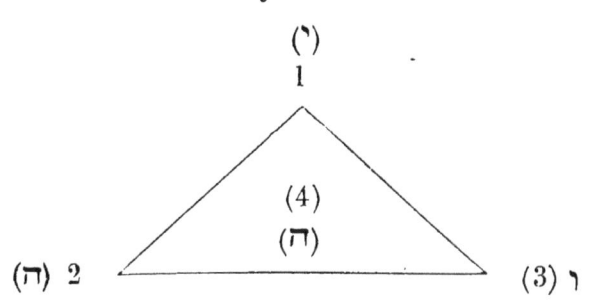

```
               (י)
                1
               /\
              /  \
            (4)   \
            (ה)    \
  (ה) 2  /_____\  (3) ו
```

The active term 1 is at the head of the triangle, the two other terms are at the other angles.

This ternary can also be represented in its affinities with *Yod-he-vau-he*—

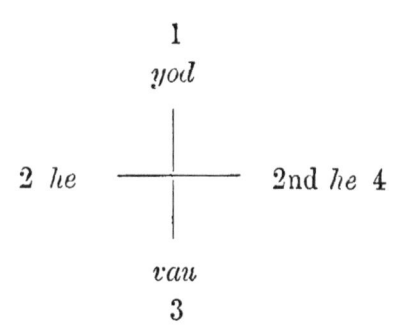

```
              1
             yod
              |
  2 he  ——————+—————— 2nd he 4
              |
             vau
              3
```

SECOND TERNARY.—We have stated that the 4 becomes the *Yod* or active term in the following sequence.

This is realized in the figure below—

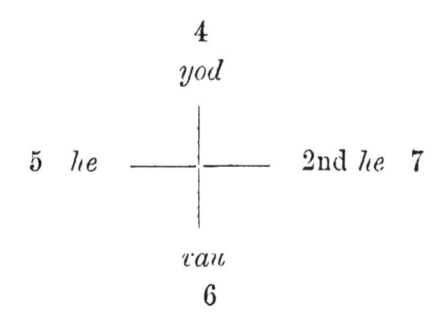

```
              4
             yod
              |
  5 he  ——————+—————— 2nd he 7
              |
             vau
              6
```

The 4 representing the *Yod*, therefore, acts with regard to 5 and 6, as the 1 acted with regard to 2 and 3, and we obtain another ternary.

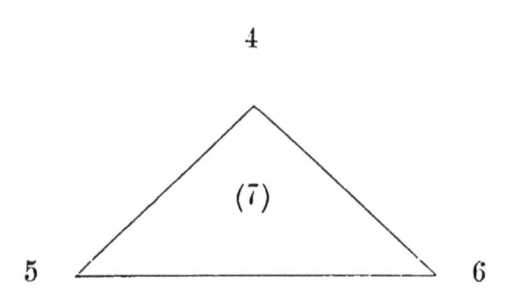

```
          4
         /\
        /  \
       / (7) \
      /      \
     /_____\
    5          6
```

The 7 acts here as the 4 acted previously, and the same rule applies to all the series in the arcana.

FIRST SEPTENARY.—The application of one law to very different terms has led us so far; we must not abandon this system, but persevere and say—

If in one ternary exist an *active* term = *yod*, a *passive* term = *he*, and a *neuter* term = *vau*, resulting from the two first, why should not the same result be found in several ternaries taken together?

The first ternary is active and corresponds to *yod*; the second ternary is passive and corresponds to *he*; the reaction of one ternary upon another gives birth to a third ternary or *vau*.

Let us make a figure representing this—

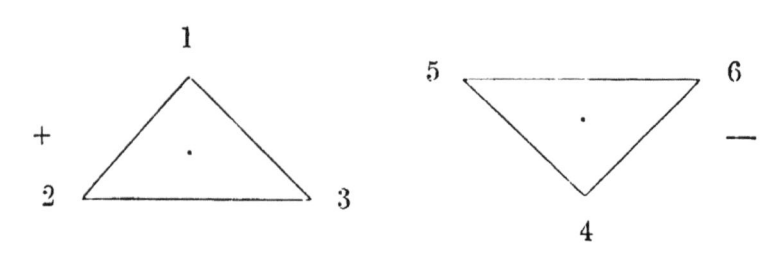

```
          1                 5 _____ 6
         /\                  \         /
     +  /  \                  \   .   /   —
       / .  \                  \     /
      /_____\                  \   /
     2        3                  \ /
                                  4
```

THE KEY TO THE MAJOR ARCANA.

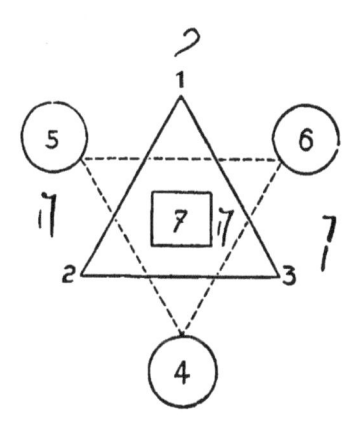

The 7 therefore forms the element of transition between one *septenary* and another.

If we define the analogy between this first septenary and the *Yod-he-vau-he*, we shall find—

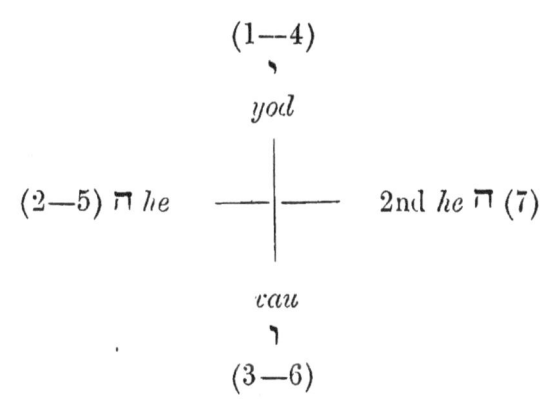

$$
\begin{array}{c}
(1-4) \\
\text{yod} \\
(2-5)\ \text{he} \quad \longmapsto \quad \text{2nd } he\ (7) \\
\text{vau} \\
(3-6)
\end{array}
$$

A deduction may be made in passing, from which a great deal of information may be derived, if it be carefully studied: the 4 being only the 1, considered *negatively*, the 5 is only the 2 considered negatively, whilst the 6 is the negative of 3. It is always *the same number* under *different aspects*.

We have therefore defined a first septenary, formed of two opposing ternaries.

THE TAROT.

We have seen that this septenary also reproduces *Yod-he-vau-he*.

SECOND SEPTENARY.—The law that applies to the first ternaries is also true for the others, and following the same method we obtain a second septenary, thus formed—

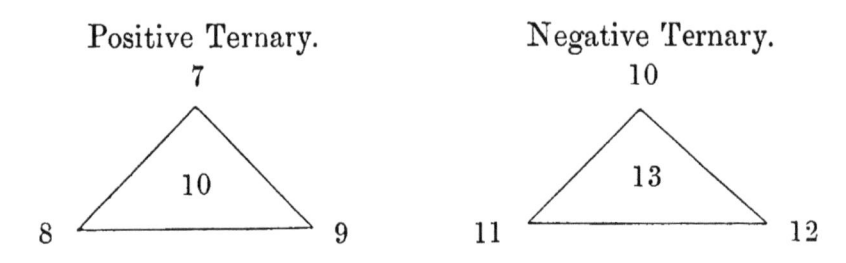

Positive Ternary.   Negative Ternary.

```
        7                              10
       /\                              /\
      /10\                            /13\
     /____\                          /____\
    8      9                        11     12
```

The two ternaries, positive and negative, will balance each other to give birth to a second septenary and to its term of transition 13. Thus—

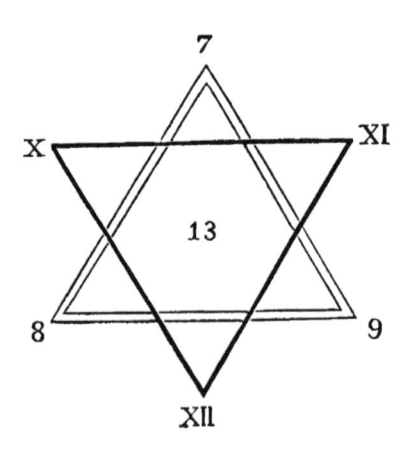

```
              7
             /\
        X   /  \   XI
         \ / 13 \ /
          X      X
         / \    / \
        8   \  /   9
             \/
             XII
```

THE KEY TO THE MAJOR ARCANA.

General figure—

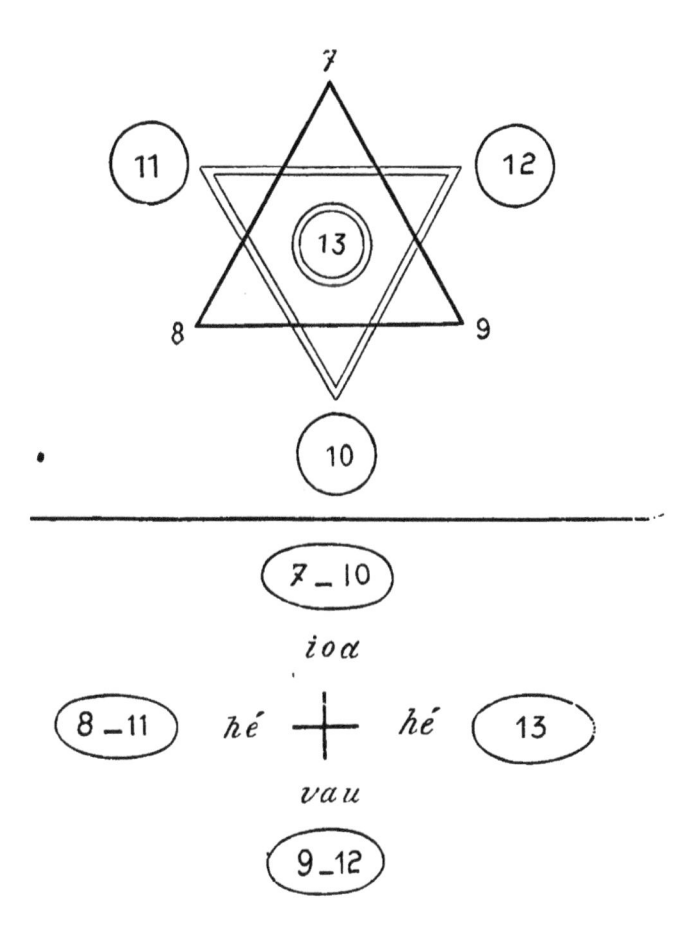

figure: Star of David with 7 at top vertex, 8 and 9 at lower side vertices, 11 and 12 at upper side circles, 13 in center, 10 below

$7-10$
i o α

$8-11$ hé $+$ hé 13
v a u
$9-12$

But if the two ternaries respectively act as positive and negative, why should not the two septenaries do the same?

The first septenary, taken as a whole, will therefore be *positive*, relatively to the second septenary, which will be *negative*.

The first septenary corresponds to *yod*, the second to *he*.

THIRD SEPTENARY. The third septenary is thus formed—

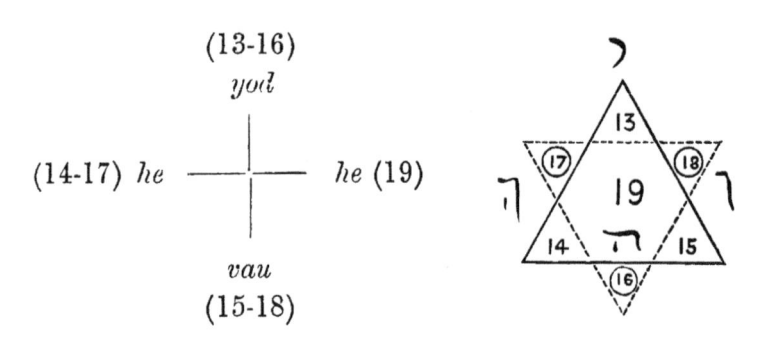

```
            (13-16)
              yod
               |
(14-17) he ---+--- he (19)
               |
              vau
            (15-18)
```

If the first septenary is positive and the second negative, the third will be neuter, and will correspond with *vau*.

We should have therefore, definitely—

1st, A POSITIVE SEPTENARY = *Yod*.
2nd, A NEGATIVE SEPTENARY = *He*.
3rd, A NEUTER SEPTENARY = *Vau*.

Yet each septenary contains one term which belongs to the preceding septenary, and one which belongs to the following septenary.

Thus the 7 is the 7th term of the first septenary and the 1st term of the second. 13 is the last term of the second septenary and the 1st of the third, etc.

The result is that three terms remain to be classed. These are—

$$19 - 20 - 21$$

These three terms form the last ternary, the ternary of transition between the *major arcana* and the *minor arcana*, a ternary which corresponds to the second *he*, and which may be thus represented—

THE KEY TO THE MAJOR ARCANA.

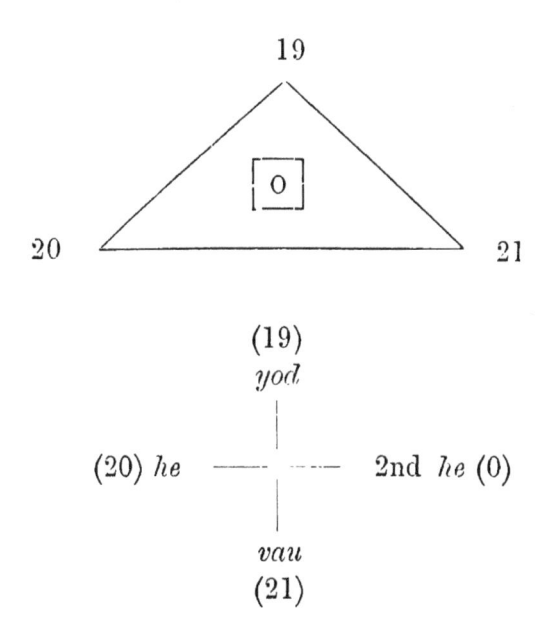

```
              19
              /\
             /  \
            / ┌─┐\
           /  │o│ \
          /   └─┘  \
         /_____ \
        20           21
```

```
           (19)
           yod
            │
(20) he ────┼──── 2nd he (0)
            │
           vau
           (21)
```

The last numbered card, which ought correctly to bear the number 22 (or its Hebrew correspondent), closes the Tarot by a marvellous figure, which represents its constitution to those who can understand it. We will return to it presently. Therefore, in the major arcana, the great law is thus definitely represented. (See next page.)

The first septenary corresponds to the Divine World, to Yod.

The second to Man.

The third to Nature.

Finally, the last ternary indicates the passage from the creative and providential world to the created and fatal world.

This ternary establishes the connection between the *major* and *minor arcana*.

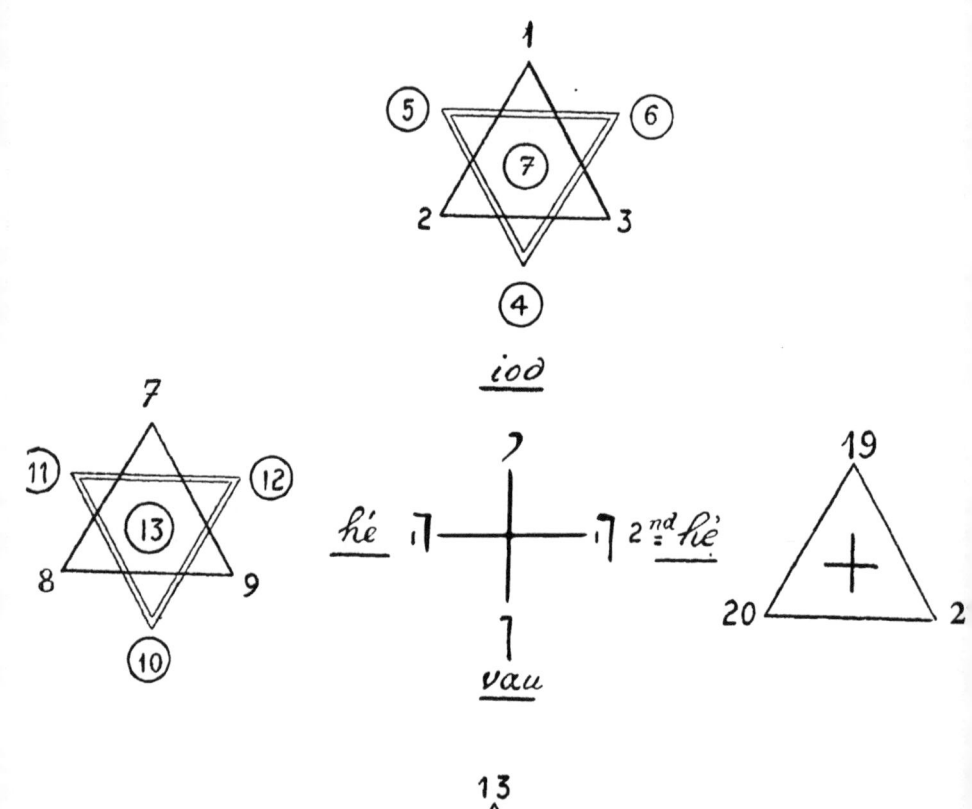

THE TAROT.

iod

hé ה ה *2ⁿᵈ hé*

vau

CHAPTER VII.

CONNECTION BETWEEN THE MAJOR AND MINOR ARCANA.
GENERAL AFFINITIES.

KEY OF THE TAROT.

Domination of the 1st Septenary—Affinities of the 2nd Septenary in the Tarot, Card by Card—Ditto of the 3rd Septenary—General Affinities—Affinities of *Yod, He, Vau*, and of the 2nd *He*. General figure giving the Key to the Tarot.

CONNECTION BETWEEN THE MAJOR AND MINOR ARCANA.

THE *Pentacles* on one side, the *Ternary of transition* on the other, establish the connection between the major and minor arcana.

This connection is found in the general affinities of the four letters of the tetragrammaton.

The 1st septenary, which corresponds to *yod*, governs all the correspondents of *yod* in the minor series, that is to say—

        The 4 Kings.
        The 4 Aces.
        The 4 Fours.
        The 4 Sevens.

Each element of the septenary governs different terms, thus—

1st Septenary.

The arcana 1 and 4 govern *King*-1.4.7 of Sceptres.
— 2 and 5 — — of Cups.
— 3 and 6 — — of Swords.
The arcanum 7 — — of Pentacles.

Moreover—

The 1st arcanum especially governs the positive terms of the series, *i. e.*—

Arcanum | The King of Yod or of Sceptres (+).[1]
1 (+) | The King of Vau or of Swords (—).

The 4th arcanum especially governs the negative terms of the series—

Arcanum | The King of He ... Cups (+).
4 (—) | The King of the 2nd He + Pentacles (—).

By applying the same law to the other arcana we find—

Arcanum | Ace of Yod (+) Sceptres.
(+) 2 | Ace of Vau (—) Swords.

Arcanum | Ace of He (+) Cups.
(—) 5 | Ace of He (—) Pentacles.

Arcanum 3 | 4 of Sceptres (+).
(+) | 4 of Swords (—).

Arcanum 6 | 4 of Cups (+).
(—) | 4 of Pentacles (—).

Arcanum 7 | All the transitional terms.
(∞) | 7 (∞).

---

[1] The signs +, —, ∞ indicate : the sign + the *positive* terms, the sign — the *negative* terms, the sign ∞ the *neuter* terms.

THE MAJOR AND MINOR ARCANA.

SECOND SEPTENARY.—The second septenary, corresponding to *He*, governs all the correspondents of the first *He*, in the minor series, that is to say—

    The 4 Queens.
    The 4 Twos.
    The 4 Fives.
    The 4 Eights.

Each element of the second septenary has the following lominations—

Arcanum 7 (+) { Queen of Sceptres, (+) / Queen of Swords, (—) }   Arcanum 10 (—) { Queen of Cups, (+) / Queen of Pentacles, (—) }

Arcanum 8 (+) { Two of Sceptres, (+) / Two of Swords, (—) }   Arcanum 11 (—) { Two of Cups, (+) / Two of Pentacles, (—) }

Arcanum 9 (+) { Five of Sceptres, (+) / Five of Swords, (—) }   Arcanum 12 (—) { Five of Cups, (+) / Five of Pentacles, (—) }

    Arcana 13 (∞) { All the 8, (∞) }

THIRD SEPTENARY.—The third septenary corresponds to *Vau*, and rules over—

    The 4 Knights.
    The 4 Threes.
    The 4 Sixes.
    The 4 Nines.

THE TAROT.

Each element of this septenary thus rules over—

Arcanum 13 (+) { Knight of Sceptres, (+) / Knight of Swords, (−) } Arcanum 16 (−) { Knight of Cups, (+) / Knight of Pentacles, (−) }

Arcanum 14 (+) { Three of Sceptres, (+) / Three of Swords, (−) } Arcanum 17 (−) { Three of Cups, (+) / Three of Pentacles, (−) }

Arcanum 15 (+) { Six of Sceptres, (+) / Six of Swords, (−) } Arcanum 18 (−) { Six of Cups, (+) / Six of Pentacles, (−) }

Arcanum 19 (∞) { All the nines, (∞) }

TERNARY OF TRANSITION.—The ternary of transition rules over—

The 4 Knaves.
The 4 Tens.

Each of its elements thus rules over—

Arcanum 19 (∞) (+) { Knave of Sceptres, (+) / Knave of Swords, (−) } Arcanum 20 (∞) (−) { Knave of Cups, (+) / Knave of Pentacles, (−) }

Arcanum 21 (+) { All the 10, (∞) }

Value of the signs +, —, and ∞.

The signs which follow each card in the preceding lists define the exact value of the card. One example will suffice to make this clearly understood.

THE MAJOR AND MINOR ARCANA.

Each term can be taken in two principal acceptations: in the positive (+) or in the negative (—). The same rule applies to the sub-divisions of these terms.

For instance, the correspondents of the first septenary are 1 and 4.

1 is the positive (+).
4 is the negative (—).

1 governs two minor arcana: the King of Sceptres and the King of Swords.

The King of Sceptres is positive.
The King of Swords is negative.

The definite value of these terms would therefore be—

1st King of Sceptres.

Positive (+) of the positive (+);
or
King of Sceptres
+   +

2nd King of Swords.

Negative (—) of the Positive (+);
or more simply
King of Swords
+   —

The same rule applies to the other terms in combining the sign which follows the *major arcanum* with that which follows *the term under consideration*.

The value of each of the 78 cards of the Tarot is thus defined.

GENERAL AFFINITIES.

AFFINITIES TO *Yod*.

	Positive.	*Negative.*
Major Arcana	Arcanum 1 — 7 — 13	Arcanum 4 — 10 — 16
Minor Arcana	King of Sceptres Ace 4 7 King of Swords Ace 4 7	King of Cups Ace — 4 — 7 — King of Pentacles Ace — 4 — 7 —

AFFINITIES TO THE 1ST *He*.

	Positive.	*Negative.*
Major Arcana	Arcanum 2 — 8 — 14	Arcanum 5 — 11 — 17
Minor Arcana	Queen of Sceptres Two — Five — Eight — Queen of Swords Two — Five — Eight —	Queen of Cups Two — Five — Eight — Queen of Pentacles Two — Five — Eight —

AFFINITIES TO *Vau*.

	Positive.	*Negative.*
Major Arcana	Arcanum 3 — 9 — 15	Arcanum 6 — 12 — 18

THE MAJOR AND MINOR ARCANA.

Minor Arcana
{
Knight of Sceptres — Knight of Cups —
Three — Three —
Six — Six —
Nine — Nine —
Knight of Swords — Knight of Pentacles
Three — Three —
Six — Six —
Nine — Nine —
}

AFFINITIES TO THE 2ND *He.*

Positive.   *Negative.*
Arcanum 19   Arcanum 20
Knave of Sceptres   Knave of Cups
— of Swords   — of Pentacles

Equilibrium.

Arcana | 21—22 |

Ten of Sceptres
— of Swords
— of Cups
— of Pentacles

GENERAL FIGURE OF THE CONSTRUCTION OF THE TAROT, SHOWING ALL THE AFFINITIES.

The absolute law.

Yod He Vau He

is in the centre of the figure.

Each of the letters of the tetragrammaton governs one quarter of the circle which contains its affinities.

The different colours indicate the especial dominion of each arcanum.

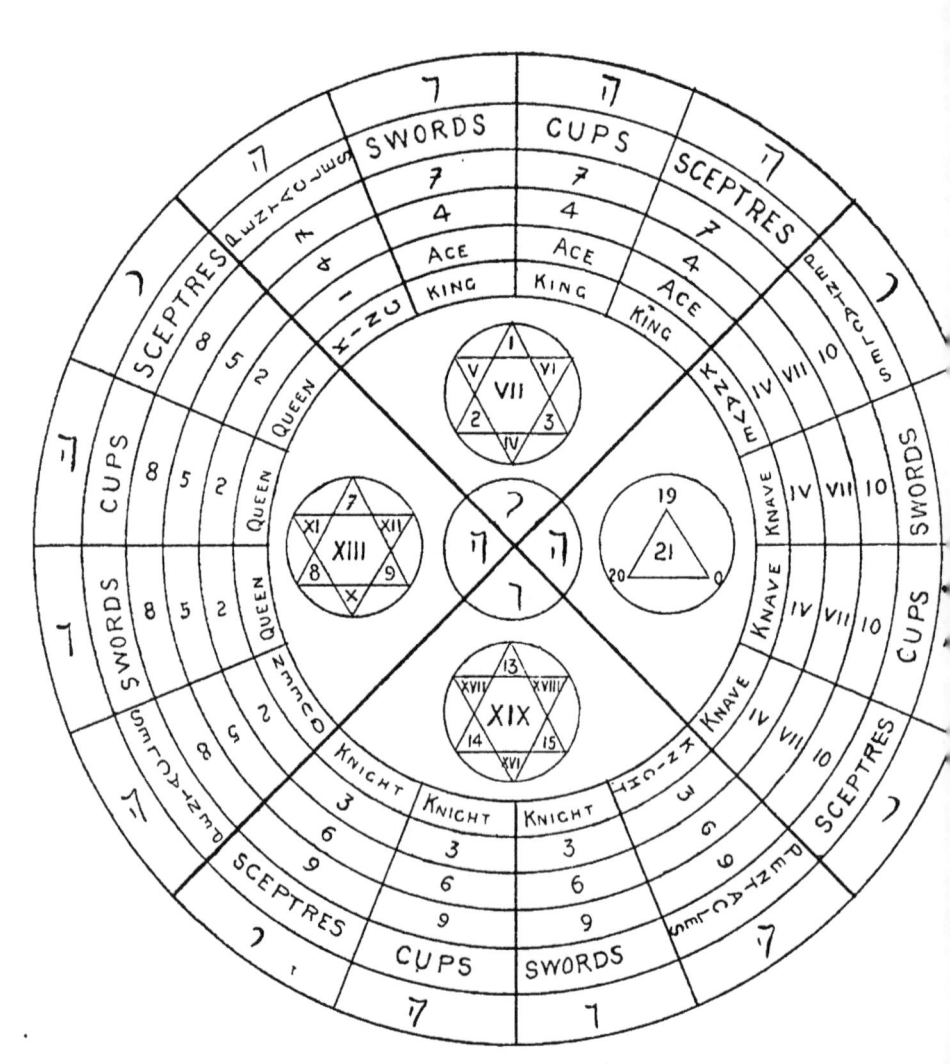

GRAND GENERAL FIGURE OF THE TAROT.—*Arrangement of Series.*

PART II.

SYMBOLISM IN THE TAROT.
APPLICATION OF THE GENERAL KEY TO SYMBOLISM.

CHAPTER VIII.

INTRODUCTION TO THE STUDY OF SYMBOLISM.

The Symbols—The Primitive Terms—Key of Symbolism—Definition of the Sense of one of the Symbols—The General Law of Symbolism.

INTRODUCTION TO THE STUDY OF SYMBOLISM IN THE TAROT.

OUR study of the Tarot and its numerical arrangement has given us the *general key*, which should be applied to all the further developments of which our subject may be susceptible.

The symbols should therefore exactly follow the evolution of the numbers, and this we shall find them do. However, as we shall now study each of the cards of the Tarot in turn, and as the reader's attention may be a little diverted by all these details, we have determined to commence by a short introduction to the study of the symbolism of the Tarot, an introduction in which we shall say a few words upon the grouping of the symbols.

This point explained, we can pass on to further details, which we shall terminate by a synthetic recapitulation. We thus hope to obtain the greatest possible light upon these difficult subjects.

The analysis of the word *Yod-he-vau-he* has given us

the general law upon which the whole Tarot is constructed. This law is thus represented—

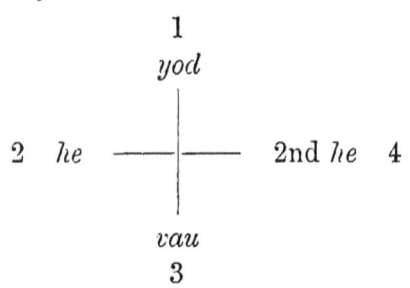

$$\begin{array}{c} 1 \\ yod \\ 2\ he \ \text{———|———}\ 2\text{nd}\ he\ \ 4 \\ vau \\ 3 \end{array}$$

We must therefore first define the four primitive terms in our symbols, which form the law exactly applicable to the whole symbolism.

And, in fact, we find these four terms in our four first cards; the general sense of these terms being—

1 — Creator or Divine.
2 — Preserver or Astral.
3 — Transformer or Physical and Diffuser.
4 — Generator or Transitional becoming Creator.

This law corresponds in all points with our sacred word, thus—

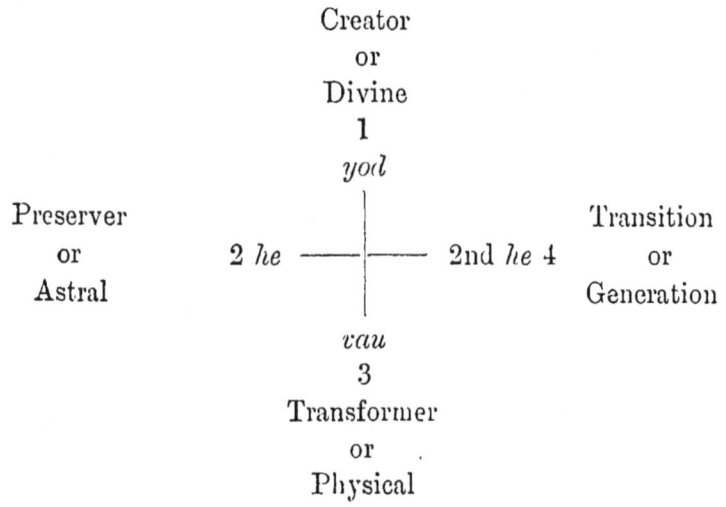

$$\begin{array}{c} \text{Creator} \\ \text{or} \\ \text{Divine} \\ 1 \\ yod \end{array}$$

Preserver or Astral $2\ he$ ———|——— $2\text{nd}\ he\ 4$ Transition or Generation

$$\begin{array}{c} vau \\ 3 \\ \text{Transformer} \\ \text{or} \\ \text{Physical} \end{array}$$

INTRODUCTION TO THE STUDY OF SYMBOLISM. 73

We shall see that this law applies exactly to each of the cards which possess three meanings.

A superlative or Divine meaning.
A comparative or Magic-Astral meaning.
A positive or Physical meaning, responding to a transition.

GENERAL STUDY OF THE FOUR FIRST CARDS.

Key to the Symbolism of the Tarot.

The four first cards of the major arcana form, symbolically as well as numerically, a complete sequence, which corresponds with the sacred word *Yod-he-vau-he*.

For the first card expresses the *active absolute*, and corresponds with *Yod*.

The second card denotes the *reflex* of the first, the *passive absolute;* it corresponds with the *first He*.

The third indicates the median term, the convertible transforming term, corresponding to *Vau*.

Lastly, the fourth card is a term of transition between the preceding series and the one that follows it.

The symbolic series of the Tarot is therefore completely represented by the four first cards, exactly as the numerical sequence is represented by the four first numbers. This fact produces a very important consideration, namely, that all the symbols of the Tarot are but transformations of the *three first*, and that the latter will supply us with the *general law* of symbolism, a law which will enable us to determine mathematically the sense of each card that follows.

But we can go still further.

Since the second card is the reflex of the first, and is formed by the first considered *negatively*, and since the third card results from the two others, *it suffices to be perfectly acquainted with the first card of the Tarot to determine mathematically the sense of all the others.*

Some details upon this subject are necessary.

The general law of the four first cards is as follows—

 1 — Positive. Creator.
 2 — Negative. Reflex of the first. Preserver.
 3 — Neuter, enveloping the two others. Transformer.
 4 — Passage from one series to another.

We can then represent the series in this way—

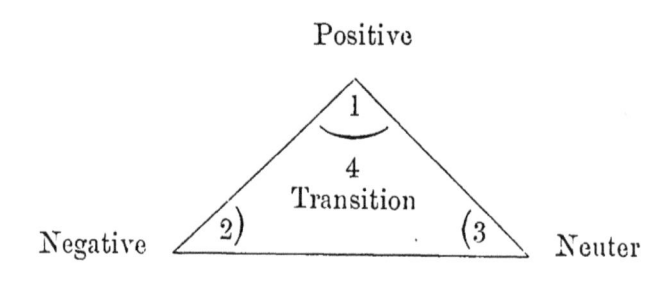

```
                Positive
                  /1\
                 / 4 \
              /Transition\
     Negative /2)_____(3\ Neuter
```

And what is true for each of the terms of a ternary is also true for the ternary taken *as a whole*, and this leads us to new considerations.

For the first ternary would be positive, corresponding to *Yod*, the active, the creator.

The second ternary would be negative, and would correspond to the first *He*, i. e. that all the terms of this ternary would be reflections of the terms of the first, just as the second card was the reflex of the first.

This gives us—

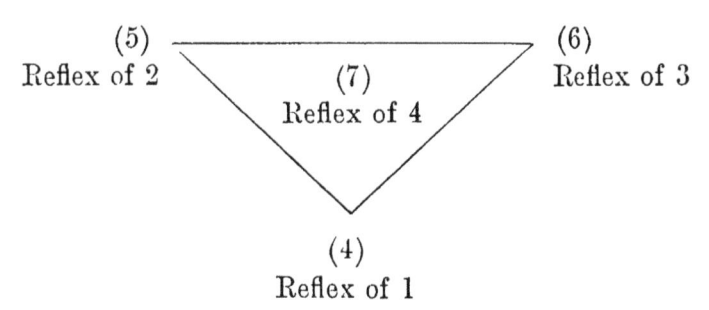

```
      (5)  ─────────────  (6)
   Reflex of 2    (7)    Reflex of 3
               Reflex of 4
                   \/
                  (4)
               Reflex of 1
```

We can thus determine the meaning of the arcana 4, 5, 6, 7 in the three worlds, since we know the meaning of the arcana 1, 2, 3, 4.

We need only refer to the study of the Tarot by numbers, to find the symbols, which correspond respectively to *Yod*, to *He*, to *Vau*, and to the second *He*.

But if the second ternary is the reflex of the first, the same rule applies to the septenaries.

All the cards of the second septenary will therefore be the symbolical reflection of those of the first.

All the cards of the third septenary are representatives of the third term, or of transformation.

We have then—

The 1*st septenary*,
> Which represents the *active Creation*. The Divine Osiris-Brahma, or the Father.

The 2*nd septenary*,
> Which represents *Preservation*. The Astral, Isis, Vishnu, the Son.

The 3*rd septenary*,
> Which represents *Transformation*, Physics, Horus, Siva, the Holy Spirit.

The three first arcana will therefore give the sense of all the others according to the following figure:

FIGURE
SHOWING THE SENSE OF EACH OF THE 22 MAJOR ARCANA.

yod positive or creative series	1.	4.	7.	10.	13.	16.	19.
1st *he* negative or preservative series	2.	5.	8.	11.	14.	17.	20.
vau neuter or transforming series equilibrium	3.	6.	9.	12.	15.	18.	21.
2nd *he* transitional series	4 = (1) + = positive negative		+ —		+ —		∞
	yod positive or creative series		*he* negative or preservative series		*vau* neuter or transforming series equilibrium		2nd *he* transitional series

This figure is very important, for it enables us to see at once the symbolical value of any card in the Tarot, by working in the following way—

INTRODUCTION TO THE STUDY OF SYMBOLISM.

O DISCOVER À PRIORI THE SYMBOLICAL VALUE OF ANY CARD IN THE TAROT.

We must see—

(1*st*) Which Hebrew letter is written to the left in the *orizontal* column, which contains the card under conideration.

(2*nd*) Which Hebrew letter is written *at the foot* of the *ertical column*, containing the card.

(3*rd*) Which sign (+ or —) governs the secondary ertical column, containing the card in question.

EXAMPLE:

I wish to determine the sense of the 5th arcanum.

I look to the left and find the Hebrew letter *he*.

This shows that the 5th arcanum is the *he* of what?

In order to know, I look at the vertical column and find *yod*.

The 5th arcanum is the *he* of *yod*, but that is not enough, so I look at the secondary column which contains the sign (—) negative.

I thus obtain a definite description of the 5th arcanum.

The fifth card of the Tarot is—

The He of Yod considered negatively.

This is a synthetic formula comprehensible to those only who are used to manipulating the sense of the word *Yod-he-vau-he*.

It is therefore necessary to give further explanations.

He represents the *reflex*.

We may therefore say, more explicitly—

The 5th arcanum is:

The reflex of *yod* considered negatively. But what is *yod* considered negatively?

To find this out, I look in my left column at the letter *yod*, I seek in the secondary vertical column the sign (—) negative, and at the intersection of these two lines I find the 4th arcanum.

The *yod* considered negatively is the 4th arcanum.

This leads me to conclude—

That the 5th arcanum is the reflex of the 4th arcanum.

All the arcana can be explained in this way by each other, according to the above rules.

This tableau is the key of the *Ars Magna* of Raymond Lulle.

CORRESPONDENCE BETWEEN THE CARDS OF THE TAROT.

To obtain the origin and derivation of any card in the Tarot, it suffices to take the third card before it, and the third card after it.

Thus the 8th arcanum is derived from the 5th arcanum, and gives rise to the 11th arcanum.

5	8	11
Universal life.	Elementary existence.	Reflected and transitory life.

**

From this it ensues that, when two cards added together give an *even* number, we need only take the half of the number to discover the card which serves to *unite* those under consideration.

Thus, in order to discover the link which binds the 4th arcanum to the 6th, *i.e.* the universal vivifying fluid, to universal love, I add together $4+6=10$, and I take one-half of the number obtained $\frac{10}{2} = 5$.

The 5th arcanum (universal life) therefore unites the two opposites.[1]

The passage of the vivifying fluid (4) into love (6) is performed through the medium of universal life (5).

Since each card of the Tarot has three meanings, it is easy to philosophize by means of our pack, without taking too much trouble about it.

*
* *

Another result of this rule is, that each card of the Tarot has a complementary in any card bearing a number which, added to its own, gives a total of 22.

For instance, what is the complementary card of the 1st arcanum?

It is the 21st arcanum, since $21 + 1 = 22$. What is the transition from 1 to 21?

According to what we have just stated it is $21 + 1 = \frac{22}{2} = 11$.

The 11th arcanum (reflected and transitory life) therefore forms the transition between the 1st arcanum (creative principle) and the 21st arcanum (universal generation).

To find the card that serves as complementary to any other, we must therefore subtract the number of the card in question from 22.

For instance to find the complementary card to 14—

$$22 - 14 = 8.$$

The 8th arcanum is therefore complementary to the 14th. We have made this digression because all these details

---

[1] The Hebrew alphabet thoroughly establishes this affiliation for the letters corresponding to these three numbers. (See 8th arcanum.)

will be most useful to us presently. We can now return to the study of our major arcana.

Let us once more recall the manner in which the four first arcana have given us the key to the symbolism of all the others, according to their affinities with the sacred word, as follows—

THE GENERAL LAW OF THE SYMBOLISM OF THE TAROT.

Positive
(1)
yod

Negative | *Transition*
Reflex of   (2) *he* ——|—— 2nd *he* (4)   *yod* of the
yod | following series

vau
(3)
Neuter
Union of *yod* and of *he*

CHAPTER IX.

HISTORY OF THE SYMBOLISM OF THE TAROT.

INQUIRY INTO ITS ORIGIN.

The Tarot is an Egyptian Book—Its Transformations—Mantegna's Pack—Venetian Tarot—Florentine Tarot—Bolognese—Hindu Tarot—Chinese Tarot—Modern Tarots—Etteila—Marseilles—Besançon—Watillaux—Oswald Wirth—Italian and German Tarots—Constitution of the Symbolism of the Tarot—The 16 primitive Hieroglyphic Signs—The 22 Hebrew Letters.

ORIGIN OF THE SYMBOLISM OF THE TAROT.

As we have already stated, each card of the Tarot represents a symbol, a number, and an idea.

We have endeavoured to avoid empiricism as far as possible in the course of these explanations; and therefore we first studied the numbers, for they are the most settled element, and give the most unvarying results in their combinations.

Relying firmly upon the basis which we have thus constructed, we can now study the symbols with absolute assurance.

We hope that for this purpose you have procured the Tarot[1] of Marseilles, the most correct in its symbolism, or

[1] See p. 89, the price of the Tarots and the addresses where they may be procured.

else the twenty-two keys designed by Oswald Wirth; perhaps—and this is really almost indispensable—you have both of them.

You need, then, only deal the cards upon the table, to see at once that the personages depicted upon them all wear *dresses of the Renaissance* period.

And yet, is this pack of cards of ancient origin? It does not appear so.

Look at your figures more attentively and you will soon perceive Egyptian symbols [the triple cross (No. 5), ibis (No. 17)] combined with these Renaissance costumes.

They at once prove that the Tarot of Marseilles is really the exact representation of the primitive Egyptian Tarot, slightly altered to the epoch denoted by the costumes. Only the gypsies possess the primitive pack intact.

The studies of those learned men who have investigated the Tarot have confirmed this fact by the strongest evidence. And the works of Chatto,[1] Boiteau,[2] and above all of Merlin,[3] show us that history corroborates our assertion.

Merlin conducted his researches very scientifically, and succeeded in discovering the original of our Tarot of Marseilles in an Italian Tarot at Venice, the father of all the later packs.

He believes also that he has discovered the origin of this Venetian Tarot in the philosophical pack of *Mantegna*.

But he cannot determine the origin of this pack, because

[1] Chatto, *Facts and Speculations on the Origin and History of Playing Cards in Europe.* 8vo. London, 1848.
[2] Boiteau, *Les Cartes à Jouer et la Cartomancie.* 4to. Paris, 1854.
[3] Merlin, *Origine des Cartes à Jouer, recherches nouvelles sur les Naïbis, les Tarots et sur les autres Espèces de Cartes.* A work ornamented with 70 illustrations. 4to. Paris, 1869.

HISTORY OF THE SYMBOLISM OF THE TAROT.

he one that Merlin believed to be the source of the Tarot is on the contrary a *reproduction*, made by one of the Initiates. The *Ars Magna* of Raymond Lulle was produced in the same way; it is drawn entirely from the Tarot.

We have given for reference the *pack of Mantegna*, known in the trade as the *cards of Baldini*, as well as the packs of the Italian Tarots, from which most of ours are derived.

The tableau [1] which indicates the connection between the Tarot packs and that of Mantegna ought to be reversed, and on the contrary show the cards of Mantegna derived from the Tarot, as we have stated.

Here are the figures of the Tarots. (See page 84.)

[1] Page 86.

MANTEGNA'S PACK.

E	D	C	B	A
1 The beggar.	11 Calliope.	21 Grammar.	31 Astronomy.	41 Moon.
2 The knave.	12 Urania.	22 Logic.	32 Chronology.	42 Mercury.
3 The artisan.	13 Terpsichore.	23 Rhetoric.	33 Cosmology.	43 Venus.
4 The merchant.	14 Erato.	24 Geometry.	34 Temperance.	44 Sun.
5 The Nobleman.	15 Polyhymnia.	25 Arithmetic.	35 Prudence.	45 Mars.
6 The Knight.	16 Thalia.	26 Music.	36 Strength.	46 Jupiter.
7 The Doge.	17 Melpomene.	27 Poetry.	37 Justice.	47 Saturn.
8 The King.	18 Euterpe.	28 Philosophy.	38 Charity.	48 8th sphere.
9 The Emperor.	19 Clio.	29 Astrology.	39 Hope.	49 Chief agent.
10 The Pope.	20 Apollo.	30 Theology.	40 Faith.	50 First cause.

E = Positions in life.
D = Muses and Arts.
C = Sciences.
B = Virtues.
A = The system of the Universe.

A = Trumps.
B = Sceptres.
C = Cups.
D = Pentacles.
E = Swords.

HISTORY OF THE SYMBOLISM OF THE TAROT.

ORIGIN OF THE OTHERS.

Minchiate of Florence, 97 cards, of which 40 are Tarots.	Venetian Tarot, 78 cards, of which 21 are Tarots.	Tarot of Bologna, 62 cards, of which 21 are Tarots.
0 The Foolish Man.	0 The Foolish Man.	0 The Foolish Man.
1 The Juggler.	1 The Juggler.	1 The Juggler.
2 The Grand Duke.	2 The High Priestess	2 The High Priestess.
3 The Emperor of the West.	3 The Empress.	3 The Empress.
4 The Emperor of the East.	4 The Emperor.	4 The Emperor.
5 Love.	5 The Pope.	5 The Pope.
6 Temperance.	6 The Lovers.	6 Love.
7 Strength.	7 The Chariot.	7 The Chariot.
8 Justice.	8 Justice.	8 Temperance.
9 The Wheel of Fortune.	9 The Hermit.	9 Justice.
10 The Chariot.	10 The Wheel of Fortune.	10 Strength.
11 The Old Man, with an Hour-glass.	11 Strength.	11 Fortune.
12 The Hanged Man.	12 The Hanged Man.	12 The Old Man.
13 Death.	13 Death.	13 The Hanged Man.
14 The Devil.	14 Temperance.	14 Death.
15 Hell.	15 The Devil.	15 The Devil.
16 Hope.	16 The Lightning-struck Tower.	16 Thunder.
17 Prudence.		
18 Faith.		
19 Charity.		
20 Fire.		
21 Water.		
22 The Earth.		
23 Air.		
24 The Scales.		
25 The Virgin.		
26 The Scorpion.		
27 The Ram.		
28 Capricornus.		
29 Sagittarius.		
30 Cancer.		
31 Pisces.		
32 Aquarius.		
33 The Lion.		
34 The Bull.		
35 The Twins.		
36 The Star.	17 The Star.	17 The Star.
37 The Moon.	18 The Moon.	18 The Moon.
38 The Sun.	19 The Sun.	19 The Sun.
39 The Universe.	20 The Last Judgment.	20 The Universe.
40 Fame.	21 The Universe.	21 The Angel.

CORRESPONDENCE BETWEEN THE PRIMITIVE ITALIAN PACKS AND THE MODERN TAROT—

Modern Tarot.	Mantegna.					
The King	King			No. 8 of Mantegna		
The Knight	Knight			6	—	
The Knave	Knave			2	—	
The Emperor	4 of the Tarot is the IX series E of Mantegna					
The Pope	5	—	X	—	E	—
Temperance	14	—	34	—	B	—
Strength	11	—	36	—	B	—
Justice	8	—	37	—	B	—
The Moon	18	—	41	—	A	—
The Sun	19	—	44	—	A	—
The Foolish Man (unnumbered)		Beggar		No. 1 Mantegna		
The Star	17		Venus	42	—	
The Chariot	7		Mars	10	—	
The Hermit	9		Saturn	47	—	
The Universe	21		{ Jupiter	46	—	
			{ First cause	50	—	

If, however, the existence of purely Egyptian symbols in these so-called Italian Tarots do not convince the reader, a few words on the transformation of the Tarot in the East, and in other countries of Europe besides Italy, will completely enlighten him on the subject.

HINDU TAROTS.

In spite of Merlin's assertions, the Tarot represents the summary of the scientific knowledge of the ancients. This is unquestionably proved by Chatto's researches amongst Orientals on this subject.

In fact the Indians possess a game of chess, the *Tchatu-*

ranga, evidently derived from the Tarot, from the manner in which the men are arranged in four series.

Elephants, chariots, horses, foot-soldiers.

The Mussulmen of India also possess a pack of cards that is derived from the old symbols of the Tarot: the *Gungeifu* or *Ghendgifch*.

This game is composed of eight series of twelve cards each, divided in this way—

Superior Section or Bishbur:	*Inferior Section* or Kunbur:
Crowns	Harps
Moons	Suns
Sabres	Royal diplomas
Slaves.	Bales of Merchandise.

CHINESE TAROT.

An inexperienced eye might find some difficulty in recognizing the Tarot in these games, but the Chinese have given us an irrefutable argument in favour of our assertion, in the arrangement of their Tarot, which is represented by the figure on page 88.

We have placed the correspondences of the minor and major arcana, and of the four letters of the tetragrammaton, above this figure.

A description of this Chinese pack will be found in Court de Gébelin (*Le Monde Primitif*), and in the work of J. A. Vaillant.

With regard to the foreign Tarots, we possess nearly all of them at the present time, and this induces us to name the various editions of the Tarot which we are now able to consult.

	MINOR ARCANA.			MAJOR ARCANA.	
yod	*he*	*vau*	*he*		
1	15	29	43	57	71
2	16	30	44	58	72
3	17	31	45	59	73
4	18	32	46	60	74
5	19	33	47	61	75
6	20	34	48	62	76
7	21	35	49	63	77
8	22	36	50	64	
9	23	37	51	65	
10	24	38	52	66	
11	25	39	53	67	
12	26	40	54	68	
13	27	41	55	69	
14	28	42	56	70	

MODERN TAROTS.

The following are the most important of these modern Tarots—

        The Tarot of Etteila.
        The Italian Tarot.
        The Marseilles Tarot.
        The Tarot of Besançon.

HISTORY OF THE SYMBOLISM OF THE TAROT.

The double-headed Tarot of Besançon.
The Tarot of Watillaux.
The German Tarot.
The Tarot of Oswald Wirth.

THE FRENCH TAROT PACKS.

The *Tarot of Etteila* is of no symbolic value, it is a bad mutilation of the real Tarot.

This pack is used by all our fortune-tellers. Its sole interest lies in the strangeness of its figures. It can be obtained for 5 or 8 francs from all the great card-sellers in Paris.

The *Tarot of Watillaux*, or pack of the princess Tarot, reproduces the minor arcana very correctly. It is worth consideration on this account.

The *Italian Tarot, that of Besançon and of Marseilles*,[1] are unquestionably the best which we now possess, particularly the latter, which fairly reproduces the *Primitive symbolical Tarot*.

FOREIGN PACKS OF TAROTS.

Besides the Italian we must quote the *German Tarot*, in which the symbols of the minor arcana are different.
For

The Cups are represented by		The Hearts
The Pentacles	—	The Bells
The Swords	—	The Leaves
The Sceptres	—	The Acorns

However, this Tarot is a very bad one.

---

[1] These Tarots are to be found in Paris, 20 Rue de la Banque, M. Pussey, at 4 francs; and one is published in London by Mr. George Redway, 15 York Street, Covent Garden.

THE TAROT OF OSWALD WIRTH.

It became necessary to have a Tarot pack in which the symbolism was definitely established. This work, suggested by Eliphas Levi, who defined the principles on which it was to be based, has been accomplished by Mr. Oswald Wirth.

This clever occultist, aided by the advice of Stanislas de Guaita, has designed the series of the twenty-two major arcana. These drawings reproduce the Tarot of Marseilles, with the symbolical modifications suggested by the researches of Eliphas Levi upon this important question.

Owing to the kindness of M. Poirel, who assisted the work by printing these designs, we now possess a marvellous symbolic document in the *Tarot of Oswald Wirth*.

It is therefore wise, as we have already said, for those who wish to study the Tarot very thoroughly, to procure the *Tarot de Marseilles*, and that of *Oswald Wirth*.

We shall use them both presently in our explanation of the symbolical meaning of each card.

But before passing to the study of these symbols, card by card, we must see if there are no means of positively defining the symbolism of the Tarot.

HOW CAN WE HOPE TO DEFINE THE SYMBOLISM OF THE TAROT CONCLUSIVELY?

We have already and sufficiently explained that the Tarot represents the ancient or occult science in every possible development.

If we then wish to find a solid basis for the study of the symbols represented in the 22 major arcana, we may put the Tarot on one side for an instant, and devote ourselves to this ancient science. It alone can enable us to attain our end, not in *finding* the explanation of the symbols, but in leading us to *create* them one by one, by reducing them from fixed and general principles.

We shall thus commence work of quite a new character, whilst avoiding, so far as possible, falling into those errors which arise from the effort to explain the symbols of the Tarot by themselves, instead of seeking for their solution at their original source.

The first step in the search for these particular symbols leads us to discuss the grave problem of the origin of symbolism itself.

We cannot enter upon, much less solve, this question by ourselves; we shall therefore quote the opinions of several writers upon this subject. Truth, having Unity for its criterion, the agreement of various conclusions in one point will be a valuable guide for us.

Claude de Saint-Martin, the unknown philosopher, states in his book, the *Livre des Rapports*, that the primitive alphabet is composed of sixteen signs. He received these data, so far as we can judge, from intuitive revelation, joined to the teaching of the Illuminism, of which he was one of the members.

Lacour, in his book on the Elohim or Gods of Moses, has inductively determined the existence of a primitive alphabet, also composed of sixteen signs. Another author, *Barrois*, pursuing inquiries of quite a different nature, also reaches the conclusion of the existence of sixteen primitive signs in his system of Dactylology.

But the labours of *Court de Gébelin*, and above all of *Fabre d'Olivet*, are the most remarkable in this respect. In his *Langue Hébraïque Restituée*, this learned Initiate established the existence of primitive hieroglyphic signs from which the Hebrew letters are derived.

All these writers, starting from very different points, agree in their conclusions, and this gives us a strong argument in favour of the truth of their inquiries.

But it matters very little to us whether these 16 primitive signs are the direct origin, either of the Hebrew, Sanscrit, Chinese, or Greek letters. The identity of source tends strongly to identity of results, and any one of these derivative alphabets will answer our purpose.

The Hebrew alphabet, composed of 22 letters, seems preferable to us, on account of the concordance between the number of its letters and that of the Arcana in our Tarot.

We shall therefore adopt, as the starting-point of our study, the Hebrew alphabet of 22 letters, derived from the 16 primitive hieroglyphic signs.

This conclusion is scarcely reached, when fresh light shines upon us from all sides.

Guillaume Postel[1] reveals to us the connection between the Hebrew letters and the Tarot; *Van Helmont fils*,[2] *Claude de Saint-Martin*,[3] *Fabre d'Olivet*,[4] all confirm our opinion; lastly, *Eliphas Levi*[5] also throws the weight of his marvellous learning into the question.

But we are more surprised to find that the *Sepher Yetzirah*,[6] an old book of the Kabbalah, which contains a study upon the formation of the Hebrew alphabet, arrives at a division of the letters which exactly corresponds with

---

[1] Clavis.
[2] *Origin of Language* (Latin).
[3] *Tableaux naturels des rapports qui existent entre Dieu, l'homme et l'Univers.*
[4] *La Langue Hébraïque Restituée.*
[5] *Rituel de la Haute Magie.*
[6] Translated into English by Dr. Wynn Westcott.

the astrological data contained in an old manuscript in the Vatican, upon which *Christian*[1] based his horoscopic works.

One single and identical conclusion arises from all these different points of view: the value of the Hebrew letter as a symbol.

In it we possess a real symbol, of which we can ascertain not only the meanings, but also the origin.

We could then make a Tarot exclusively composed of Hebrew letters and of numbers, but this is not our object; we are seeking to discover in the symbolism of the Hebrew characters the symbolism of the Tarot, and we shall thus realize our intention of ascertaining deductively the value of the figures of the Tarot and the reason they have been chosen.

THE HEBREW LETTERS AS THE BASIS OF THE SYMBOLICAL TAROT.

We shall now study the Hebrew letters one by one, in determining successively—

1st. The hieroglyphic value of each one of them according to its origin (Fabre d'Olivet, Barrois);

2nd. Its symbolic value derived from this hieroglyphic (Fabre d'Olivet, Eliphas Levi, Christian);

3rd. Its astronomical value (Christian and the *Sepher Yetzirah*).

Once acquainted with these data, it will be easy for us to deduce from them the application of the letters to the symbols of the Tarot.

But before we enter upon this study, it is necessary to say a few words upon the Hebrew alphabet in general and its constitution.

[1] *Histoire de la Magie.*

The alphabet of the Hebrews is composed of 22 letters; these letters, however, are not placed by chance, one after the other. Each of them corresponds with a number according to its rank, with a hieroglyphic according to its form, with a symbol according to its affinities with the other letters.

As we have already said, all the letters are derived from one amongst them, the *yod*.[1] The *yod* has generated them in the following manner (see *Sepher Yetzirah*)—

1st. Three mothers:

The A	(Aleph)	א
The M	(The Mem)	מ
The Sh	(The Shin)	ש

2nd. Seven doubles (double because they express two sounds, the one positive strong, the other negative soft):

The B	(Beth)	ב
The G	(Gimel)	ג
The D	(Daleth)	ד
The Ch	(Caph)	כ
The Ph	(Pe)	פ
The R	(Resh)	ר
The T	(Tau)	ת

3rd. Lastly, twelve simple, formed by the other letters.

To render this clearer, we will give the Hebrew alphabet here, indicating the quality of each letter and its rank. (See page 95.)

We have now given a fixed principle for symbolism in the Hebrew letter, and need not fear being deceived by the false interpretation of a costume, or of an incorrect figure. The Hebrew letter will be always there, to enlighten us upon obscure or difficult points.

[1] See above (p. 19): Study upon the word *Yod-he-vau-he*.

HISTORY OF THE SYMBOLISM OF THE TAROT.

We can therefore safely return to the Tarot, which we have left to make this digression.

NUMBERS IN ORDER	HIEROGLYPHIC	NAMES	VALUE IN ROMAN LETTERS	VALUE IN THE ALPHABET
1	א	aleph	A	mother
2	ב	beth	B	*double*
3	ג	gimel	G	*double*
4	ד	daleth	D	*double*
5	ה	he	E	simple
6	ו	vau	V	simple
7	ז	zain	Z	simple
8	ח	heth	H	simple
9	ט	teth	T	simple
10	י	Yod	I	simple and principle
11	כ	kaph	CH	*double*
12	ל	lamed	L	simple
13	מ	mem	M	mother
14	נ	nun	N	simple
15	ס	samech	S	simple
16	ע	ayin	GH	simple
17	פ	phe	PH	*double*
18	צ	tzaddi	TS	simple
19	ק	qoph	K	simple
20	ר	resh	R	*double*
21	ש	shin	SH	mother
22	ת	tau	TB	*double*

CHAPTER X.

THE SYMBOLICAL TAROT.

THE FIRST SEPTENARY, 1ST TO 7TH ARCANA. THEOGONY.

Scheme of Work—Key to the 1st Septenary—The 1st Card of the Tarot the Origin of all the others—The three Principles of the Absolute—The Trinity—Figure of the first Card and its Affinities—The High Priestess and the Beth—The Gimel and the Empress—The Daleth and the Emperor—The He and the Pope—The Van, the Lovers—Summary of the 1st Septenary—Constitution of God.

STUDY OF EACH OF THE 22 MAJOR ARCANA.

Scheme of Work.

WE shall now apply this general law of symbolism to each of the twenty-two major arcana.

We must here beg for the reader's careful attention in spite of the length of the subject under consideration. We shall make every effort to be as clear as possible, and therefore we shall first explain the scheme which we have adopted in the study of each of the cards of the Tarot.

(1st) We shall always start from the hieroglyphic sign which has given birth to the Hebrew letter. Court de Gébelin is the author whom we shall consult chiefly upon this subject.

(2nd) We shall explain from the hieroglyphic character

all the ideas that can be progressively deduced from it, and which characterize the Hebrew letter considered as a sign. Kircher and Fabre d'Olivet are our authorities in this work.

(3rd) When we have once defined the ideas signified by the Hebrew letter, we shall search for the application of these ideas in the symbolic figure of the Tarot.

Eliphas Levi,[1] Christian,[2] and Barrois[3] will aid us in our inquiries.

(4th) Lastly, we shall determine the meaning which must be attributed to the card of the Tarot, according to its numerical and symbolical affinities with all the others, in applying to it the general law of symbolism. This portion of our work is strictly personal.

(5th) We shall end the study upon each of the cards by a figure showing all that we have said.

We must warn the reader that the perusal of the recapitulations only will be of no use as a means of understanding the card of the Tarot, and that the best way will be to carefully follow the successive explanations of each card, with the Tarot before him.

We cannot end this opening chapter without alluding to the basis upon which we have established the astronomical relations of each card of the Tarot.

One of the most ancient books of the Kabbalah which we possess, the *Sepher Yetzirah*,[4] says that the three mother letters of the Hebrew alphabet correspond with the three worlds, the seven doubles with the seven planets, and the twelve simple with the twelve signs of the zodiac.[5]

---

[1] *Rituel de la Haute Magie.*   [2] *Histoire de la Magie.*
[3] *Dactylologie ou Langage Primitif.*
[4] Translated into French by Papus.
[5] See Franck, *The Kabbala*, Paris, 8vo.

Now in studying the astrological manuscript published by Christian, we have discovered that the numbers attributed to the planets by the author of this manuscript exactly correspond with the *double* Hebrew letters. The numbers attributed to the twelve signs of the zodiac exactly correspond with the simple letters.

We considered that this absolute agreement between two documents of such different origin deserved our serious attention, and we' have therefore given with each letter its astronomical correspondence.

THE SYMBOLICAL TAROT.

KEY OF THE FIRST SEPTENARY.

ARRANGEMENT OF THE FIGURES FOR STUDY.

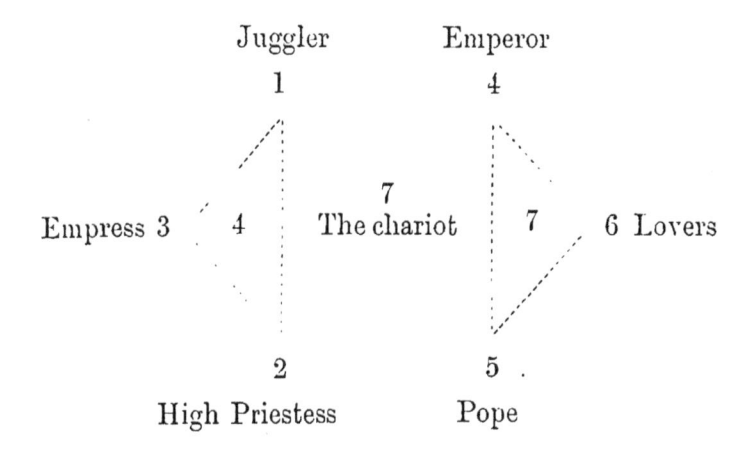

```
                Juggler           Emperor
                   1                 4

                         7
  Empress 3     4     The chariot     7     6 Lovers


                   2                 5
              High Priestess        Pope
```

CHARACTER OF THE FIGURES.

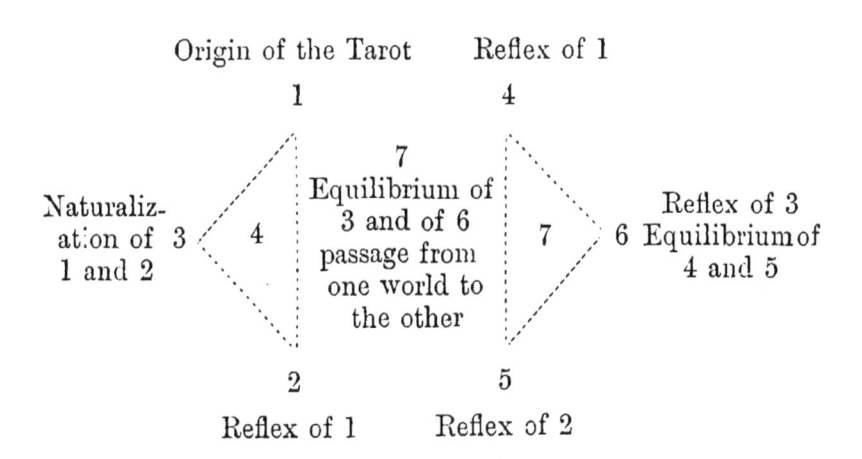

```
              Origin of the Tarot    Reflex of 1
                       1                  4

                              7
                         Equilibrium of
  Naturaliz-                3 and of 6                Reflex of 3
  ation of  3      4       passage from       7    6 Equilibrium of
  1 and 2                   one world to                4 and 5
                            the other

                       2                  5
                   Reflex of 1       Reflex of 2
```

THE FIRST CARD OF THE TAROT.

ORIGIN OF THE SIGNIFICATION OF ALL THE OTHERS.

We see from our preceding work that if we know the exact meaning of the first card of the Tarot we can, from that, discover the signification of all the others.

We cannot approach this subject without great hesitation. The hope of ascertaining the truth is, in fact, troubled by the possibility of making a mistake which might have very serious results.

The work which we have already accomplished will, however, enable us to decipher the meaning of the symbolism of the first card of the Tarot almost mathematically, but the general meaning only; whilst we know that each card must have not one, but *three meanings*.

We must discover three sufficiently general principles to be applied to every order of human knowledge; for this should be the object of the Tarot.

In this case we will, as usual, resort to those eminent authors who have treated these questions from different points of view, and the agreement between their teachings will give us new light to illuminate our path.

The Pole HŒNÉ WRONSKI,[1] who died of hunger in the suburbs of Paris, was perhaps one of the most powerful intellects produced by the 19th century. He asserted that he had discovered the formula of the absolute, and his works are unquestionably a summary of one of the most elevated syntheses that we have ever seen. We need not discuss the doctrines of Wronski, but will only say a few words upon the three primitive elements which enter into his law of creation.

[1] See *l'Occultisme Contemporain* (M. Carré).

Wronski places at the origin of all creation three elements, which he designates by the names—

Of Neuter Element (E. N.)
Of Element of Being (E. B.)
Of Element of Wisdom (E. W.)

The Neuter Element represents the Absolute, Reality resulting from the total neutralization of the two other elements by each other.

The Element of Wisdom represents the CREATIVE FACULTY with its especial characteristics, autogeny and spontaneity.

The Element of Being represents the PERMANENT FACULTY with its characteristics, autothesis and inertia.

Principle of the Creation or Element of Wisdom.
Principle of Preservation or Element of Being.
Principle of Neutralization or Neuter Element.

These are the three terms upon which Wronski establishes the foundations of Reality, and, consequently, of all the systems of creation. We must remember these conclusions.

FABRE D'OLIVET, in his researches upon the first principles which direct everything,[1] determines the existence of three elements, which he names Providence, Destiny, and Human Will.

Providence is the principle of ABSOLUTE LIBERTY, of the creation of beings and things.

Destiny is the principle of ABSOLUTE NECESSITY, of the preservation of beings and of things.

Lastly, the *Human Will* is a neuter principle intermediate between the two: the principle of mobility and CHANGE in all their forms. Now it is not necessary to be

---

[1] See *The Golden Verses* of Pythagoras, and the *Histoire Philosophique du Genre Humain.*

very learned to perceive the absolute agreement which exists between the two authors; the one, Wronski, reached his conclusions by mathematics, the other, d'Olivet, attained his by profound study of antiquity and its mysteries. The words used may vary, but the idea is fundamentally the same.

Wronski's Element of Wisdom (E. W.), the *principle of the creation*, is the same thing as the Providence of d'Olivet, who thus places it as the principle of the creation.

Wronski's Element of Being (E. B.), the *principle of the permanent faculty*, exactly represents what d'Olivet calls Destiny, and which he concludes to be the principle of preservation.

Lastly, d'Olivet's human Will corresponds in all points with Wronski's Neuter Element.

Here then are two very different systems, which lead to the same signification. But our conclusions do not stop here.

If we study these three primitive principles more attentively we shall find in the first: Providence or the Element of Wisdom, represented in philosophy by the word *God*.

Destiny or Being shows us its identity with the immutable laws which govern the *Universe*.

Lastly, it does not require much study to prove to us that the human Will responds to Man.

God, Man, and the Universe.

This is the basis of all the esoteric philosophy of the ancients, and not only Wronski and Fabre d'Olivet agree in their conclusions respecting this mysterious ternary;

THE SYMBOLICAL TAROT.

occult science itself proclaims its identity with these principles by the mouth of all its disciples. *Hermes Trismegistus*, the *Holy Kabbalah, Neo-Platonicism* and the *Alchemists* through *Pythagoras* and all the Greek philosophers assert the division of the Great All into THREE ENTITIES OR WORLDS.

In less remote ages *Guillaume Postel*[1] gives the key of the Tarot without explaining it, and the basis of this key is formed by this mysterious entity—

DEUS, HOMO, RÓTA.

Trithemie and his pupil *Cornelius Agrippa*[2] also give us this fecund and sublime trinity in all their analogical figures.

The Jesuit *Kircher*[3] describes this division into three worlds as the basis of the Egyptian mysteries.

Lastly, *Claude de Saint-Martin* has written a book entirely based upon the keys of the Tarot, and it is entitled—*Tableau Naturel des rapports qui unissent* DIEU, L'HOMME, ET L'UNIVERS.

Let us question India upon the law of the absolute, she replies—

Trimurti: BRAHMA, SIVA, VISHNU.

Let us ask China for the great secret of her philosophy, and she will give us the *Tri-grams of Fo-Hi*.

Address ourselves to one of the ancient initiated Egyptians, he will tell us—

[1] Clavis.
[2] *La Philosophie Occulte* (La Haye).
[3] *Œdipus Ægyptiacus.*

Osiris, Isis, Horus.

The founder of *Greek Cosmogony*, the disciple of the science of Egypt, *Hesiod*, also transmits this law to us, and they all confirm Louis Lucas when he states:[1] "I feel that hidden beneath this mystical formula of the Trinity is one of the most important scientific laws that man has ever discovered."

God, Man, and the Universe, these are the most general principles that we can attain, and they constitute the three meanings of the first card of the Tarot.

It remains for us to ascertain first, whether these meanings respond to the primitive hieroglyphic, and then to determine how far they extend through the whole Tarot.

[1] See *Le Roman Alchimique*.

THE SYMBOLICAL TAROT.

THE JUGGLER.

THE JUGGLER.

1. א

1st Hebrew letter (Aleph).

ORIGIN OF THE SYMBOLISM OF THE FIRST CARD OF THE TAROT.

The Aleph hieroglyphically expresses *Man* himself as a collective unity, the master principle, ruler of the earth.

From this hieroglyphic meaning are derived ideas of the *Unity* and of the *principle which determines it*, ideas which give to Aleph its value as the sign of Power and Stability.

Man, or the Microcosm, the Unity and the Principle in all the worlds, is the meaning of the primitive hieroglyphic, which, as we see, exactly renders the general ideas which we have established.

But attentive consideration of this first card of the Tarot will enlighten us still further.

Symbolism of the First Card of the Tarot.

THE JUGGLER.

If you take the first card of the Tarot and examine it attentively, you will see that the form of the juggler depicted upon it corresponds in all points with that of the letter Aleph. If we now apply to the study of this card the principles of the elucidation of symbolism, according to the *Traité Élémentaire de Science Occulte*, we at once find new explanations of it.

The top of the figure is occupied by the divine sign of Universal Life ∞ placed upon the head of the Juggler.

The bottom of the figure represents the Earth ornamented with its productions, the symbol of Nature.

Lastly, the centre is occupied by the Man himself, placed behind a table covered with divers objects.

The right and left of the figure are occupied by the hands of the Juggler, one of them bent towards the Earth, the other raised towards Heaven.

The position of the hands represents the two principles, active and passive, of the Great All, and it corresponds with the two columns *Jakin* and *Bohas* of the temple of Solomon and of Freemasonry.

Man with one hand seeks for God in heaven, with the other he plunges below, to call up the demon to himself, and thus unites the divine and the diabolic in humanity. In this way the Tarot shows us the *rôle* of universal mediator accorded to the Adam-Kadmon.

If we wish to make a summary of the meaning of the symbol, so far as we have now deciphered it, we can represent it in this way—

	Top		Head	
RIGHT				LEFT
(*Arm lowered*)	CENTRE	Human	*Body*	(*Arm raised*)
Necessity				Liberty
Evil	BOTTOM	Natural	*Feet*	Good

Yet the symbolism of this first card of the Tarot does not end here.

The Juggler holds the wand of the Mage in the left hand, which he raises, and the four great symbols of the Tarot are placed before him.

The Cup, the Sword, the Pentacles or Talisman, which, as we have already seen, exactly correspond with the letters of the Tetragrammaton—

Sceptre or Yod, symbol of the active Principle pre-eminent, and of God.

Cup or He, symbol of the passive Principle pre-eminent, or of the Universe.

Sword, Cross or Vau, symbol of the Equilibrist Principle pre-eminent, or of Man.

Pentacles or 2nd He, the cyclic symbol of Eternity, which unites the three first Principles in one Whole.

From the human point of view these symbols correspond with the four great human castes.

The men of Yod, or the Inventors, the Producers. The Nobility of Intellect.

The men of He, or the depositaries of the great truths discovered by the men of *Yod*: the Savants, the Judges. Professional nobility.

The men of Vau, or the guardians and defenders of the former: the Warriors. Nobility of the sword.

The men of the 2nd He, the multitude from which the other classes are continually recruited: the People.

The four great symbols are placed upon the table at random, and Man rules them and must arrange them; in the twenty-first arcana we shall find these symbols arranged in a cross.

We already know that the first card of the Tarot is completed by the twenty-first $(21+1=22)$, and we see why, if this first card represents *Microcosm*, the last would represent *Macrocosm*, and the eleventh card, which serves as the universal link to all the complements of the Tarot, represents the *Vital reflex Current*, which serves as a link between the worlds.

But we must not anticipate, so we will return to our first arcanum.

This symbol is the first of the whole Tarot,[1] and it bears the Unity as its characteristic number.

The Unity-principle, the origin of which is impenetrable to human conceptions, is placed at the beginning of all things. We cannot seize the origin of this primal cause, which we are content to assert according to the absolute law of analogies so well expressed by Eliphas Levi—

"Je crois à *l'inconnu* que Dieu *personnifie*,
Prouvé par l'être même et par l'immensité,
Idéal SURHUMAIN de la philosophie,
Parfaite Intelligence et Suprême Bonté."[2]

If we cannot follow this Unknown in its principle, it is

---

[1] It is curious to notice, when examining the position of the hands of the personages in the Tarot of Marseilles, how often this position represents the alphabetical letter to which the figure corresponds, according to *Barrois* (system of dactylology or primitive language). The arcana 1, 2 and 5 are especially noticeable in this respect.

[2] "I believe in *the unknown*, which God *personifies*,
Proved by existence itself and by immensity,
SUPERHUMAN *Ideal* of all philosophy,
Perfect Intelligence and Supreme Benignity."

least easy to us to follow it in its consequences, and therefore our study will be only the development of the unity-principle in creation, related according to the cosmogony of ancient initiation.

God, *Man*, and the *Universe* are, then, the three meanings of our first card, and we will now say a few words upon the application of these data to all the other cards of the pack.

EXTENSION OF THE THREE GREAT PRINCIPLES THROUGH THE TAROT.

The three meanings of the first card respectively represent—

    The Creator or *Yod*.
    The Receiver or *He*.
    The Transformer or *Vau*.

Lastly, the transition to the second *He*, which is not under consideration at present.

But the first card of the Tarot, taken *as a whole*, represents the *Creator or Yod*, the second card taken as a whole will therefore represent the *Receiver or He*, and the third the *Transformer or Vau*. Each of them will also show the four aspects of *Yod-he-vau-he* in the idea which it expresses.

But what is true of the ternary, is also true of the septenary, so that the first Septenary, taken as a whole, will represent the CREATOR.

The second septenary will represent the RECEIVER.

The third the TRANSFORMER.

Lastly, the ternary of transition will represent the return of effects to causes, and of consequences to the principle.

Let us condense this all by saying—

1st *septenary* represents God.
2nd *septenary*   —   Man.
3rd *septenary*   —   the Universe.

Moreover, each of these elements is contained in the two others in all points of their manifestations.

GENERAL RECAPITULATION.

We have now to recapitulate all the acceptations of the first card in a general figure. As each card in the Tarot will have the same recapitulation, we think it may be useful to explain the scheme followed in this arrangement.

At the head of the figure will be found the Hebrew number and letter of the card. Below it, the name usually given to the card in the Tarot.

To the right of the figure are the significations in the *Three Worlds*: Divine, Human, and Natural.

Below these three significations is found the *absolute key* to each card, according to the figure of the revolutions of the word *Yod-he-vau-he*. The Hebrew letters placed upon the upper line of this key indicate the origin of the card under consideration, the Hebrew letters placed above it indicate the exact meaning of the card.

THE SYMBOLICAL TAROT.

1. א
The Juggler.

AFFINITIES		SIGNIFICATIONS
		Key to the Card *yod* / yod
Primitive Hieroglyphic	Man	The divine creator or GOD the Father OSIRIS
Kabbalah	Kether	
Astronomy	No affinity	
		yod of yod / yod-yod
		The divine preserver MAN ADAM
		he of yod / yod-yod
OBSERVATIONS		The divine transformer THE ACTIVE UNIVERSE NATURA NATURANS[1]
		vau of yod / yod-yod
		2nd *he of yod* / yod-yod

[1] According to Spinoza the only free cause and substance of all modes or phenomena, conscious and unconscious, past, present, and to come. [A. P. M.]

THE HIGH PRIESTESS.   THE HIGH PRIESTESS.

2. ב

2nd Hebrew letter (Beth).

ORIGIN OF THE SYMBOLISM OF THE SECOND CARD OF THE TAROT.

The Beth hieroglyphically expresses the mouth of man as the organ of speech. Speech is the production of man's inner self. Therefore Beth expresses that inner self, central as a dwelling, to which one can retire without fear of disturbance. From this ideas arise of a Sanctuary, an inviolate abode for man and for God. But the Beth also expresses every production that emanates from this mysterious retreat, every internal activity, and from it issue ideas of Instruction, of the higher Knowledge, of Law; of Erudition, of occult· Science or Kabbalah.

Beth corresponds with the number 2, and astronomically with the moon. This number has given birth to all the passive significations emanated from the Binary, hence the ideas of reflection, of Woman; applied to the Moon relatively to the Sun, and to Woman relatively to Man.

THE SECOND CARD OF THE TAROT.
The High Priestess.

God himself, or God the Father, reflects himself, and gives birth to God the Man, or God the Son, the negative relatively to his creator. As we have seen, man is the divine receiver, therefore this second card of the Tarot will express all the ideas of the first conceived negatively.

The first card represents a man standing; this, on the contrary, bears the figure of a *seated woman*.

> (First idea of passivity) by the woman and by her position.

The man, endowed with all the attributes of Power, was placed in the midst of nature.

The woman is adorned with all the attributes of Authority and persuasion, and she is placed under the porch of the temple of Isis, between two columns.

> Idea of a sacred dwelling, of a divine recipient.
>
> The two columns, like the arms of the Juggler, express the Positive and the Negative.

The woman is crowned with a tiara, surmounted by the lunar crescent, she is enveloped in a transparent veil falling over her face. On her breast she bears the solar cross, and upon her knees lies an open book, which she half covers with her mantle.

This is the picture of Isis, of Nature, whose veil must not be raised before the profane. The book indicates that the doctrines of Isis are hidden; but she divulges to the magi the secrets of the true Kabbalah, and of occult science. We must admire this profound symbol.

I

The first card expressed Osiris in the three worlds; this second gives us the signification of Isis, the companion of Osiris—

In God it is the reflex of Osiris, the reflex of God the Father, Isis, or God the Son.

In Man it is the reflex of Adam of the absolute man: Eve, the woman, life (הוה).

In the Universe it is the reflex of *natura naturans*: it is *natura naturata*.[1]

2. ב

The High Priestess.

AFFINITIES		SIGNIFICATIONS
Hieroglyphic—	The Mouth of Man	Reflex of God the Father or Osiris
Kabbalah	*Chocmah*	GOD
Astronomy	*The Moon* ☾	the Son
Day of the Week	Monday	ISIS
Hebrew letter	Beth (Double)	*yod of he* he he
		Reflex of Adam
		EVE
		the woman
		he of he he he
OBSERVATIONS		Reflex of Natura naturans
		NATURA NATURATA
		vau of he he he
		2nd *he of he*

[1] That which follows from the divine nature.

THE SYMBOLICAL TAROT.

THE EMPRESS.

THE EMPRESS.

3. ג

3rd Hebrew letter (Gimel).

ORIGIN OF THE SYMBOLISM OF THE THIRD CARD OF THE TAROT.

The hieroglyphic meaning of the letter Gimel is the throat, the hand of man half closed in the act of prehension. Hence it signifies all that incloses, all that is hollow, a canal, an inclosure. The throat is the spot where the words conceived in the brain are formed, or I might almost say embodied, therefore the Gimel is the symbol of the material envelopment of spiritual forms, of organic generation under all its forms, of all the ideas springing from the corporeal organs or their actions.

Generation is the mystery by which the spirit unites itself to matter, by which the Divine becomes Human.

The signification of Venus-Urania, to which this card corresponds, is easily understood by the above explanations.

THE THIRD CARD OF THE TAROT.

The Empress.

This symbol would therefore signify ideas of generation, of embodiment in all the worlds.

A woman seen full face.

The human being becomes corporeal in the womb of a woman.

This woman is represented with wings, or in the centre of a radiating sun.

The idea of the spirituality of the vivifying Principle of all beings.

She holds an eagle in her right hand.

The eagle is the symbol of the soul and of life (Holy Spirit).

In the left hand she bears a sceptre forming the astrological sign of Venus.

The sceptre is held in the *left* hand to indicate the *passive* influence, which Nature, Venus-Urania, or the woman exercises in the generation of beings.

She wears a crown with twelve points, or twelve stars.

The sign of the diffusion of the vivifying Principle through all the worlds and of the sun, through the Zodiac.

The third card of the Tarot shows the result of the reciprocal action of the two first terms neutralizing each other in one principle. It is the *Neuter Element* of Wronski, the basis of every system of reality.

The absolute creative force, or Osiris, and the absolute preservative force, or Isis, neutralize themselves in the equilibrist force, which contains in itself the two very different properties of the two first forms.

In God this would be the equilibrium of the Father and of the Son, or—

God the Holy Ghost
HORUS
The universal vivifying force.

In Man this would be the equilibrium of the Adam-Eve—

Adam-Eve
or HUMANITY.

In the Universe this would be the equilibrium of *Natura naturans* and of *Natura naturata*—

THE WORLD
Conceived like a being.

3. ג

The Empress.

AFFINITIES		SIGNIFICATIONS *vau* / vau
Primitive Hieroglyphic	The hand in the act of prehension	God the Holy Ghost Horus THE UNIVERSAL VIVIFYING FORCE *yod of vau* vau-vau
Kabbalah	BINAH	
Astronomy	Venus ♀	
Day	Friday	
Hebrew letter	Gimel (double)	
		Adam Eve HUMANITY *he of vau* vau-vau
OBSERVATIONS		THE WORLD *vau of vau* vau-vau
		2nd *he of vau* vau-vau

THE SYMBOLICAL TAROT. 119

The creative principle and the receptive principle, ving, by their mutual action, given birth to the transming principle, a complete entity is created.

The term which now follows will correspond with the 2nd *he* of the sacred word, and will consequently indicate passage from one series to the other.

| THE EMPEROR. | THE EMPEROR. |

4. ד

4th Hebrew letter (Daleth).

GIN OF THE SYMBOLISM OF THE FOURTH CARD OF THE TAROT.

The hieroglyphic meaning of Daleth is the womb. It ;gests the idea of an object giving plentiful nourishnt, the source of future growth. The child is the living link, which in its neutrality reunites the opposition of the sexes; the Daleth therefore denotes abundance springing from division.

Like the 1, it is a sign of active creation; but this creation is the result of previous actions easily determinable, whilst the origin of the Unity is inaccessible to human conceptions. The Daleth expresses a creation made by a created being according to divine laws.[1]

The Daleth should be the image of the active vivifying principle of the Universe, Jupiter, the reflex of the Primal cause.

THE FOURTH CARD OF THE TAROT.

The Emperor.

This symbol should express in the *active* form all that the preceding card expressed in the *passive*.

A man seated in profile.

> The man indicates the active; his position, however, shows that this activity is engendered by a superior term. The 1st arcanum, the Juggler, the *active absolute*, was represented *standing*, looking to the front; the 4th arcanum, *active relative*, is seated in profile.

This man holds in his right hand the sceptre, the symbol of generation or of Venus ♀.

> The sceptre is held in the *right hand*, to indicate the *active* influence, which the vivifying principle exercises in nature, by opposition to the formative principle (arc. 3).

The man is bearded and wears a helmet with twelve points (six on each side). He is seated upon a cubic stone, which bears the figure of an eagle.

---

[1] See the *second He*, and the study upon the number 4.

THE SYMBOLICAL TAROT. 121

The helmet indicates the rule of the Divine Will in the Universe, and its universal action in the creation of Life (eagle).

The position upon the cubic stone indicates realization in all the worlds.

(1st) Realization of the Divine Word by the creation.

(2nd) Realization of the ideas of the Being shared by the quadruple work of the spirit—

  Affirmation,—Negation,
  Discussion,
  Solution.

(3rd) Realization of the actions conceived by the Will.

The man's legs are crossed, his body forms a triangle ⇑.

Domination of the Spirit over Matter.

Considered more attentively, the figure reproduces the mbol of Jupiter 2+, represented by the fourth card of e Tarot.

The fourth card of the Tarot corresponds to the *second* e, and therefore bears two very distinct aspects.

It first expresses a term of transition uniting the first ries (active and passive forces, the link between the two rces) to the following series; the passage from one world the other.

But it also represents this term of transition, itself coming the first term in the following series. As the llowing series taken as a whole is negative relatively to e first, the fourth symbol represents the active influence the first series 1, 2, 3, in the second series 4, 5, 6.

The 4 therefore expresses the reflections of the first rd in all its details. It acts towards the first series actly as the second card acted towards the first.

This interprets its meaning—

In the Divine. Reflex of God the Father—
THE WILL.

In the Human. Reflex of Adam—
THE POWER.

In the Natural. Reflex of Natura naturans—
THE UNIVERSAL CREATIVE FLUID.
The soul of the Universe.

4. ד

The Emperor.

AFFINITIES	SIGNIFICATIONS
Primitive Hieroglyphic { The Womb	Reflex of God the Father THE WILL
Kabbalah CHESED	
Astronomy Jupiter	Reflex of Adam THE POWER
Day Thursday	
Hebrew letter Daleth (double)	
OBSERVATIONS	Reflex of *Natura naturans* The universal creative fluid THE SOUL OF THE UNIVERSE

THE SYMBOLICAL TAROT. 123

THE POPE.   THE POPE.

5. ה

5th Hebrew letter (He).

ORIGIN OF THE SYMBOLISM OF THE FIFTH CARD OF THE TAROT.

The hieroglyphic meaning of He is aspiration, breath. It is by aspiration that life is incessantly maintained and created. Hence springs the idea of *all that animates* attributed to He.

But life specializes the being, by rendering it different from any other; hence the idea of the being itself attributed to this letter.

However, the action of life does not stop here. It is also the mediating principle, which attaches the material body to the divine spirit, in the same way that man unites God and Nature; life is to the man (*aleph*) what man is to the universe, pre-eminently the mediate principle.

Here we find the origin of the ideas of *bond*, of the reunion of opposing principles, of religion, attributed to He.

This letter is simple; astronomically it corresponds with the igneous sign of the Ram, which it explains.

THE FIFTH CARD OF THE TAROT.

The Pope.

This symbol expresses the following ideas—

   (1st) Idea of Life, of animation,
   (2nd) Idea of Being,
   (3rd) Idea of Reunion.

The Initiate of the mysteries of Isis is seated between the two columns of the sanctuary. He leans upon a triple cross, and makes the sign of Esoterism with his left hand.

> The triple Cross represents the triple *Lingam* of Indian theogony; that is to say, the penetration of the creative power throughout the Divine, the Intellectual, and the Physical Worlds, which causes all the manifestations of universal life to appear (first idea).
>
> The two columns symbolize: on the right, the Law; on the left, the Liberty to obey and to disobey, the essence of Being (second idea).

The Initiate wears a tiara. Two crowned men kneel at his feet, one clothed in red, the other in black.

> Here we find the *active* form of the symbolism expressed *in passive* form by the second card. The same idea of Esoterism, of secret Instruction, reappears; but the Tuition is now *practical and oral*, it no longer requires a book (third idea).

As we see, this card is the complement of the second;

he same rule applies to all the cards, when the total of heir number makes 7. Thus—

3		4
The Empress	is completed by	The Emperor
	4 + 3 = 7	
	7 = 28 = 10 = 1	
2		5
The High Priestess	is completed by	The Pope
	2 + 5 = 7	
1		6
The Juggler	is completed by	The Lovers
	1 + 6 = 7.	

The fifth card of the Tarot corresponds with the letter *ıe* of the sacred word. It is the direct reflection of the 4th arcanum, and the indirect reflection of the 2nd arcanum. It therefore signifies—

In the Divine. Reflex of the Will—
INTELLIGENCE
(characteristic of God the Son).

In the Human. Reflex of the Power—
AUTHORITY
(characteristic of the Woman).
Religion. Faith.

In Nature. Reflex of the Soul of the World, or of the Universal creative fluid—
THE UNIVERSAL LIFE
(characteristic of *Natura naturata*).

5. ה

The Pope.

AFFINITIES		SIGNIFICATIONS
Primitive Hieroglyphic	{ Breath	Reflex of the Will
		INTELLIGENCE
Kabbalah	Pechad	
Astronomy	The Ram	Reflex of Power
Month	March	AUTHORITY
Hebrew letter	He (simple)	RELIGION—FAITH
OBSERVATIONS		Reflex of the soul of the world
		THE UNIVERSAL LIFE

Universal life is the negative part of the vivifying universal fluid. Their reciprocal action will give rise to the *universal attraction* or *universal Love* represented by the 6th arcanum.

THE SYMBOLICAL TAROT. 127

THE LOVERS.   THE LOVERS.

6. ו

The 6th Hebrew letter (Vau).

ORIGIN OF THE SYMBOLISM OF THE SIXTH CARD OF THE TAROT.

The hieroglyphic sign for the Vau is the eye, all that relates to light and brilliancy. The eye establishes the link between the external world and ourselves; by it light and form are revealed to us. The dominant idea expressed by this letter will therefore be that *of a connection, of a link between antagonists.* We have already dwelt at some length upon the Vau, but we think it may be useful to quote Fabre d'Olivet's observations upon this letter *in extenso*—

"This sign is the image of the deepest and most inconceivable mystery, the image of the knot which reunites, or of the point which separates, the nothing from the being. It is the universal convertible sign, which forms the passage from one nature to the other; communicating on one side with the sign of light and of spiritual sense ו (a pointed Vau), which is but a higher form of itself; on the other hand linking itself in its degeneration with Ayin (ע), the sign of darkness and of the material senses, which again is but a lower form of itself."

The Vau is the second simple letter; astronomically it represents the second sign of the zodiac, the Bull.

THE SIXTH CARD OF THE TAROT.

The Lovers.

This symbol represents reunion, antagonism, with all their consequences.

A beardless youth (our Juggler of the 1st arcanum), but without a hat, is *standing* motionless in the angle where two roads meet. His arms form a diagonal cross upon his breast.

> The repetition of the 1st arcanum under another form. Here the man is not one of the Initiates. He does not know how to direct the magnetic currents of the Astral Light; he is therefore plunged in the *antagonism* of the different ideas which he cannot master.

Two women, one on his right, the other on his left, each with one hand upon his shoulder, point to the two roads. The woman on the right has a circle of gold upon her head, the one on the left is dishevelled and crowned with vine leaves.

> The two arms of the Juggler, expressing the positive and negative, the two columns of the temple of Isis, expressing necessity and liberty, are here personified by the two women, who represent Vice and Virtue.

The future of the young man depends upon the road which he chooses, whether he becomes one of the Initiates, the Mage of the 1st arcanum (the spiritual ꜥ), or the rash thunder-stricken personage of the 16th arcanum (the ע).

The spirit of Justice floats above this group in a radiant o; he bends his bow and aims the arrow of Punishment the personification of Vice.

A profound symbol indicating that if man chooses the path of Virtue he will not be left unaided, but that Providence will ally itself to his will and assist him to overcome vice.

In short, this hieroglyphic expresses the struggle ,ween the passions and conscience, the antagonism of as.

But this antagonism is also the most powerful natural ,ducer that exists in the world, when it resolves itself o Love, which attracts the opponents and unites them ever.

This sixth card of the Tarot must be regarded under ɔ aspects, which tend to the same signification.

1. As 3 of the 4, that is to say, as representing the ɩ arcanum, or the reflection of 1 considered in its ation to union.

2. As balancing 4 and 5; this is shown in the triangle med by the second ternary—

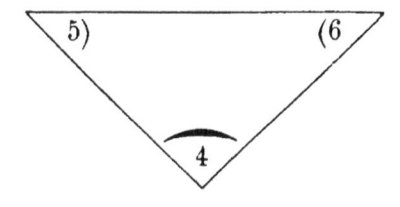

$$\begin{matrix} 5) & & (6 \\ & 4 & \end{matrix}$$

Each card balances the two others.

The 4 balances the 5 and the 6.
The 5 — the 4 and the 6.
The 6 — the 4 and the 5.

Its signification proceeds from this:—

In the Divine. The Equilibrium between Will and Intelligence—

BEAUTY

(characteristic of the Holy Spirit).

In the Human. The Equilibrium between Power and Authority—

LOVE

(characteristic of Humanity).

CHARITY.

In Nature. The Equilibrium between the Universal soul and the Universal life—

THE UNIVERSAL ATTRACTION.

Universal Love.

6. ו

The Lovers.

AFFINITIES		SIGNIFICATIONS
Primitive Hieroglyphic } The eye, The ear		Equilibrium of Will and Intelligence
Kabbalah	TIPHERETH	BEAUTY
Astronomy	The Bull	
Month	April	Equilibrium of Power and Authority
Hebrew letter	Vau (simple)	
		LOVE
		CHARITY
OBSERVATIONS		Equilibrium of the Universal Soul and the Universal Life
		THE UNIVERSAL ATTRACTION
		or
		UNIVERSAL LOVE

THE TAROT.

1st Septenary.

CONSTITUTION OF GOD.

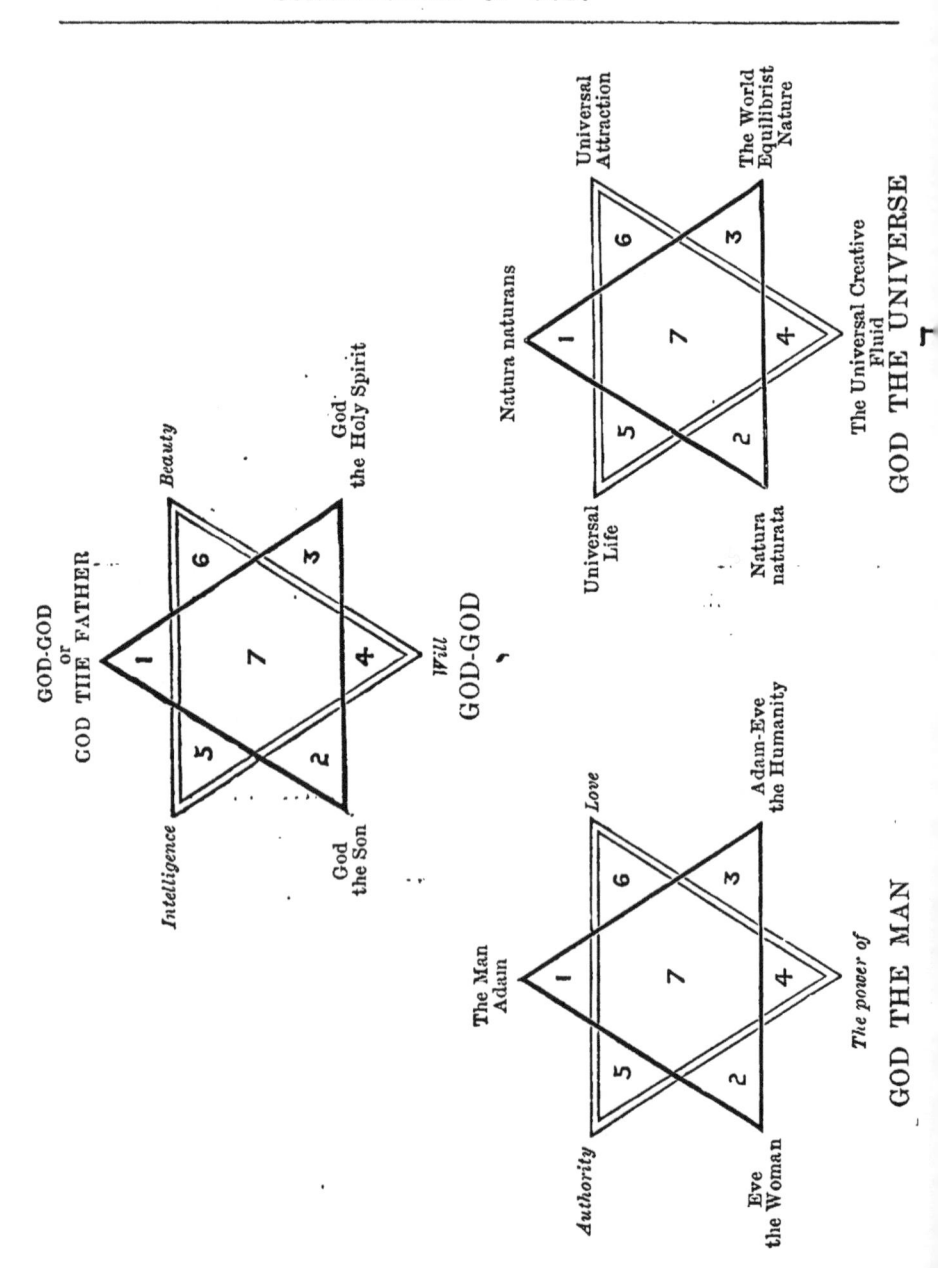

GOD-GOD or GOD THE FATHER
- Beauty
- God the Holy Spirit
- God the Son
- Intelligence
- Will
- (points 1–7)

GOD-GOD

GOD THE UNIVERSE
- Universal Attraction
- The World Equilibrist Nature
- The Universal Creative Fluid
- Natura naturata
- Universal Life
- Natura naturans

GOD THE MAN — *The power of*
- Love
- Adam-Eve the Humanity
- Eve the Woman
- Authority
- The Man Adam

CHAPTER XI.

SECOND SEPTENARY. ARCANA 7 TO 13.

ANDROGONY.

Key to the 2nd Septenary—The Zain and the Chariot—The Heth and Justice—The Teth and the Hermit—The Yod and the Wheel of Fortune—The Kaph and Strength—The Lamed and the Hanged Man.
Summary of the 2nd Septenary—Constitution of Man.

KEY TO THE SECOND SEPTENARY.

ARRANGEMENT OF THE FIGURES FOR STUDY.

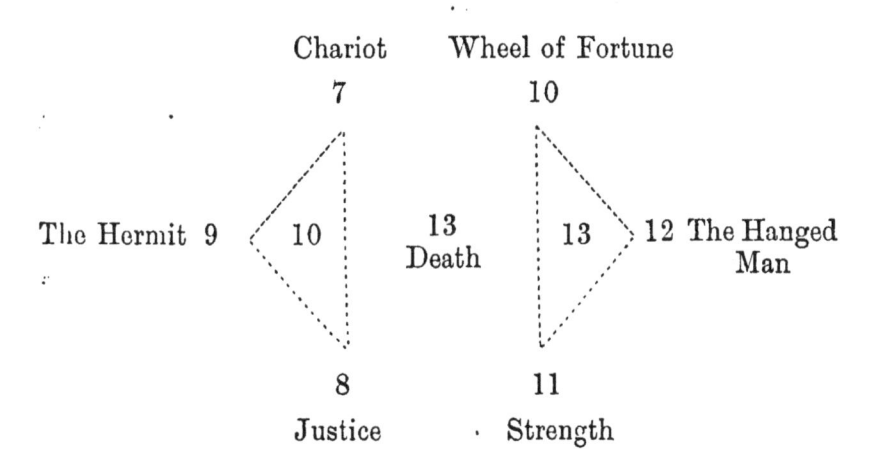

```
              Chariot     Wheel of Fortune
                 7               10

The Hermit 9    10       13          13    12 The Hanged
                        Death                     Man

                 8               11
              Justice         Strength
```

CHARACTER OF THE FIGURES.

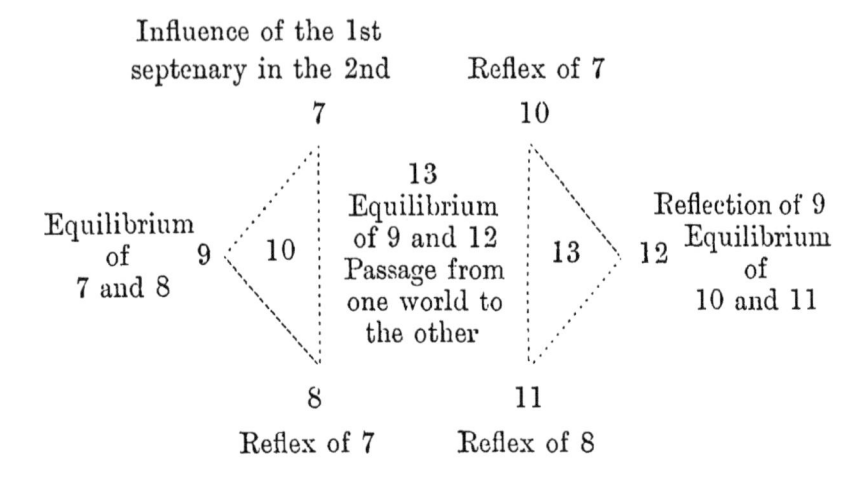

```
         Influence of the 1st
         septenary in the 2nd        Reflex of 7
                  7                      10

Equilibrium          ⟨ 10 ⟩    13              ⟨ 13 ⟩   Reflection of 9
    of        9              Equilibrium                Equilibrium
  7 and 8                    of 9 and 12         12         of
                             Passage from               10 and 11
                             one world to
                              the other
                  8                      11
              Reflex of 7            Reflex of 8
```

The 1st septenary has shown us the *World of principles*, or of the Creation under all its aspects; we shall now study the *World of laws*, or of Preservation.

---

7. ז

7th Hebrew letter (Zain).

ORIGIN OF THE SYMBOLISM OF THE SEVENTH CARD OF THE TAROT.

Hieroglyphically the Zain expresses an arrow, and therefore it suggests the idea of a *weapon*, of the instrument which man uses *to rule and conquer*, and to attain his object.

The Zain expresses victory in all the worlds. As a simple letter it corresponds with the astronomic sign of the Twins in the Zodiac.

SECOND SEPTENARY.

THE CHARIOT.   THE CHARIOT.

SEVENTH CARD OF THE TAROT.

The Chariot.

The symbolism of this card corresponds in all points with the ideas which it expresses.

A Conqueror, crowned with a coronet, upon which rise three shining Pentagrams of gold, advances in a cubical chariot, surmounted by an azure, star-decked canopy supported by four columns.

> This symbol reproduces the 1st and 21st arcana in another order of ideas. The four columns represent the four animals of the 21st arcanum, and the four symbols of the 1st arcanum, symbols of the *quaternary* in all its acceptations.
>
> The Conqueror, who occupies the centre of the four elements, is the man who has vanquished and directed the elementary forces: this victory is confirmed by the cubical

form of the chariot, and by the Pentagrams, which crown the Initiate.

The Conqueror has three right angles upon his cuirass, and he bears upon his shoulders the Urim and Thummim of the sovereign sacrificant, represented by the two crescents of the moon on the right and left; in his hand is a sceptre surmounted by a globe, a square, and a triangle. Upon the square, which forms the front of the chariot, we see the Indian *lingam*, surmounted by the flying sphere of Egypt.

Two sphinxes, one white, the other black, are harnessed to the chariot.

This symbol represents the sacred septenary in all its manifestations. The word *Yod-he-vau-he* is portrayed upon the front of the chariot by the winged globe, to indicate that the septenary gives the key to the whole Tarot. The two sphinxes correspond to the two principles, active and passive. The Conqueror corresponds especially with the *Sword* and the *Vau* of the sacred name.

The 7th card of the Tarot shôws the influence of the creation in the preservation of the Divine in the Human. It represents the *Yod* or the God of the 2nd septenary.

THE GOD *of the 2nd septenary.*
Man performing the function or God the Creator.
THE FATHER.

The law of the 2nd septenary.
REALIZATION.
(Reflex of the Power.)

The Man of the 2nd septenary.
Nature performing the function of Adam.
THE ASTRAL LIGHT.

SECOND SEPTENARY.

7. ז

The Chariot.

AFFINITIES		SIGNIFICATIONS
Primitive Hieroglyphic } Arrow		Man performing the function of God the creator
Kabbalah	Hod	THE FATHER
Astronomy	The Twins	The Realizer
Month	May	
Hebrew letter	Zain (simple)	Law
		THE REALIZATION
OBSERVATIONS		
		Nature performing the function of Adam
		THE ASTRAL LIGHT

The passage from one world to the other is scarcely performed, when we see the same law in action that we found in the 1st septenary. The second term of this series will be *the reflection* of the first, just as the second term of the first series also reflected the first. However, since this 2nd septenary is the central one, we shall find as the foundation of all its constituent arcana, the idea of mediation or equilibrium. This is shown by the eighth card.

JUSTICE.   JUSTICE.

8. ח

8th Hebrew letter (Heth).

ORIGIN OF THE SYMBOLISM OF THE EIGHTH CARD OF THE TAROT.

Hieroglyphically the Heth expresses a field. From it springs the idea of anything that requires labour, trouble, an effort.

Continued effort results in the establishment of an equilibrium, between the destruction of the works of man accomplished by nature, when left to herself, and the preservation of this work. Hence the idea of *balancing power*, and consequently of Justice attributed to this letter.[1]

---

[1] This letter, an intermediary between ה (He) and כ (Kaph), the one designating life, absolute existence, the other the relative life, assimilated existence, is the sign of *elementary existence:* it is the image of a kind of equilibrium, and attaches itself to ideas of effort, of labour, and of normal and legislative action.—FABRE D'OLIVET.

SECOND SEPTENARY. 139

Astronomically the Heth corresponds to the sign of Cancer in the zodiac.

THE EIGHTH CARD OF THE TAROT.

Justice.

The ideas expressed by this symbol are of *Equilibrium* in all its forms.

A woman seen full face, and wearing an iron coronet, is seated upon a throne. She is placed between the two columns of the temple. The solar cross is traced upon her breast.

> Here we find the continuation of the symbolism of the 2nd and 5th arcana. The seated woman occupies the centre between the columns, the first idea of the equilibrium between Good and Evil.

She holds a sword, point upwards, in her right hand, and a balance in her left.

> Occult science (2), at first theoretical, has become practical (5), and has been taught verbally. Now it appears in all the pitilessness of consequences, terrible for the false Magi (the Sword), but just toward the true Initiates (Balance). The signification of this arcanum is central between the 5th (ה He) and the 11th (כ Kaph) arcana.

This card is the complement of the eleventh, as the fifth was of the second. In the 1st septenary all the cards which, by addition, formed the number 7, completed each other; in the 2nd septenary all the cards which, added together, form 19, act in the same way.

7		12
The Chariot	is completed by	The Hanged Man
	7 + 12 = 19	
	19 = 10 = 1	
8		11
Justice	is completed by	Strength
	8 + 11 = 19	
9		10
The Hermit	is completed by	The Wheel of Fortune
	9 + 10 = 19	

The eighth card of the Tarot represents the conception in *preservative* of the second card. It synthetizes in itself the meaning of the second and of the fifth card of the Tarot, and represents the reflex of the seventh. It signifies—

1. *In the Divine.* God the Son of the 2nd septenary. The woman fulfilling the functions of God the Son.

The Mother.

Reflex of the Father. Preserver of God the Son in Humanity.

2. Passive law of the 2nd septenary.

Justice.

Reflex of Realization and Authority.

3. *The woman of the 2nd septenary.* Nature fulfilling the function of Eve.

Elementary Existence.

Reflex of the Astral Light. Preservation of Natura naturata in the World.

SECOND SEPTENARY.

8. ח
Justice.

AFFINITIES	SIGNIFICATIONS
Primitive Hieroglyphic } A Field	The woman fulfilling the functions of God the Son
Kabbalah NIZAH	
Astronomy Cancer	THE MOTHER
Month June	
Hebrew letter Heth (simple)	Law
	JUSTICE

OBSERVATIONS	Nature performing the function of Eve
	ELEMENTARY EXISTENCE

The elementary existence is the means by which the astral vivifying fluid or *astral light* (7) manifests itself through the ether or *astral matter* (9). This is demonstrated by the following arcanum.

THE HERMIT.   THE HERMIT.

9. ט

9th Hebrew letter (Teth).

ORIGIN OF THE SYMBOLISM OF THE NINTH CARD OF THE TAROT.

Hieroglyphically the Teth represents a roof, and suggests the idea of a place of safety, a protection. All the ideas arising from this letter are derived from the alliance of safety and protection given by wisdom.

Astronomically the Teth corresponds with the zodiacal sign of the Lion.

NINTH CARD OF THE TAROT.

The Hermit.

The following ideas are connected with this card—

    1. Protection.
    2. Wisdom, Circumspection.

An old man walking supported by a stick. He carries before him a lighted lamp, half hidden by the great mantle which envelopes him.

This symbol is midway between the sixth and the twelfth.

Protection is indicated by the mantle which envelops the old man.

Wisdom by the half-hidden lamp.

The stick indicates that the Sage is always armed to fight against Injustice or Error.

By comparing this card with two others, the sixth and the twelfth, we shall see that the beardless young man in the former (6th) has chosen the right path. Experience won in the labour of life has rendered him a prudent old man, and prudence united to wisdom will safely lead him to the higher level, which he is anxious to attain (12th card). The arrow shot by the genius in the sixth arcanum has become his support, and the effulgent aureole which surrounded the genius is now imprisoned in the lamp which guides the Initiate. This is the result of his prolonged efforts.

The ninth card of the Tarot represents the third conceived as preserver and recipient. It also balances the seventh and the eighth.

1. Humanity fulfilling the function of God the Holy Spirit.

The human creative force.

Human Love.

The preserving power of Humanity. The equilibrium of the Father and the Mother.

. 2. Equilibrium of Realization and Justice.

Prudence.
(Silence.)

3. Nature accomplishing the function of humanity. Equilibrium of the Astral Light and Elementary Existence.

The Natural Preserving Force.

The Astral Fluid.

9. ט

The Hermit.

AFFINITIES		SIGNIFICATIONS
Primitive Hieroglyphic } A Roof		Humanity accomplishing the functions of God the Holy Spirit
Kabbalah	Iesod	
Astronomy	The Lion	HUMAN LOVE
Month	July	
Hebrew letter	Teth (simple)	PRUDENCE
		Silence
OBSERVATIONS		
		The natural Preserving Force
		THE ASTRAL FLUID

SECOND SEPTENARY. 145

The astral fluid therefore represents the universal ·eservation of the active forces in nature. Here ends ιe first ternary of the septenary of Preservation. We all now see the reflections of all these terms in the llowing ternary.

THE WHEEL OF FORTUNE.   THE WHEEL OF FORTUNE.

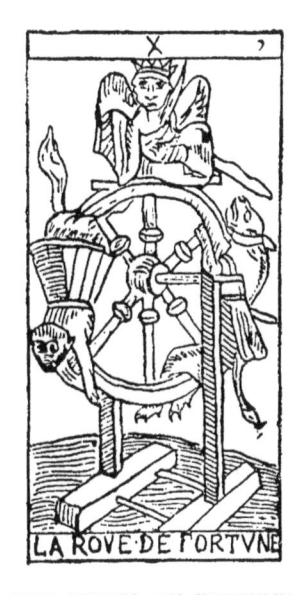

10. י

10th Hebrew letter (Yod).

:IGIN OF THE SYMBOLISM OF THE TENTH CARD OF THE TAROT.

The hieroglyphic meaning of the Yod is the finger of an; the forefinger extended as a sign of command. This tter has therefore become the image of potential manistation, of spiritual duration; lastly of the eternity of me, with all the ideas relating to it.[1]

[1] See the study of the word *Yod-he-vau-he.*

L

146   THE TAROT.

The Yod is a simple letter; astronomically it corresponds with the zodiacal sign of the Virgin.

TENTH CARD OF THE TAROT.

The Wheel of Fortune.

Two principal ideas are expressed by this symbol—

1. The idea of Command, of Supremacy.
2. The idea of the duration, of the eternal action of time.

The wheel of fortune suspended upon its axis. To the right *Anubis*, the genius of good ascending; to the left *Typhon*, the genius of evil descending, the *Sphinx* is balanced upon the centre of the wheel, holding a sword in its lion claws.

The first idea is expressed by the ternary, Anubis or positive, Typhon or negative, the balanced Sphinx the ruler.

The second idea is expressed by the wheel, a line without beginning or end, the symbol of eternity.

The 10th arcanum is midway between the 7th and 13th arcana.

$$7 + 13 = 20 \quad \frac{20}{2} = 10.$$

It expresses the incessant equilibrium, which modifies the creative realizations of the septenary by the necessary destruction by Death (arcanum 13). The three arcana, 7, 10, 13, correspond exactly with the *Hindu* trinity or *Trimurti*.

$$\begin{array}{lcl} \text{Brahma} = \text{Creator} & = & \text{Arcanum 7.} \\ \text{Siva} = \text{Destroyer} & = & \text{Arcanum 13.} \\ \text{Vishnu} = \text{Preserver} & = & \text{Arcanum 10.} \end{array}$$

SECOND SEPTENARY.

It represents the course of things according to the ternary law, which directs all the divine manifestations.

The tenth card of the Tarot commences the negative portion of the 2nd septenary, and expresses the notion of the septenary considered in its reflections.

It will therefore represent—

1. Reflex of will (see 4th arcanum).

    NECESSITY.

    The *Karma* of the Hindus.

2. Reflex of power and of realization.

    MAGIC POWER.

Fortune.

(To will.)

3. Reflex of the universal soul.

    FORCE POTENTIAL IN ITS MANIFESTATION.

10.
The Wheel of Fortune.

AFFINITIES		SIGNIFICATIONS
Primitive Hieroglyphic } The Forefinger		NECESSITY
Kabbalah MALCHUT		The *Karma* of the Hindus
Astronomy The Virgin		MAGIC POWER
Month August		Fortune
Hebrew letter Yod (simple)		*To Will*
OBSERVATIONS		Reflection of the universal soul FORCE POTENTIAL IN ITS MANIFESTATION

The absolute creative force has varied successively in the universal vivifying Fluid (4), and the astral Light (7); now it is represented by force potential in its manifestation. We shall see this force fully displayed in the following arcanum.

STRENGTH.   STRENGTH.

11. כ

11th Hebrew letter (Kaph).

ORIGIN OF THE SYMBOLISM OF THE ELEVENTH CARD OF THE TAROT.

The hieroglyphic meaning of the Kaph is the hand of man, half closed and in the act of prehension, like the Gimel. But the Kaph is reinforcement of the Gimel, so that we might say that it designates the hand of man in the act of *grasping strongly*. Ideas of strength are therefore applied to this letter.

SECOND SEPTENARY.

The number 11, the first after the decade, gives a different value to the Kaph, which designates a reflected transitory life, a kind of mould, which receives and restores every variety of form.

It is derived from the letter Heth, ח (8), which is itself derived from the sign of absolute life, He ה (5). Thus, allied on one side to the sign of elementary life (see the 8th arcanum), it joins to the signification of the letter Heth (ח) that of the organic sign ג (Gimel) (3rd arcanum), of which too it is merely a reinforcement.

The Kaph is a double letter, corresponding astronomically with March and Tuesday.

THE ELEVENTH CARD OF THE TAROT.

Strength.

Only two ideas are expressed by this arcanum—

1. The idea of strength.
2. The idea of vitality.

A young girl calmly closing a lion's mouth without any visible effort.

(First idea.)

This young girl wears the vital sign ∞ upon her head.

(Second idea.)

The 11th arcanum is midway between the 5th and 14th arcana. In it we find the symbolism of the 8th arcanum transformed to the physical plane. It is, in fact, the image of the power given by the sacred science (2nd arcanum) when justly applied (8).

The eleventh card of the Tarot shows us all the negative or reflective significations of the fifth, that is to say—

1. Reflex of the Intelligence (5).

    LIBERTY.

2. Reflex of Authority, of Faith.

    COURAGE.

    (To dare.)

3. Reflex of the Universal Life. Manifestation of the strength of the preceding arcanum.

  REFLECTED AND TRANSITORY LIFE.

11. כ

Strength.

AFFINITIES	SIGNIFICATIONS
Primitive Hieroglyphic { The Hand in the act of grasping	Reflex of the Intelligence
Astronomy Mars ♂	LIBERTY
Day Tuesday	
Hebrew letter Kaph (double)	Reflex of Authority, of Faith COURAGE (*To dare*)
OBSERVATIONS	Reflex of Universal Life Reflex and Transitory Life

SECOND SEPTENARY. 151

The strength, already potential in its manifestations, has shown its full force in the 11th arcanum; it will balance itself in the following arcanum.

THE HANGED MAN.   THE HANGED MAN.

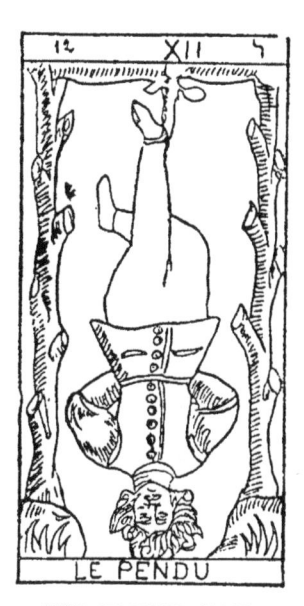

12. ל

12th Hebrew letter (Lamed).

ORIGIN OF THE SYMBOLISM OF THE TWELFTH CARD OF THE TAROT.

Hieroglyphically the Lamed designates the arm, and therefore it is connected with anything that stretches, that raises, that unfolds like the arm, and has become *the sign of expansive movement*. It is applied to all ideas of extension, of occupation, of possession. As a last sign, it is the image of the power derived from elevation.

Divine expansion in humanity is produced by the

prophets and revelation, and this inspires the idea of the *revealed law*. But the revelation of the law involves punishment for him who violates it, or elevation for him who understands it; and here we find the ideas of punishment, of violent death, voluntary or involuntary.

The Lamed, a simple letter, astronomically corresponds with the zodiacal sign of the Balance.

TWELFTH CARD OF THE TAROT.

The Hanged Man.

A man hanging by one foot to a gibbet, resting upon two trees, each bearing six branches, which have been cut off.

The man's hands are tied behind his back, and the fold of his arms forms the base of a reversed triangle, of which his head forms the point. His eyes are open and his fair hair floats upon the wind. His right leg crosses his left and so forms a cross.

> This young man is again the Juggler whose transformations we have already followed in the 1st, 6th, and 7th arcana.
>
> Like the sun placed in the midst of the signs of the Zodiac (six on each side, the lopped branches), our young hero is again suspended between two decisions, from which will spring, no longer his physical future, as in the 6th arcanum, but his spiritual future.

The 12th arcanum fills the centre between the 6th arcanum (Wisdom) and the 15th (Fatality). These arcana represent the two women of the 6th arcanum, regarded in the spiritual sense.

This Hanged Man serves for an *example* to the presumptuous, and his position indicates *discipline*, the absolute submission which the human owes to the Divine.

Considered alchemically, the Hanged Man shows the sign of personality.

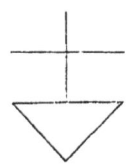

$$\underset{\triangledown}{\overset{\mid}{+}}$$

In the hermetic grade of the Rosy-Cross (18th degree of the Freemasonry of Scotland) one of the signs of recognition consists in crossing the legs like those of the Hanged Man. It is needless to say that the origin and meaning of this sign is quite unknown to the Freemasons.

The twelfth card of the Tarot represents Equilibrist Power. It neutralizes the oppositions of the tenth and eleventh cards.

1. Equilibrium of Necessity and Liberty—

CHARITY.—Grace.

(Preserving power of Love.)

2. Equilibrium of Power and Courage. Reflex of Prudence—

ACQUIRED EXPERIENCE.

(Knowledge.)

3. Equilibrium of the potential Manifestation (10), and of reflected Life (11). Reflex of the astral Fluid.

EQUILIBRIST FORCE.

12. ל

The Hanged Man.

AFFINITIES	SIGNIFICATIONS
Primitive Hieroglyphic } The Arm outstretched	**CHARITY** Grace
Astronomy — The Balance	
Month — September	**ACQUIRED EXPERIENCE** (Knowledge)
Hebrew letter — Lamed (Simple)	
OBSERVATIONS.	**EQUILIBRIST FORCE**

Modifying force is the last term of the 2nd septenary. By it the Astral will *realize itself* to pass into the physical, from the world of preservation and reception (2nd septenary) into the world of transformation (3rd septenary).

SECOND SEPTENARY.

CONSTITUTION OF MAN.

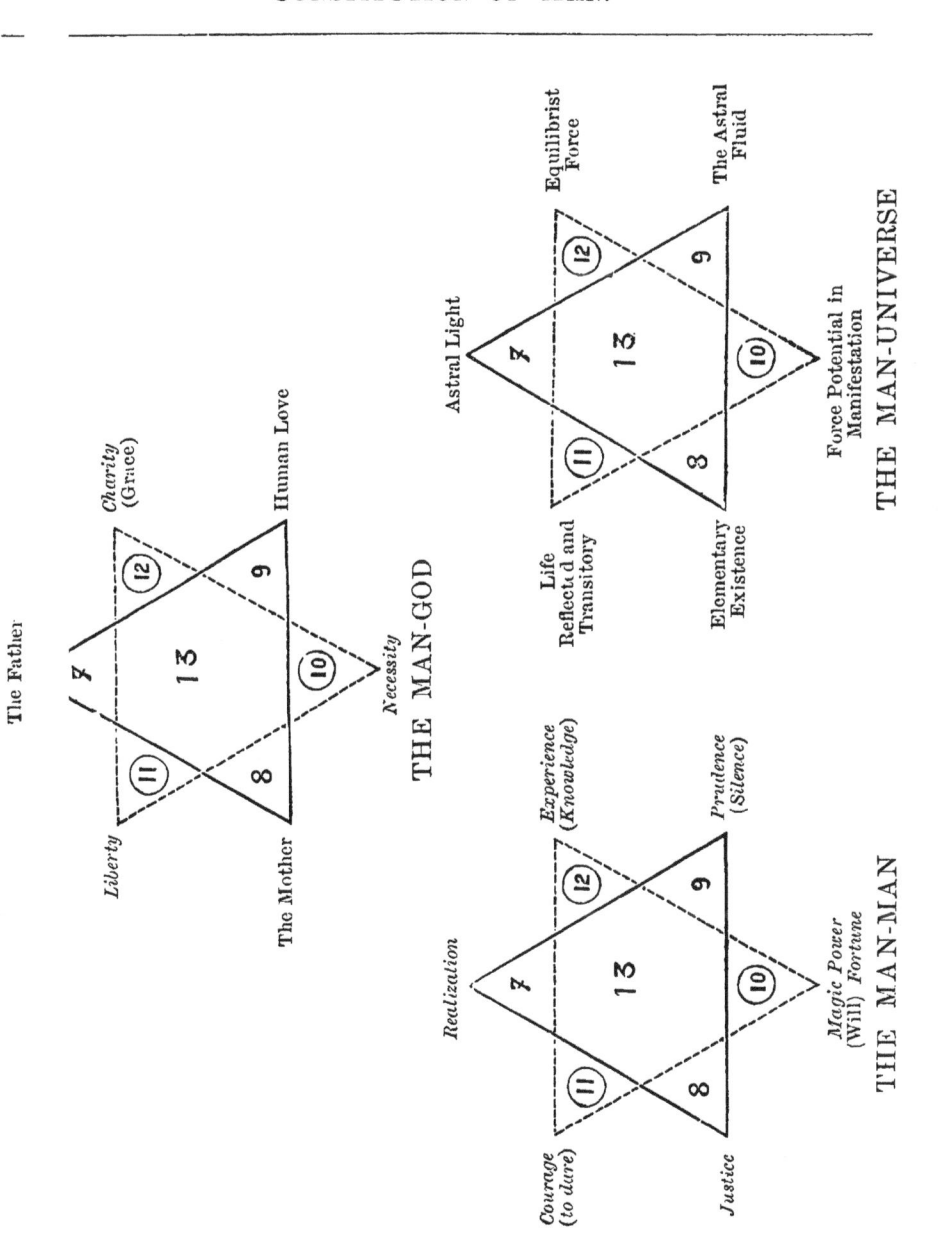

THE MAN-GOD

- The Father
- Liberty
- The Mother
- *Charity (Grace)*
- Human Love
- *Necessity*

THE MAN-MAN

- *Realization*
- *Courage (to dare)*
- *Justice*
- *Experience (Knowledge)*
- *Prudence (Silence)*
- *Magic Power (Will) Fortune*

THE MAN-UNIVERSE

- Astral Light
- Life Reflected and Transitory
- Elementary Existence
- Equilibrist Force
- The Astral Fluid
- Force Potential in Manifestation

CHAPTER XII.

THIRD SEPTENARY. ARCANA 13—19.

Key of the 3rd Septenary—The Mem and Death—The Nun and Temperance—The Samech and the Devil—The Ayin and the Lightning-struck Tower—The Tzaddi and the Moon.
Summary of the 3rd Septenary—Constitution of the Universe.

KEY TO THE THIRD SEPTENARY.

ARRANGEMENT OF THE FIGURES FOR STUDY.

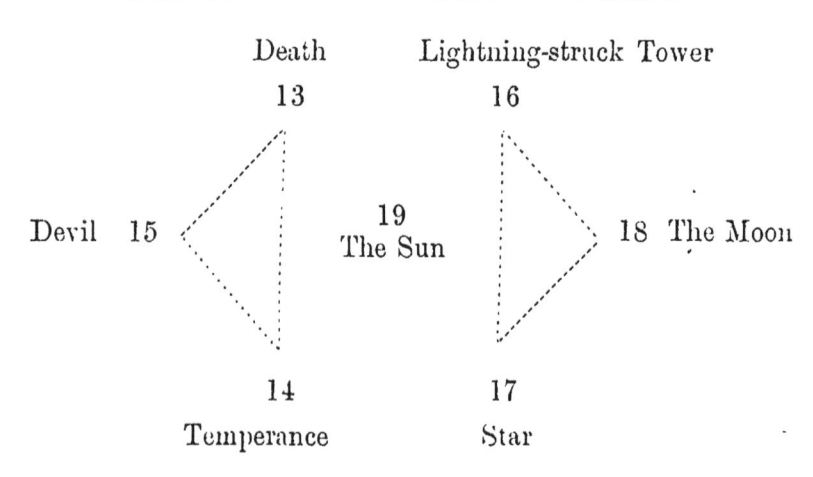

```
            Death           Lightning-struck Tower
             13                      16
              /\                     /\
             /  \                   /  \
Devil  15 <      \     19         /      > 18 The Moon
             \    \  The Sun     /    /
              \    \            /    /
               \    \          /    /
                \  /            \  /
                 14              17
              Temperance         Star
```

THIRD SEPTENARY.

CHARACTER OF THE FIGURES.

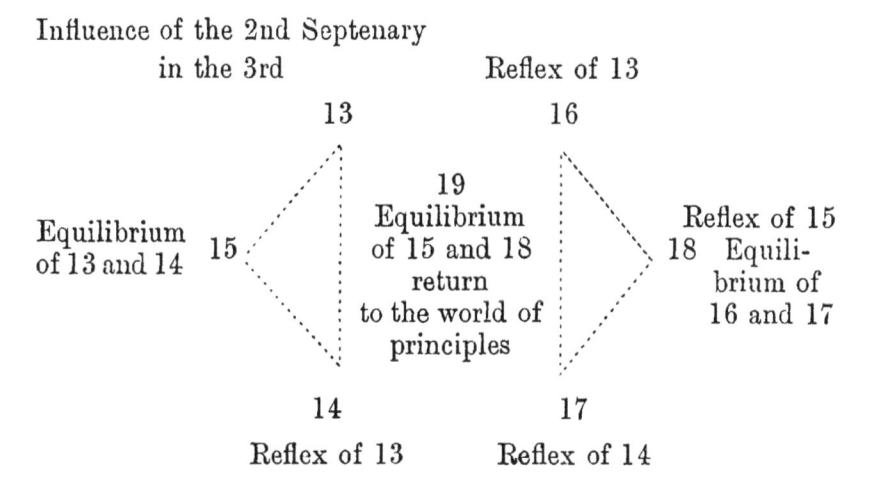

```
Influence of the 2nd Septenary
     in the 3rd              Reflex of 13
                   13                16
                         19
Equilibrium              Equilibrium           Reflex of 15
of 13 and 14   15        of 15 and 18       18 Equili-
                         return                brium of
                         to the world of       16 and 17
                         principles

                   14                17
              Reflex of 13       Reflex of 14
```

The first septenary has shown us the *World of Principles*, or of the Creation.

The second has developed the *World of Laws*, or of Preservation.

The third will now show us the *World of Facts*, or of Transformation. We shall now see how the circulation of the forces of the two first septenaries is established.

158 THE TAROT.

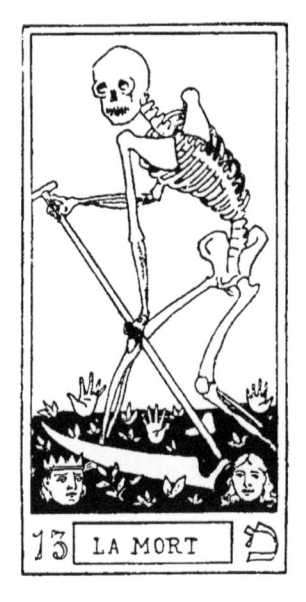

DEATH.

13. מ

13th Hebrew letter (Mem).

ORIGIN OF THE SYMBOLISM OF THE THIRTEENTH CARD OF THE TAROT.

The hieroglyphic meaning of the Mem is a woman, the companion of man, it therefore gives rise to ideas of fertility and formation. It is pre-eminently the maternal and female, the local and plastic sign, the image of external and passive action. Employed at the end of words, this letter becomes a collective sign ם (final Mem). In this case it develops the being in unlimited space.

Creation necessitates equal destruction in a contrary sense, and therefore the Mem designates all the regenerations that have sprung from previous destruction, all transformations, and consequently death, regarded as the passage from one world to the other.

The Mem is one of the three Mother letters.

THIRTEENTH CARD OF THE TAROT.

Death, or the Skeleton Mower.

The ideas expressed by this arcanum are those of destruction preceding or following regeneration.

A skeleton mows down heads in a field, from which hands and feet spring up on all sides, as the scythe pursues its work.

> The works of the head (conception) become immortal as soon as they are realized (heads and feet).

The 13th arcanum is explained by the 10th (Fortune) and by the 16th (Destruction), between which it stands.

$$10 + 16 = 26 \quad \frac{26}{2} = 13.$$

13 is therefore the centre between the Yod (Principle of the creation) and the Ayin (16), Principle of destruction.

The 13th arcanum is completed by the 18th, its complementary, as the fifth was of the second, and the twelfth of the seventh. (See the 8th and the 5th arcana.)

13		18
Death	is completed by	The Moon
	$13 + 18 = 31$	
	$31 = 4 = 10 = 1$	
14		17
Temperance	is completed by	The Stars
	$14 + 17 = 31$	
15		16
The Devil	is completed by	Destruction
	$15 + 16 = 31$	

THE TAROT.

The thirteenth card of the Tarot is placed between the invisible and the visible worlds. It is the universal link in nature, the means by which all the influences react from one world to the other. It signifies—

1. God the transformer—

THE UNIVERSAL TRANSFORMING PRINCIPLE.

Destructive and creative.

2. The negative of realization—

DEATH.

3. The Astral light accomplishing the function of the Creator—

THE UNIVERSAL PLASTIC FORCE.

(Balancing death and the transforming force.)

13. מ

Death.

AFFINITIES	SIGNIFICATIONS
Primitive Hieroglyphic } The Woman	THE UNIVERSAL TRANSFORMING PRINCIPLE
Hebrew letter Mem (one of the 3 mothers)	Destroyer and Creator
	DEATH .
OBSERVATIONS	THE UNIVERSAL PLASTIC FORCE

TEMPERANCE.　　　　　　TEMPERANCE.

14. נ

14th Hebrew letter (Nun).

ORIGIN OF THE SYMBOLISM OF THE FOURTEENTH CARD OF
THE TAROT.

The hieroglyphic sense of the Nun is the offspring of the female; a son, a fruit of any kind, all things produced. This letter has therefore become the image of the being produced or reflected, the sign of individual and corporeal existence.

As a final it is the sign of augmentation ן (Nun as a final), and gives to the word which receives it all the individual extension of which the thing expressed is susceptible.

Astronomically the Nun corresponds with the zodiacal sign of the Scorpion.

In short the Nun expresses the production of any combination, the result of the action of the ascending or creative forces, and of the descending or destructive forces figured by the star of Solomon.

FOURTEENTH CARD OF THE TAROT.

Temperance.

The following ideas are expressed by this symbol—

1. Combination of different fluids.
2. Individualization of existence.

The genius of the Sun pours the fluid of Life from a golden vase into a silver one.

(First idea.)

This essence passes from one vase to the other without one drop being spilt.

(Second idea.)

The fourteenth card represents the young girl whom we have already seen in the 11th arcanum, and whom we shall see again in the 17th.

The vital current placed upon her head in the 11th arcanum here passes from one vase into another, but will spread further in the 17th arcanum.

The fourteenth card of the Tarot shows us the fluid, hitherto carefully preserved, now freely circulated in nature.

1. Combination of active and passive fluids. Entry of Spirit into Matter, and reaction of Matter upon the Spirit—

INVOLUTION.

THIRD SEPTENARY.

2. Reflex of Justice in the material world—
    TEMPERANCE.
3. Fixation of reflex Life. Incarnation of Life—
    INDIVIDUAL AND CORPOREAL LIFE.

14. נ

Temperance.

AFFINITIES		SIGNIFICATIONS
Primitive Hieroglyphic } A Fruit		INVOLUTION (The Spirit descends towards Matter)
Astronomy	The Scorpion	
Month	October	
Hebrew letter	Nun (simple)	TEMPERANCE
OBSERVATIONS		INDIVIDUAL AND CORPOREAL LIFE

THE DEVIL.   THE DEVIL.

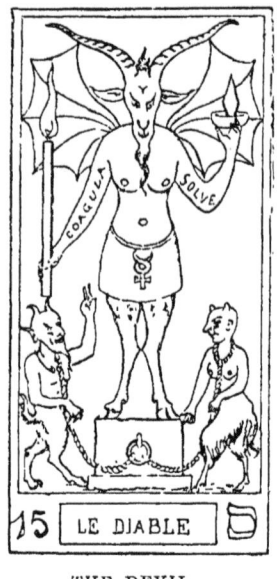

15. ס

15th Hebrew letter (Samech).

ORIGIN OF THE SYMBOLISM OF THE FIFTEENTH CARD OF THE TAROT.

The Samech expresses the same hieroglyphic sign as the Zain (7th arcanum), that is to say, an arrow; a weapon of any kind; but to this idea is here added that of the arrow making a circular movement, of any circle defining and delimiting a circumscription.

This idea of an impassable circle has given birth to that of Destiny, of Fatality, circumscribing the limits of the circle in which the human will can act freely; so that the Serpent forming a circle of his own body, biting his own tail, has always been the symbol of this Fatality, of this Destiny, encircling the world in its embrace. It is the image of the year (the ring), and of the fatal and settled revolutions of time.

As a letter, the Samech is the link (Zain) reinforced and turned back upon itself. As a simple letter, it corresponds with the zodiacal sign of Sagittarius.

FIFTEENTH CARD OF THE TAROT.

The Devil.

In every cosmogony the Devil represents the mysterious astral force, the origin of which is revealed to us by the hieroglyphic of Samech.

But a little attentive consideration of the symbol will show us that it contains several of the details which we have already seen in other figures of the Tarot, but under a different aspect.

If we place the Juggler by the side of the Devil we shall see that the arms of the two personages are using the same gesture, but in an inverse sense. The Juggler points his right hand towards the Universe, his left hand towards God; on the other hand the Devil raises his right hand into the air, whilst his left points to the earth. Instead of the magic initiating wand of the Juggler, the Demon holds the lighted torch, the symbol of black magic and of Destruction.

By the side of the Devil, and balanced by him, are two personages reproducing the same symbolism that we find in the two women of the Lovers (6), and in the two supports of the gibbet of the Hanged Man (12).

The universal vivifying force represented by the 3rd arcanum has here become the universal destroying force. The sceptre of Venus-Urania has become the Demon's torch, the Angel's wings have changed into the hideous pinions of the God of Evil.

The 3rd arcanum symbolizes the Holy Spirit, or the Providence of Fabre d'Olivet.

The 15th arcanum symbolizes the False Spirit, or the Destiny of Fabre d'Olivet.

$$15 + 3 = \frac{18}{2} = 9.$$

The 9th arcanum, which fills the centre between the two figures, symbolizes Prudence, or the Human Will of Fabre d'Olivet.

The Devil has materialized upon his head the universal fluid which surrounded the head of the Juggler; this is indicated by the two six-pointed horns which adorn him.

He stands upon a cube placed upon a sphere, to indicate the domination of Matter (the cube) over the Spirit (the Sphere).

The fifteenth card of the Tarot derives its signification from its own symbolism—

1. DESTINY (chance).
2. FATALITY, the result of the *fall* of Adam-Eve.
3. The astral fluid, which individualizes.

NAHASH, the Dragon of the Threshold.

THIRD SEPTENARY.

15. ס
The Devil.

AFFINITIES	SIGNIFICATIONS
Primitive Hieroglyphic } Serpent Astronomy Sagittarius Month November Hebrew letter Samech (simple)	DESTINY Chance
	FATALITY Result of the fall of Adam-Eve
OBSERVATIONS	NAHASH The Dragon of the Threshold

THE FIRE OF HEAVEN.
(*Lightning.*)

THE LIGHTNING-STRUCK TOWER.

16. ע

16th Hebrew letter (Ayin).

ORIGIN OF THE SYMBOLISM OF THE SIXTEENTH CARD OF THE TAROT.

The Ayin expresses the same hieroglyphic as the Vau (6), but materialized. It is the sign of *Material sense.* Again degenerated, it expresses all that is crooked, false, perverse, and bad.

Astronomically this letter corresponds with the zodiacal sign of Capricornus.

SIXTEENTH CARD OF THE TAROT.

The Lightning-struck Tower.

This card bears the picture of a tower, with its battlements struck by lightning; two men, one crowned, the other uncrowned, are falling with the fragments of broken masonry; the attitude of the former recalls the shape of the letter Ayin.

This card contains the first allusion to a material building in our pack, but we shall find the same symbol reproduced in the 18th and 19th arcana.

Here it signifies the invisible or spiritual world, incarnated in the visible and material world.

The 16th card represents the material fall of Adam. He will gradually become more materialized until the 18th arcanum, in which he attains the maximum of his materialization.

The significations of this figure are all derived from this idea of fall, of the materialization of the spiritual letter (Vau).

1. Materialization of God the Holy Spirit. (See 3rd arcanum.)

Entrance of the Holy Spirit into the visible World. The Holy Spirit acting like the God of matter.

DIVINE DESTRUCTION.

2. The materialization of the Adam-Eve, who have been spiritualized until now.

Entrance of the Adam-Eve into the visible World—

THE FALL.

3. Materialization of the Universe-principle—

THE VISIBLE WORLD.

16. ע

The Lightning-struck Tower.

AFFINITIES		SIGNIFICATIONS
Primitive Hieroglyphic	} Link (Vau) materialized	DIVINE DESTRUCTION
Astronomy	Capricornus	
Month	December	THE FALL
Hebrew letter	Ayin (simple)	
OBSERVATIONS		THE VISIBLE WORLD

THIRD SEPTENARY.

THE STARS.

17. פ

17th Hebrew letter (Phe).

ORIGIN OF THE SYMBOLISM OF THE SEVENTEENTH CARD OF THE TAROT.

The Phe expresses the same hieroglyphic meaning as the Beth (2nd card), but in a more *extended* sense. For, whilst the Beth signifies the mouth of man as the organ of speech, the Phe represents the produce of that organ: Speech.

It is the sign of speech and of all connected with it. The *Word in action* in nature with all its consequences.

Astronomically this letter responds to Mercury the God of Speech and of scientific or commercial diffusion, the God of Universal exchange between all beings and all worlds.

Phe is a double letter.

SEVENTEENTH CARD OF THE TAROT.

The Star.

The ideas expressed by this symbol are those—

1. Of the expansion of fluids.
2. Of their eternal renewal.

A nude female figure pours the Water of Universal Life from two cups.

> The genius of the Sun (14th arcanum) has now descended to earth under the form of this young girl, the image of eternal Youth. The fluids, which she formerly poured from one vase to the other, she now throws upon the ground (first idea).

This young girl is crowned with seven stars; in the midst of them shines a very large and brilliant one. Near her an ibis (or sometimes a butterfly) rests upon a flower.

> Here we find the symbol of immortality. The soul (ibis or butterfly) will survive the body, which is only a place of trial (the ephemeral flower). The courage to bear these trials will come from above (the stars).

The fall of the Divine and of the Human into the Material has scarcely taken place, when a mysterious voice whispers courage to the Sinner, by showing him future re-instatement through trial.

This card exactly balances the evil effects of the preceding one, and from it we derive the following significations—

1. *Opposition to destruction.* No destruction is final. Everything is eternal and immortal in God—

THIRD SEPTENARY. 173

IMMORTALITY.

Creation of the human soul.

2. The fall is not irreparable. This is whispered to us by the intuitive sentiment we name

HOPE.

3. The Visible Universe contains the source of its Divinization in itself. This is

THE FORCE WHICH DISPENSES THE ESSENCE OF LIFE,

which gives it the means of perpetually renewing its creations after destruction.

17. פ

The Star.

AFFINITIES		SIGNIFICATIONS
Primitive Hieroglyphic	Speech (the mouth and the tongue)	IMMORTALITY
Astronomy	Mercury	
Day	Wednesday	HOPE
Hebrew letter	Phe (double)	
OBSERVATIONS		THE FORCE WHICH DISPENSES THE ESSENCE OF LIFE

THE MOON.

THE MOON.

18. צ

18th Hebrew letter (Tzaddi).

ORIGIN OF THE SYMBOLISM OF THE EIGHTEENTH CARD OF THE TAROT.

The hieroglyphic idea connected with the Tzaddi is the same as that of the Teth (9th card); but it chiefly signifies a *term*, an aim, an end. It is a final concluding sign, relating to all the ideas of term, of secession, division and aim.[1]

The Tzaddi is a simple letter; it corresponds with the zodiacal sign of Aquarius.

[1] Placed at the commencement of a word it indicates the movement which leads towards the end; placed at the end it marks the term itself to which it has tended; it then receives this form, ץ. It is derived from the letter Samech ס (15) and the letter Zain ז (7), and it marks the secession of one or the other.

THE EIGHTEENTH CARD OF THE TAROT.

The Moon.

We have now traversed the steps which the spirit descends in its gradual and utter fall towards the material world. All is now ended; the spirit is completely materialized, and the change is indicated by the eighteenth card.

A meadow feebly lighted by the moon.

> The light, the symbol of the soul, no longer reaches us directly; the material world is only lighted by *reflection*.

The meadow is bounded by a tower on each side. Drops of blood are falling from the moon.

> The material world is the last point which the spirit can reach, it can descend no lower; this is shown by the boundaries of the field. The drops of blood represent the descent of the Spirit into Matter.

A path sprinkled with drops of blood loses itself in the horizon. In the centre of the field a dog and a wolf are howling at the moon, a crayfish is climbing out of the water between the two animals.

> The entry of the Spirit into Matter is so great a fall that everything conspires to augment it.
>
> Servile spirits (the dog), savage souls (the wolf), and crawling creatures (the crayfish) are all present watching the fall of the soul, hoping to aid in its destruction.

1. End of divine Materialization. Final point of involution—

CHAOS.

2. End of the Materialization of man—
   THE MATERIAL BODY AND ITS PASSIONS.
3. End of physical Materialization—
   MATTER.

18. צ

The Moon.

AFFINITIES	SIGNIFICATIONS
Primitive Hieroglyphic } A Roof	CHAOS
Astronomy Aquarius	
Month January	
Hebrew letter Tzaddi (simple)	THE MATERIAL BODY AND ITS PASSIONS
OBSERVATIONS	
	MATTER

Involution, that is to say, the descent of the Spirit into Matter, ends with the 3rd septenary.

The three last cards of the Tarot will show us how all the emanated forces gradually return to their common principle by *evolution*.

CONSTITUTION OF THE UNIVERSE.

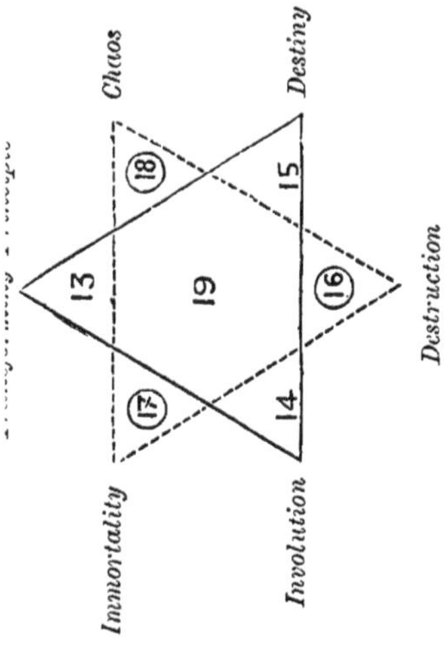
Chaos
Destiny
Destruction
Involution
Immortality
13
15
19
14
17
18
16

THE UNIVERSE-GOD.

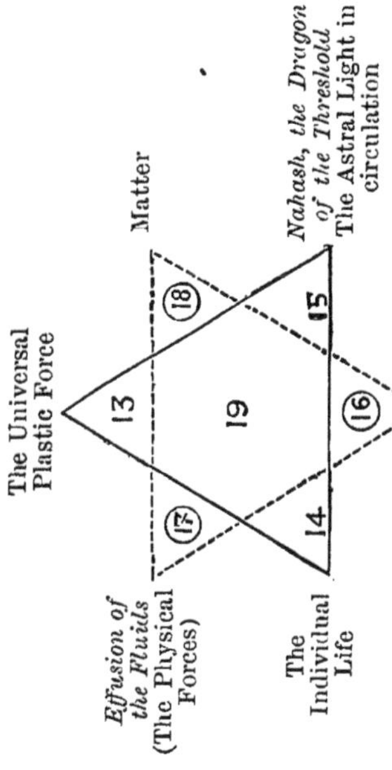
Matter
Nahash, the Dragon of the Threshold
The Astral Light in circulation
The Universal Plastic Force
The Visible World
Effusion of the Fluids (The Physical Forces)
The Individual Life
13
15
19
14
17
18
16

THE UNIVERSE-UNIVERSE

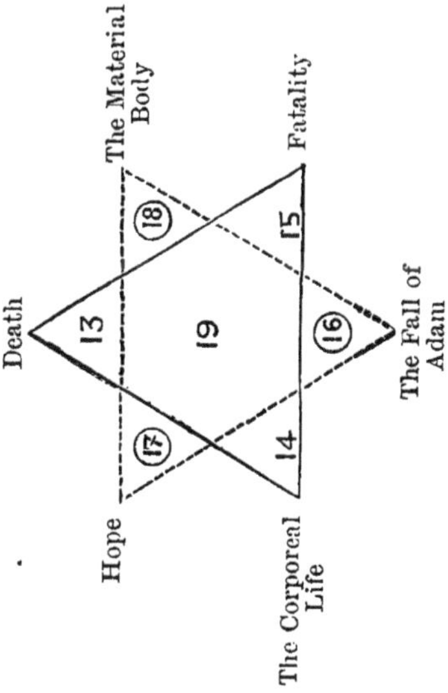
The Material Body
Fatality
Death
The Fall of Adam
Hope
The Corporeal Life
13
15
19
14
17
18
16

THE UNIVERSE-MAN

CHAPTER XIII.

GENERAL TRANSITION. ARCANA 19 TO 21.

The Qoph and the Sun—The Resh and the Judgment—The Shin and the Fool—The Vau and the Sun.
The Ternary of Transition.

THE SUN.   THE SUN.

19. ק

19th Hebrew letter (Qoph).

ORIGIN OF THE SYMBOLISM OF THE NINETEENTH CARD OF THE TAROT.

HIEROGLYPHICALLY the Qoph expresses a sharp weapon, everything that is useful to man; defends him; makes an effort for him.

The Qoph is therefore a particularly compressive, astringent, and cutting sign; it is the image of agglomerative, restricting form, and this gives rise to the idea of *material existence*.

This letter represents the letter כ (Kaph, 11) entirely materialized, applying itself to purely physical objects. Here is the progression of the sign—

ה (He, 5).   Universal life.
ח (Cheth, 8).   Elementary existence. The effort of nature.
כ (Kaph, 11).   Assimilated life, tending to material forms.
ק (Qoph, 19).   Material existence, becoming the medium of forms.

This is a simple letter; it corresponds with the sign of the Gemini.

NINETEENTH CARD OF THE TAROT.

The Sun.

Two naked children are shut into a walled enclosure. The sun sends down his rays upon them, and drops of gold escape from him and fall upon the ground.

The spirit resumes its ascendancy. It is no longer a reflected light, as in the preceding arcanum, which illumines the figure, but the direct creative light of the God of our Universe, which floods it with his rays.

The walls indicate that we are still in the visible or material world. The two children symbolize the two creative fluids, positive and negative, of the new creature.

1. Awakening of the Spirit. Transition from the material world to the divine world. Nature accomplishing the functions of God—

THE ELEMENTS.

2. The body of man is renewed—

NUTRITION. DIGESTION.

3. The material world commences its ascension towards God—

THE MINERAL KINGDOM.

GENERAL TRANSITION.

19. ק
The Sun.

AFFINITIES	SIGNIFICATIONS
Primitive Hieroglyphic { Axe, sharp-edged weapon	THE ELEMENTS
Astronomy The Gemini Month February Hebrew letter Qoph (simple)	NUTRITION Digestion
OBSERVATIONS	
.	THE MINERAL KINGDOM

THE JUDGMENT.

THE JUDGMENT.

20. ר

20th Hebrew letter (Resh).

ORIGIN OF THE SYMBOLISM OF THE TWENTIETH CARD OF THE TAROT.

The hieroglyphic meaning of the Resh is the *head of man*, and it is therefore associated with the idea of all that possesses in itself an original, determined movement. It is the sign of motion itself, good or bad, and expresses the renewal of things with regard to their innate power of motion.

The Resh is a double letter, and responds astronomically to Saturn.

GENERAL TRANSITION.

TWENTIETH CARD OF THE TAROT.

The Judgment.

An angel with fiery wings, surrounded by a radiant halo, sounds the trumpet of the last judgment. The instrument is decorated with a cross.

A tomb opens in the earth, and a man, woman, and child issue from it; their hands are joined in sign of adoration.

How can the reawakening of nature under the influence of the Word be better expressed? We must admire the way in which the symbol answers to the corresponding Hebrew hieroglyphic.

1. Return to the divine World. The Spirit finally regains possession of itself—

ORIGINAL DETERMINED MOTION.

2. Life renews itself by its own motion—

VEGETABLE LIFE.
RESPIRATION.

3. The material world progresses one degree in its ascension towards God—

THE VEGETABLE WORLD.

20. ר

The Judgment.

AFFINITIES	SIGNIFICATIONS
Primitive Hieroglyphic { The Head of Man Astronomy Saturn Day Saturday Hebrew letter Resh (double)	ORIGINAL AND DETERMINED MOTION
	RESPIRATION Vegetable Life
OBSERVATIONS	THE VEGETABLE KINGDOM

GENERAL TRANSITION.   185

LE FOU	LE·MAT
THE FOOL.	THE MATE.

21. שׁ

21st Hebrew letter (Shin).

ORIGIN OF THE SYMBOLISM OF THE UNNUMBERED CARD OF THE TAROT.

The Shin [1] expresses the same hieroglyphic meaning as the Zain (7th arcanum) and the Samech (15th) : this is an arrow, an object directed to an aim. But the movement which was direct in the Zain (ז), and which became circular in the Samech (ס), here takes the form of a vibration from one pole to the other, with an unstable point of equilibrium in the centre. The Shin is therefore the sign of *relative duration* and of the movement relating to it, whilst the

[1] This letter is derived from its vocal י (Yod), become a consonant; and it adds to its original meaning the respective significations of the letters ז (Zain) and ס (Samech).—FABRE D'OLIVET.

Samech expresses cyclic movement, and therefore absolute duration.

Shin is one of the three mother letters.

TWENTY-FIRST (UNNUMBERED) CARD OF THE TAROT.

The Foolish Man.

A careless-looking man, wearing a fool's cap, with torn clothes and a bundle upon his shoulder, goes quietly on his way, paying no attention to a dog which bites his leg. He does not look where he is going, so walks towards a precipice, where a crocodile is waiting to devour him.

This is an image of the state to which unresisted passion will reduce a man. It is the symbol of the *Flesh* and of its gratification. From a moral point of view the following verses of Eliphas Levi well explain this symbol—

> " Souffrir c'est travailler, c'est accomplir sa tâche,
> Malheur au paresseux qui dort sur le chemin ;
> La douleur, comme un chien, mord les talons du lâche,
> Qui, d'un seul jour perdu, surcharge un lendemain." [1]

1. More rapid return to the Divine World. Personality asserts itself—

THE MOTION OF RELATIVE DURATION.

2. The intellect roughly appears under the influence of evolution—

INNERVATION. INSTINCT.

---

[1] " Sorrow lessens in work, in fulfilling a task,
Woe to the sluggard who sleeps on his way ;
Like a dog at his heels pain clings to him fast,
If he leave for to-morrow the work of to-day."

3. The matter of the world attains the maximum of its material progression—

THE ANIMAL KINGDOM.

21. שׁ

The Foolish Man.

AFFINITIES	SIGNIFICATIONS
Primitive Hieroglyphic } The Arrow Hebrew letter } The Shin (one of the 3 mothers)	THE MOTION of Relative Duration
	INNERVATION Instinct
OBSERVATIONS	
	THE ANIMAL KINGDOM

THE WORLD.

THE WORLD.

22. ת

22nd Hebrew letter (Tau).

ORIGIN OF THE SYMBOLISM OF THE TWENTY-FIRST CARD OF THE TAROT.

The Tau has the same hieroglyphic meaning as the Daleth (fourth card), the womb; but it is chiefly the sign of reciprocity, the image of all that is mutual and reciprocal. It is the sign of signs, for to the abundance of the letter Daleth ד (fourth card), and by dint of the resistance and protection of the letter Teth, ט (ninth card), it adds the idea of PERFECTION, of which it is the symbol.

In the primitive Hebrew alphabet the Teth was represented by a cross (+). This letter is double, and in astronomy it represents the Sun.

TWENTY-FIRST CARD OF THE TAROT.

The World.

A nude female figure, holding a wand in each hand, is placed in the centre of an ellipsis, her legs crossed (like those of the Hanged Man in the twelfth card). At the four angles of the card we find the four animals of the Apocalypse, and the four forms of the Sphinx: the Man, the Lion, the Bull, and the Eagle.

This symbol represents Macrocosm and Microcosm, that is to say, God and the Creation, or the Law of the Absolute. The four figures placed at the four corners represent the four letters of the sacred name, or the four great symbols of the Tarot.

    The Sceptre or *yod* = Fire.
    The Cup or *he* = Water.
    The Sword or *vau* = Earth.
    The Pentacle or *2nd he* = Air.

These affinities can be represented thus—

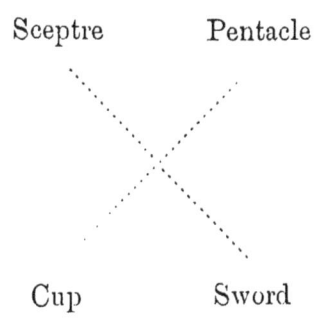

   Sceptre   Pentacle

      ✕

   Cup   Sword

Between the sacred word that signifies GOD and the centre of the figure is a circle or an ellipsis, representing NATURE and her regular and fatal course. From this comes the name of *Rota*, wheel, given to it by Guillaume Postel.

Lastly, the centre of the figure represents humanity, ADAM-EVE, the third term of the great series of the Absolute, which is thus constructed:—

    The impenetrable Absolute, the EN SOPH of the Kabbalists, the PARABRAHM of the Hindus—

The impenetrable Absolute or God   ... 1st septenary.
The soul of the Absolute or Man   ... 2nd septenary.
The body of the Absolute or the Universe 3rd septenary.

This twenty-first card of the Tarot therefore contains in itself a recapitulation of all our work, and proves to us the truth of our deductions.

A simple figure will sum up what we have said.

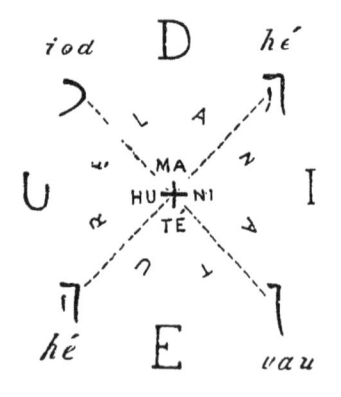

$$\begin{array}{ccc} iod & D & h\acute{e} \\ & \text{MA} & \\ U & \text{HU}+\text{NI} & I \\ & \text{TE} & \\ h\acute{e} & E & vau \end{array}$$

This symbol gives us an exact figure of the construction of the Tarot itself, if we notice that the figure in the centre represents a triangle (a head and two extended arms) surmounting a cross (the legs), that is to say, the figure of the septenary thus formed $\frac{\triangle}{+}$.

The four corners therefore reproduce the four great symbols of the Tarot. The centre represents the action of these symbols between themselves, represented by the ten numbers of the minor arcana, and the twenty-two letters of the major arcana. Lastly, the centre reproduces the septenary law of the major arcana themselves.

As this septenary is in the centre of three circles, representing the three worlds, we see that the sense of the twenty-one arcana is once more determined ($3 \times 7 = 21$).

The following figure indicates the application of the twenty-first card to the Tarot itself.

We shall also see that this card of the Tarot gives the key of all our applications of the pack to the Year, to Philosophy, to the Kabbalah, etc., etc.

THE TERNARY OF TRANSITION.

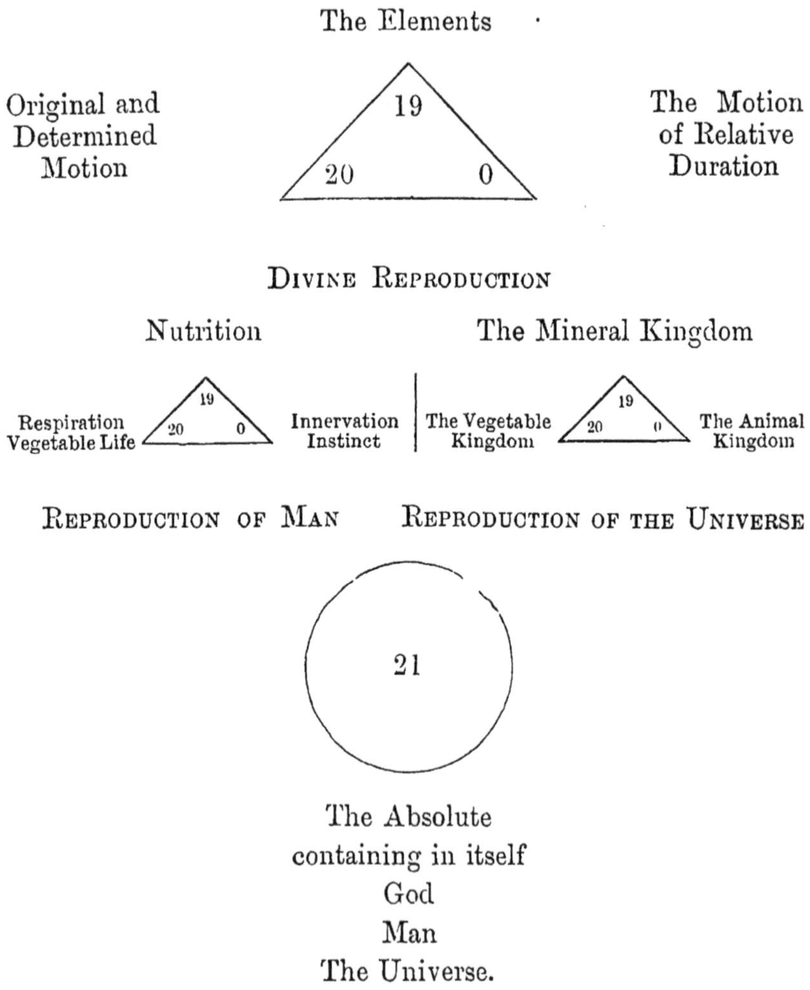

The Elements

Original and Determined Motion △ (19, 20, 0) The Motion of Relative Duration

DIVINE REPRODUCTION

Nutrition   The Mineral Kingdom

Respiration Vegetable Life △(19, 20, 0) Innervation Instinct | The Vegetable Kingdom △(19, 20, 0) The Animal Kingdom

REPRODUCTION OF MAN   REPRODUCTION OF THE UNIVERSE

(21)

The Absolute
containing in itself
God
Man
The Universe.

CHAPTER XIV.

GENERAL SUMMARY OF THE SYMBOLICAL TAROT.
THEOGONY—ANDROGONY—COSMOGONY.

Involution and Evolution. *Theogony*—The Absolute according to Wronski, Lacuria, and the Tarot—Theogony of divers Religions identical with that of the Tarot—Summary. *Androgony—Cosmogony*.
Figure containing the Symbolism of all the Major Arcana, enabling the Signification of each Card to be defined immediately.

GENERAL SUMMARY OF THE SYMBOLISM OF THE MAJOR ARCANA.

THEOGONY—ANDROGONY—COSMOGONY.

Having completed our study of the twenty-two major arcana, considered separately, we will now review as clearly as possible the knowledge which may be gathered from the preceding explanations.

We have already established from the study of the first card, that three primary principles are considered throughout their evolution: the Universe, Man, and God.

We need only recall *grosso modo* the sense of each card of the Tarot to prove the existence of a well-established progression, which starts from *God the Holy Ghost* to end in *Matter*, while passing through a number of varying

o

modalities. Another gradation leads from Matter to God, the primitive origin of all things.

This double current of the *progressive Materialization* of the Divine, or INVOLUTION, and of the *Progressive Divinization* of the Material, or EVOLUTION, has been too well studied by our eminent friend CH. BARLET, for us intentionally to vary from him in any way; we shall therefore quote his interesting work *in extenso*,[1] and thus enable the reader to see that our conclusions are absolutely identical, although we have been led to them by very different paths.

But our present object is to review as clearly as possible the meanings of the major arcana of the Tarot, regarded from a synthetic point of view. From the preceding chapters it will be seen that this study is really a COSMOGONY, or study of the creation of the *Universe*, crowned by an ANDROGONY, or study of the creation of *Man*, and even by an essay on THEOGONY, or study of the innate creation of God.

THEOGONY.

The Tarot places at the origin of all things the *Absolute* undetermined, undeterminable, the ONE, both knowing and unknowing, affirmative and negative, force and matter, unnamable, incomprehensible to man.[2]

The Unity manifests itself to itself by three terms, the highest and most general terms which the human comprehension can grasp; terms which form the basis of all theogonies, and which designate the same principles under a multitude of varying names.

[1] See p. 253.   [2] Ch. Barlet, *Initiation*, p. 10.

1. The first of these terms symbolizes *Absolute activity* in all its acceptations, the origin of all movement, of all masculine creative force.

God the Father: Osiris—Brahma—Jupiter.

2. The second of these terms symbolizes *Absolute passivity* in all its acceptations, the origin of all repose, of all feminine preserving force. It is the humid principle of nature, even as the first is the igneous principle.

God the Son: Isis—Vishnu—Juno.

The third of these terms is the most important to us. Synthetically it blends the two preceding terms in one Unity; all study should be commenced by it, for no being is conceivable unless it be considered synthetically, and the third term is the origin of all synthesis. It is *Absolute Union* in all its acceptations, the origin of all reality, of all equilibrium, of all equilibrist transforming force. It is the mercurial principle in nature balancing the two first.

God the Holy Ghost: Horus—Siva—Vulcan.

*

It is necessary to give a few explanations before we proceed further, in order that the deductions which follow may be intelligible to our readers.

We have said that no being is conceivable unless it be considered synthetically: we must now explain this sentence.

Let us take Man for our example, and follow the advice of Claude de Saint-Martin: "We must explain nature by man, and not man by nature."

Man, regarded synthetically, is composed of an *acting, animated body.*

If we would think of the being man as a body only, without reference to its animation or to its faculty of acting, its *reality* immediately disappears, it is no longer a man; we are considering but a phantom created by our spirit, a phantom which we can *analyze,* study in all its subdivisions, but which, since it conveys no *synthetic* idea, does not really exist.

If in the same way we wish to imagine by itself the principle which animates this body, which makes it live, the reality at once disappears. It is impossible for us to separate *the life* from the idea of the body, to conceive what this thing may be which is called the human Life, if we wish to see in it a kind of metaphysical being. It is on this point that materialistic savants find the most power in their arguments against exclusively idealist thinkers.

The difficulty increases considerably if it be a question of the principle which causes this body to act—of the Will, of the Soul. Analysis here, as elsewhere, can be brought into use, but we cannot possibly conceive what the soul can be like unclothed in a *form,* that is to say, in a principle that differs from itself. We picture to ourselves a small sphere, a winged head, in fact anything, according to individual fancy, but never the soul considered individually.

On the other hand, the moment we say A MAN, these three terms, thus *synthetised,* assume consistence and become the expression of a *reality,* and a being, formed of a body, a life and a will, defines itself quite clearly.

This synthetic action, the source of all existence and of all reality, is the innate property of the third term in our Trinity of principles. This is why the study of all realities should be commenced by this third term. Henri Wronski has always adopted this method; he names this principle the *Neuter Element*, and places it at the commencement of all his studies.

* ***

Consequently, the Trinity, composed of the three terms which we have specified, should be considered under two aspects.
1. We should first look at the *synthesis* of this trinity, the cause of its reality. The third term (God the Holy Spirit) contains these conditions in itself.
2. We should then *analyze* this synthesis by dividing it into its three constituent terms, and by determining the existence of the two opposite terms, active and passive, positive and negative. We must not forget that during this analysis we destroy the *reality* of the being thus divided into fractions.

Every reality, of whatever kind it may be, is therefore composed of *three terms*, and these three terms are contained in *one sole whole*. This truth is quite as applicable to physics as to metaphysics; the works of Louis Lucas upon physics and chemistry,[1] and of Wronski in mathematics,[2] are an irresistible argument against those who think that a philosophical principle is a *foolish idea*, without any practical import.

The third term of our theogonic series, or God the Holy Ghost, therefore represents the *whole body* of God, who can be *analyzed* in this way—

[1] Louis Lucas, *La Chimie Nouvelle*, Paris, 1854. 18mo.
[2] Wronski, *Messianisme*, 1825, fol.; and above all *Apodictique Messianique*, 1876, fol.

GOD THE HOLY SPIRIT
Synthesis
3

GOD THE SON   GOD THE FATHER
Antithesis   *Thesis*
2   1

To sum up all that we have studied so far, we will say that we have discovered, first of all—

1. An indeterminable and unnamable principle, of which we are content to assert the existence only—

2. This synthetic principle, when *analyzed*, is found to consist of a Trinity thus constituted—

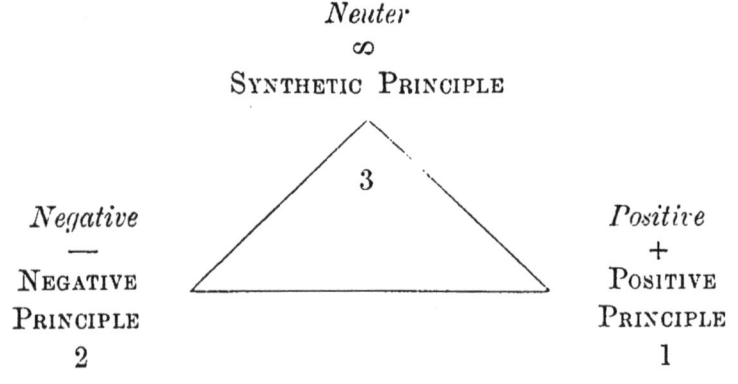

Neuter
∞
SYNTHETIC PRINCIPLE

Negative   *Positive*
—   +
NEGATIVE   POSITIVE
PRINCIPLE   PRINCIPLE
2   1

If we would use a common but very suggestive image, we should say—

The constitution of God is thus defined by the Tarot—

The Spirit of God, or *God the Father.*
The Soul of God, or *God the Son.*
The Body of God, or *God the Holy Spirit.*[1]

* * *

[1] Spirit is here taken in the sense of the *superior* and creative principle: soul in the sense of *median* and animator. Since many writers use these words in a different sense, it is useful to explain what is our meaning in this case.

GENERAL SUMMARY OF SYMBOLICAL TAROT.

We must now prove that the conclusions which we have reached through the Tarot agree in all points with those of every author who has treated the question on a higher level and with all the superior theogonies of antiquity.

1. THE PRINCIPAL AUTHORS WHO HAVE STUDIED THIS QUESTION.

We have chosen from amongst the authors who have studied this question of first principles, two writers who, starting from different points of view, support the conclusions of the Tarot: Lacuria and Wronski.

F. G. Lacuria.

This eminent writer, in his book on the *Harmonies of the Being expressed by Numbers*, starts in his deductions from the three words used by St. John: *Vita, Verbum, Lux*. He analyzes each of these words, establishes the connection that exists between it and the Christian Trinity, and defines each of the elements in this trinity—

"Here is the Trinity: the Father, who is *life* or immensity; the Son, who is *word* or form, and distinction or variety; the Holy Spirit, who is *light* and love, or unity. And these three persons are only one God. Their unity is not only in the external fact of their existence, but in the essence of things, *for they are inseparable in the thought of man;* no one can imagine one without the others" (p. 43).

"In the commencement was the BEING, the being is not undetermined, but it *is distinct* from the NON-BEING; it sees that it is the being, and these two points of view, participating in the unity of the substance which they affect, produce *by their union* THE CONSCIENCE, which is also light or harmony" (vol. ii. p. 333).

<table>
<tr><td>+
THE BEING
The Father
The Life</td><td>−
THE NON-BEING
The Son
The Word</td></tr>
</table>

∞
THE CONSCIENCE
The Holy Spirit
The Light

First principles of Lacuria.

Henri Wronski.

This author interests us doubly, for his conclusions not only agree with the data given by the Tarot, but they also throw great light upon them. Let us therefore listen to him (*Apodictique*, p. 5)—

"Thus the reality of the absolute, REALITY in itself or reality in general, is unquestionably the first determination of the very essence of the absolute, and consequently the *first principle* of reason. Without it as an indispensable condition, as we have just admitted it to be, every assertion made by reason would be valueless. And it is upon this fundamental principle of reason, upon this indestructible and in every way indispensable condition, that we shall now establish absolute philosophy itself with the same infallibility.

"In the first place this reality of the absolute, which we now recognize so profoundly, produces or creates itself; for, as we have already irrevocably concluded, the absolute, this indispensable term of reason, is that which is BY ITSELF. Thus this innate generation, this autogeny of the reality of the absolute, this creation by itself, is manifestly a *second*

GENERAL SUMMARY OF SYMBOLICAL TAROT.

determination of the very essence of the absolute; and the condition by which alone this determination can take place constitutes quite as manifestly, and in all its primitive purity, the faculty which is designated by the name of *Wisdom* (λόγος, *das Wissen*).

"We therefore discover WISDOM as the second essential attribute of the absolute; this primordial faculty which is the condition of all *creation,* or rather which is the *creative faculty* itself in its loftiest puissance, as we have now discerned it, is, if we may thus express it, the *instrument of autogeny,* that is to say, the faculty of the creation by itself. And consequently we discover in *Wisdom,* shown in this highest creative power, the *second principle* of reason, quite as infallible as the absolute itself, from which we have now deduced it.

"Moreover, in the reality of the absolute, the necessary result of its wisdom or of its innate creation is PERMANENT STABILITY, because, precisely through being what it is by itself, the absolute could not be other than itself. We can therefore understand that this permanent stability in the reality of the absolute, which is properly its *autothesis,* constitutes a *third determination* of the very essence of the absolute, and we shall easily recognize that this stability, this permanent unchangeableness, this *innate unalterability,* is only that condition of the reality which we name *Being* (ὤν, *das Seyn*).

"Thus, we discover as the third essential attribute of the absolute, *the Being,* the condition of stability in reality, and therefore of its *force* or *innate unalterability,* which in the absolute constitutes its autothesis itself. And consequently we find in the *Being,* considered almost in its autothetic origin, the *third principle* of reason, as infallible as the absolute itself, from which we have deduced it.

"We therefore already possess the three first principles of reason, which, as we have just seen, are the three first determinations of the very essence of the absolute. Moreover, if we notice on the one hand that *Wisdom* and the *Being*, taking them in all their generality, are opposed to each other, just as autogeny and autothesis—of which they form the conditions—are opposed, or spontaneity and inertia, which form their characters; and if on the other hand we notice that *Wisdom* and the *Being*, these antagonistic conditions, are neutralized in all REALITY in general, this reality—according to the deductions which we have given—being the fundamental principle of reason, its primitive basis, we shall understand that the three principles which we have discovered in the determinations of the essence itself of the absolute, are really the three *primitive principles* of the supreme Wisdom, or of Philosophy."

+	—
WISDOM	THE BEING
Autogeny	Autothesis
Principle of Motion	Principle of Stability

∞
REALITY
Principle of Existence

FIRST PRINCIPLES OF WRONSKI.

2. THEOGONIES OF DIFFERENT RELIGIONS.

We have now shown the identity of the three first principles of the Tarot with the philosophical discoveries of some modern authors. We need only revert to the study of the first arcanum to see the conclusions which Fabre d'Olivet and Claude de Saint-Martin have come to upon the same subject; and we will now say a few words upon the identity of the deductions of the Tarot with the religious ideas of various nations.

EGYPTIAN THEOGONY.

Osiris is an emanation of the Great Being; he reveals himself in three persons—

> *Amen*, who brings forth the hidden forms of things, is Power.
> *Ptah* the *demi-urgus*, the eternal workman, embodying the primitive ideas, is Wisdom.
> *Osiris*, the author of being, the source of all life, is Goodness.

"The Egyptian god is called *Amen* when he is regarded as the hidden force which brings all things to the light; he is *Ptah* when he accomplishes all things with skill and truth; lastly, when he is the good and beneficent god, he is named *Osiris.*"—JAMBLIQUE.

Indeterminable Principle
RA
Divine Trinity:

+   —
AMEN   PTAH
∞
OSIRIS

HINDU THEOGONY.

Indeterminable Principle
PARABRAHM:

+		−
BRAHMA		VISHNU
Creator		Preserver
	∞	
	SIVA	
	Transformer	

Here is an analysis of this conception applied to Cosmogony:—

PRIMITIVE HINDU COSMOGONY, ACCORDING TO THE RIG-VEDA.

There was neither being nor no-being, nor ether, nor the roof of the heavens; nothing enveloping nor enveloped. There was neither death nor immortality; nothing separated the darkness of night from the light of day.

But That One, the HE, breathed alone with HER, whose life was sustained in his breast. Of all those who have existed since that time, no other then existed. The darkness covered them like an ocean, which cannot be lightened. This universe was indistinct, like the fluids mingled with the waters; but this mass, which was covered by a crust, was at last organized by the power of contemplation.

The first wish was formed in its intelligence, and it became the original productive seed. This productive seed became *Providence* or *sensitive souls;* and *Matter* or *Elements,* SHE who was supported in his breast was the inferior part, and HE who observes was the superior part. Who can know exactly, and who in this world can assert, from whom or how this creation took place? The gods are posterior to this creation of the world.

KABBALISTIC THEOGONY.

Indeterminable Principle
EN SOPH
The Absolute
Divine Trinity:

+   —
Chocmah   Binah
Absolute Wisdom   Absolute Intelligence

∞
Kether
Absolute Equilibrist Power

We might carry these comparisons much further; but it is useless to prolong our studies unreasonably. The curious reader can refer to the works on the ancient theogonies,[1] and see the universal harmony that exists in the primitive principles of all religions.

It will be sufficient if we determine the universality of the three first principles, which we name, like the Christians, in order to be clearly understood—

+   —
God the Father   God the Son

∞
God the Holy Spirit

***

These principles once defined, we shall see them in action throughout creation.

The first principle had manifested its existence to itself in the second principle named by Christians:

---

[1] See particularly P. Renand, *Nouvelle Symbolique*, Paris, 1877. 8vo.

the Son. Lastly, these two principles had embodied themselves in the third, which gave them substance. This is why we have named the Holy Spirit the body of God.

Now the same law of creation acting in the affinities of the first principle with the second, will manifest itself in the action of the first ternary upon itself, to give birth to the following Trinity:—

God the Father, the principle of *Will*, is entirely self-reflected in the rough ADAM, the principle *of Power;* *God the Son*, the principle of *Intelligence*, is self-reflected in the gentle EVE, the principle of *Authority*. Lastly, God as a whole, or God the Holy Spirit, clothed these two mystical unities in a body, and made a reality of them in the balanced creation of Adam-Eve, or of HUMANITY.

Humanity, the image of *Love*, also contains in itself a rough, astringent principle (see Jacob Boëhm [1]), and a gentle, insinuating principle (Jacob Boëhm). The first of these principles, symbolized by Adam, is the origin of brute Force, of Power in all its manifestations. The second, symbolized by Eve, is the origin of feminine Grace, of Authority. We have seen that Power and Authority find their equilibrium in Love.

Each man, a reflected molecule of humanity made in its image, contains in himself an Adam, the source of the Will—this is the Brain; an Eve, source of the intelligence —the heart; and he should balance the heart by the brain, and the brain by the heart, to become a centre of divine love.

It is the same with man and woman, represented by Adam and Eve (הוה Eve, the life).

---

[1] Jacob Boëhm, *The Three Principles.*

GENERAL SUMMARY OF SYMBOLICAL TAROT.

But just as the Father and the Son have become realities in the Holy Spirit, as Adam and Eve are embodied in Humanity, so the third ternary will take rise in the reciprocal action of the other two.

NATURA NATURANS, or creating, will take her birth under the action and the reciprocal reaction of God the Father and of Adam, the two active and passive creative principles. Thus also appears the *Universal creative Fluid*, balancing and realizing in itself both will and power.

From this again will be born NATURA NATURATA, or preserving, realizing the union of God the Son and of Eve, at the same time that the *Universal preserving Fluid*, or *Universal Life*, will appear, balancing and realizing the Intelligence and Authority which define its innate qualities.

Lastly, the Holy Spirit and Humanity, the divine and the human bodies, unite and manifest themselves eternally in the LIVING UNIVERSE, the source of *Universal Attraction*.

For even as the Holy Spirit was the body of God, the Son his soul, and the Father his Spirit, even as Humanity was the body of Adam, Eve his life or soul, and Adam his Spirit; so also—

The Universe is the body of God;
Humanity is the soul of God;
God Himself is the Spirit of God.

From this we recognize the truth of the opinion of the Pantheists, who declared that God was the Universe; but we also see their error, when they refuse to acknowledge in him any innate consciousness. For as the consciousness of man is independent of the millions of cells which compose his body, so the consciousness of God is independent of the molecules of the Universe and of man which form its body and its soul. We might partly destroy the

Universe without in any way diminishing the Divine Personality, even as the four limbs can be cut off a man without his losing the consciousness of the integrity of his personality. This is why the conclusions of Schopenhauer and Hartmann are partly erroneous.

Before leaving this study, we must once more express our admiration for this wonderful book, this symbolical Tarot, which thus defines God—

God is the Absolute, the essence of which is impenetrable, formed of the Universe as body, of Humanity as soul, and of himself as Spirit.

GENERAL SUMMARY OF SYMBOLICAL TAROT.

THEOGONY.

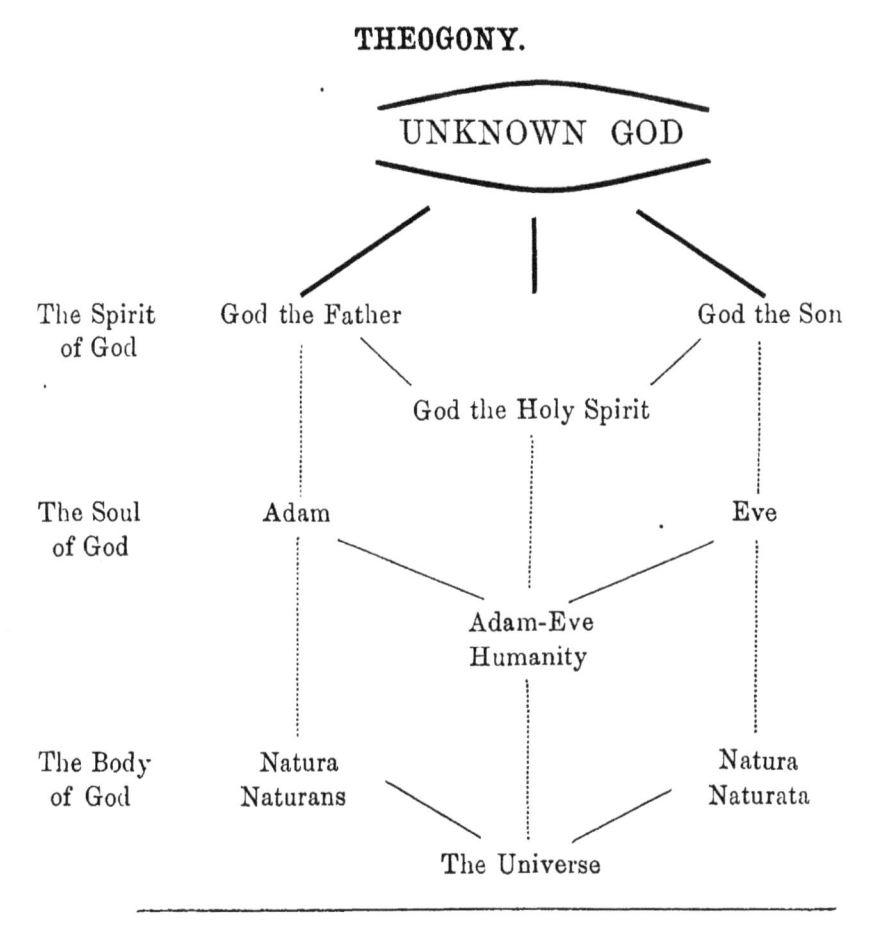

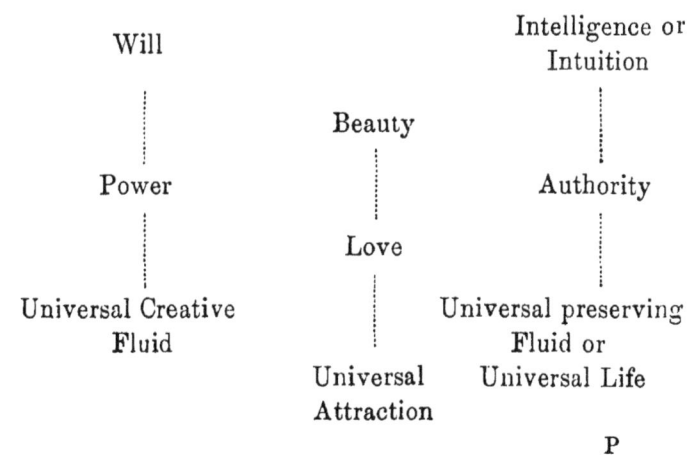

UNKNOWN GOD

The Spirit of God	God the Father		God the Son
		God the Holy Spirit	
The Soul of God	Adam		Eve
		Adam-Eve Humanity	
The Body of God	Natura Naturans		Natura Naturata
		The Universe	

Will		Intelligence or Intuition
	Beauty	
Power		Authority
	Love	
Universal Creative Fluid		Universal preserving Fluid or Universal Life
	Universal Attraction	

P

ANDROGONY.

Each man contains in himself an *Adam*, source of the Will, *i. e.* the Brain; an *Eve*, source of the Intelligence,[1] *i. e.* the Heart, and he should balance the heart by the brain, and the brain by the heart, if he would become a centre of divine love.

In Humanity, the passive Realistic principle of God Himself, the Father and the Divine Son, are represented by Man.

Man accomplishing the functions of God the creator is the FATHER; the woman accomplishing the work of God the preserver is the MOTHER; lastly, HUMAN LOVE realizes the whole Divinity in Humanity.

The human family is therefore the representation of the Divinity upon earth. The Tarot also teaches us this fact by its minor arcana (king or father, queen or mother, knight or young man, knave or child); and it was so thoroughly understood by ancient science, that the whole social organization was based upon the *family*, instead of upon the *individual*, as it is in modern times.[2] That the social organization of China has been maintained for so many centuries, is solely due to the principle of basing everything upon the family.[3]

The characteristics of the human Ternary are: Adam, Necessity, the image and reflection of Will and Power; Eve, Liberty, the image and reflection of Intelligence and Authority; and Adam and Eve, Charity, the image

---

[1] Intelligence is here taken in the sense of *Intuition*, and not in the sense usually attributed to it by the Philosophy of the Universities.

[2] See Saint-Yves d'Alveydre, *Mission des Juifs*, 1884.

[3] See Simon, *La Cité Chinoise*, 1886. 8vo.

GENERAL SUMMARY OF SYMBOLICAL TAROT.

and reflection of Love and Beauty given by the constituent terms.

REALIZATION and JUSTICE, balanced by PRUDENCE, indicate the moral constitution of Man, whilst the POSITIVE ASTRAL LIGHT (or OD), the NEGATIVE ASTRAL LIGHT (or OB), and the EQUILIBRATE ASTRAL FLUID (or AOUR), demonstrate the origin of his physical constitution.

Magic Power, *Courage*, and *Hope* manifest the moral qualities of man, whilst *Force potential in its manifestation*, *reflected Life*, and *Force balancing* the two preceding qualities, indicate the influence of the Universe in him.

Thus, the law which governs all these manifestations of God in the series of his creations is *Emanation*.

From the unique but fathomless centre emanates, in the first place, a Trinity of absolute principles which serves as a model for all the posterior emanations of the Being principle itself. Each element of this Trinity manifests itself in two great principles, of which it is the source: from the first principle, or the Father, emanate successively Adam and Nature creating, *naturans*, according to Spinoza; from the second principle, or the Son, emanate Eve and Nature *naturata*, or recipient; lastly, the third principle, or the Holy Spirit, serves as a model to the similar constitution of Adam-Eve, or Humanity and the Universe.

In this way also the *Ternary*, emanated from the mysterious Unity, soon constitutes a *Septenary* formed by the various emanations of these three Principles, like the *seven colours* of the scale of light formed by the combination of *three simple colours*, themselves emanated from one *single light;* or like the *seven notes* of the musical scale, formed by the fundamental *trinity* of sounds.

The Septenary formed of " two Ternaries in the midst of

which the Unity upholds itself," [1] is therefore the expression of a being completely constituted. This is now confirmed by the recent data given by Hindu Theosophy upon the *seven principles of Man*, and upon the *seven principles of the Universe*.[2]

We could apply the Tarot to the explanation of these data; but we feel sure that it will soon be done, and we consider it useless to lengthen our work too much.

We will therefore conclude our study upon man by pointing out his constitution as given by the Tarot, which teaches that his body comes from the Universe, his soul from the Astral plane, whilst his Spirit is a direct emanation from God.[3]

[1] *Sepher Yetzirah* (trans. Papus), chap. vi.
[2] See Sinnet, *Esoteric Buddhism*; H. P. Blavatsky, *Secret Doctrine*; and all the publications of the Theosophical Society.
[3] See for further developments the works of Paracelsus and Van Helmont.

GENERAL SUMMARY OF SYMBOLICAL TAROT.

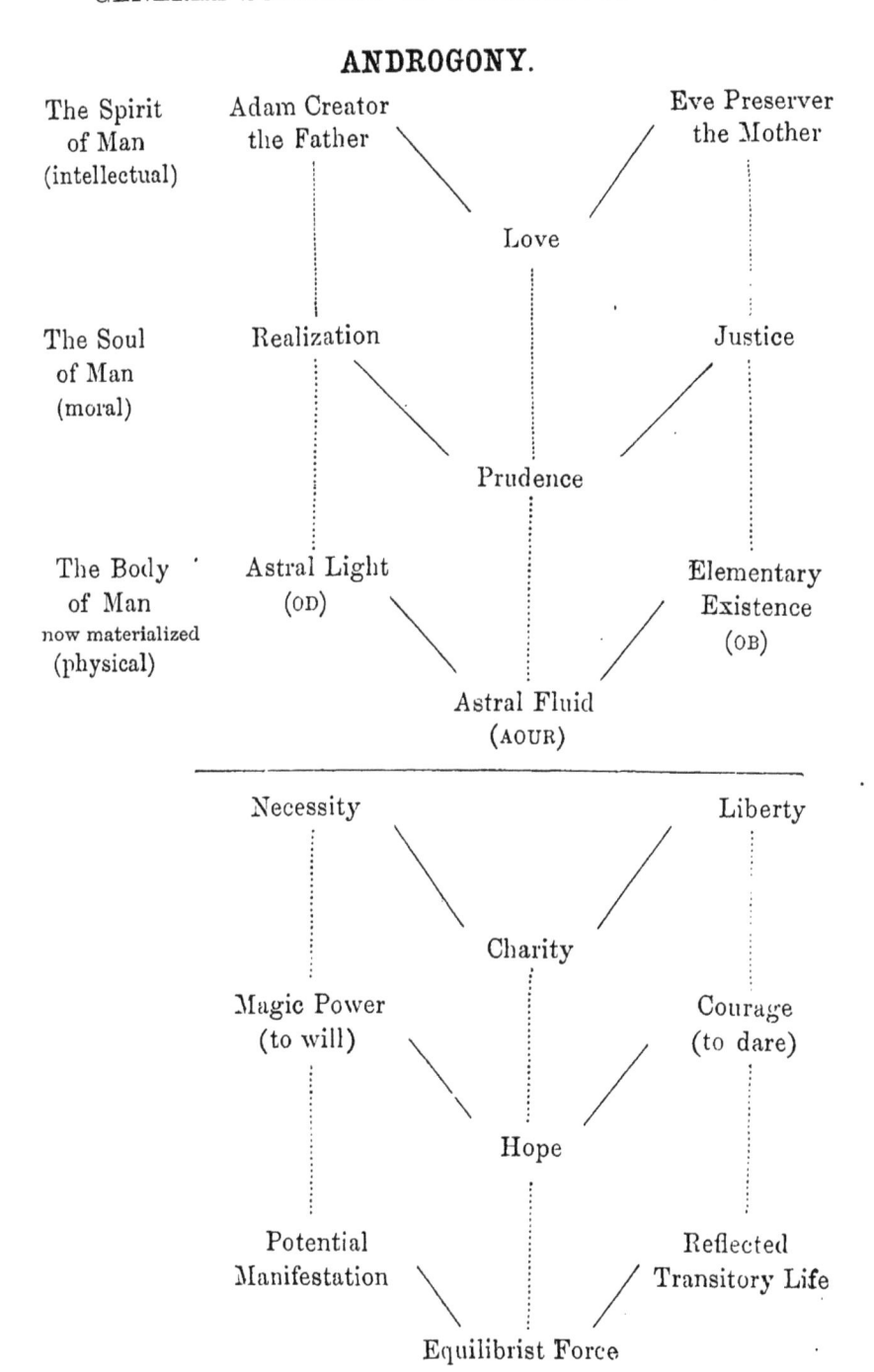

ANDROGONY.

The Spirit of Man (intellectual)	Adam Creator the Father		Eve Preserver the Mother
		Love	
The Soul of Man (moral)	Realization		Justice
		Prudence	
The Body of Man now materialized (physical)	Astral Light (OD)		Elementary Existence (OB)
		Astral Fluid (AOUR)	

	Necessity		Liberty
		Charity	
	Magic Power (to will)		Courage (to dare)
		Hope	
	Potential Manifestation		Reflected Transitory Life
		Equilibrist Force	

COSMOGONY.

As we descend the ladder of the emanations of the Absolute Being, the principles become more material and less metaphysical. The Tarot teaches us that the Universe results from the participation of the Human in the creative actions of the Divine, a profound mystery, which can throw much light upon the theological theories of the Fall. Jacob Boëhm, the sublime visionary shoemaker, and Claude de Saint-Martin, his admirer and disciple, give upon this subject some explanations which may be easily understood with the Tarot, and to which we refer curious inquirers.

God manifests himself in the Universe by his third trinitarian manifestation: *Natura naturans*, realized in the UNIVERSAL TRANSFORMING PRINCIPLE, *Natura naturata*, in INVOLUTION; and lastly in the mysterious cyclic force which we have analyzed, in reference to the 15th arcanum, and which we name the FATAL FORCE OF DESTINY. This is the God adored by materialist science, and we see that unconsciously its homage is offered to the Divinity itself under its most material form, even whilst it foolishly boasts of Atheism.

DEATH, CORPOREAL LIFE, and the DESTINY which rules their mutual connection, constitute the preserving principles of the Universe; lastly, PLASTIC FORCE, INDIVIDUAL LIFE, and the ASTRAL LIGHT IN CIRCULATION, show us the means of Transformation and of Realization used by the Cosmos.

But these are abstract principles; if we wish to see them in action we must consider the following ternary. The *Universal Transforming Principle* marks its existence by the DESTRUCTION of beings and of things; but the *Opposing Principle, Involution,* at once IMMORTALIZES Destruction by the influx of new divine currents into CHAOS.

Adam materialized his nature by the FALL of his spirit into matter, the source of *Death;* but the *Corporeal Life,* the source of HOPE, arises and provides the means of redeeming the fault, by suffering in the MATERIAL BODY.

Lastly MATTER itself appears, the final term of involution, after which recommences the grand Evolution towards the primitive centre.

It is unnecessary to say that we only wished to give a rapid sketch of the evidence of the Tarot upon Theogony, Androgony, and Cosmogony, without entering into detail. In fact these are very serious questions, which require whole volumes to themselves, and we had not the least intention of discussing them in a few pages.

COSMOGONY.

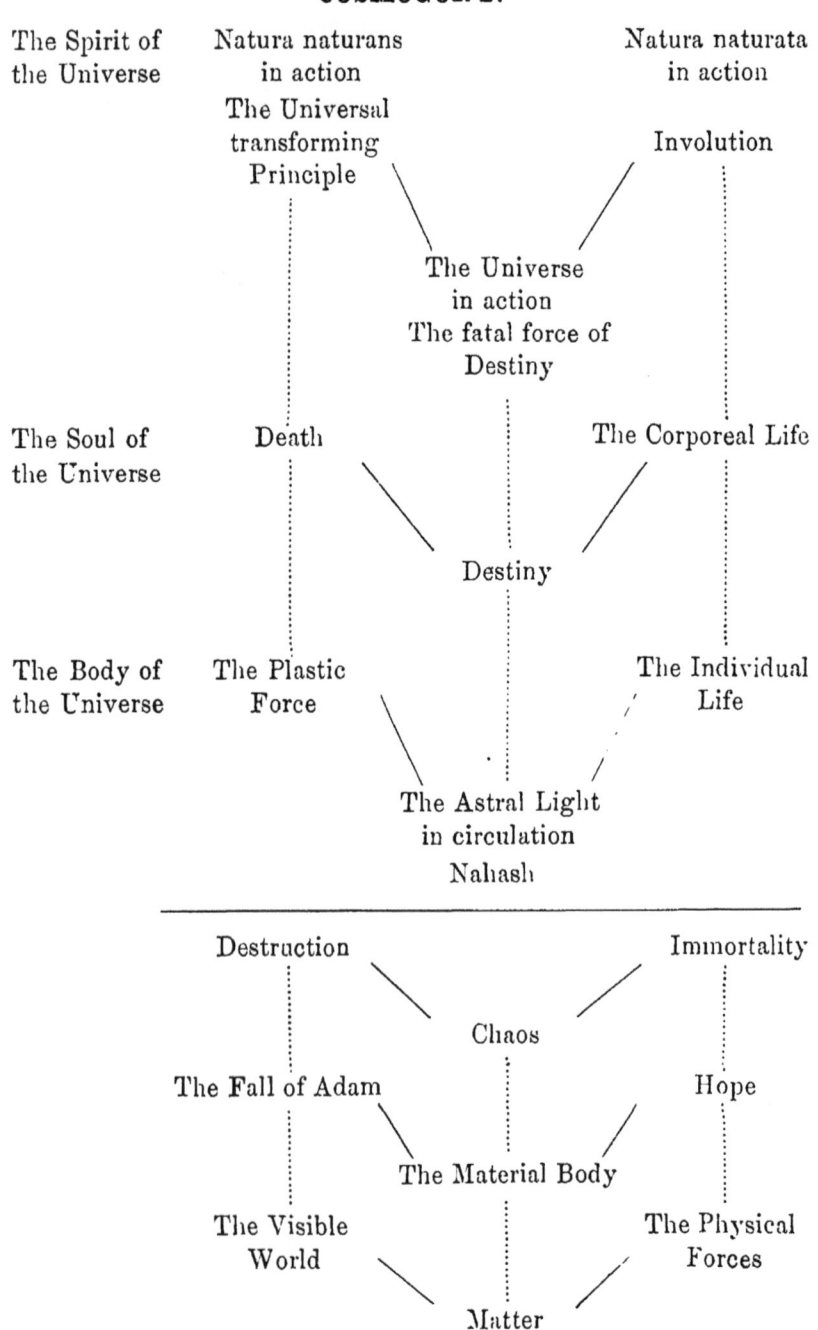

The Spirit of the Universe — Natura naturans in action — Natura naturata in action

The Universal transforming Principle — Involution

The Universe in action
The fatal force of Destiny

The Soul of the Universe — Death — The Corporeal Life

Destiny

The Body of the Universe — The Plastic Force — The Individual Life

The Astral Light in circulation
Nahash

Destruction — Immortality

Chaos

The Fall of Adam — Hope

The Material Body

The Visible World — The Physical Forces

Matter

Let us now recapitulate a little, so that we may definitely end the involution of the three grand principles:

From GOD THE FATHER have emanated successively—

Adam	Will
Natura Naturans	Power
Then their form	The Universal Creative Fluid.

Adam realized in the *Father* has produced *Realization* and the *Astral Light*; whilst the Will was realized in *Necessity*, Supreme Power is shown in *Magic Power*, and the universal creative Fluid in *Force potential in its manifestation*.

Natura naturans realized in the *Universal Transforming Principle* has produced *Death*, and the *Universal Plastic Force*, with their forms, *Destruction*, the *Fall of Adam*, and the visible world.

These are all the principles that have successively emanated from the *Father*, and which represent him. We have reproduced them in a tableau—

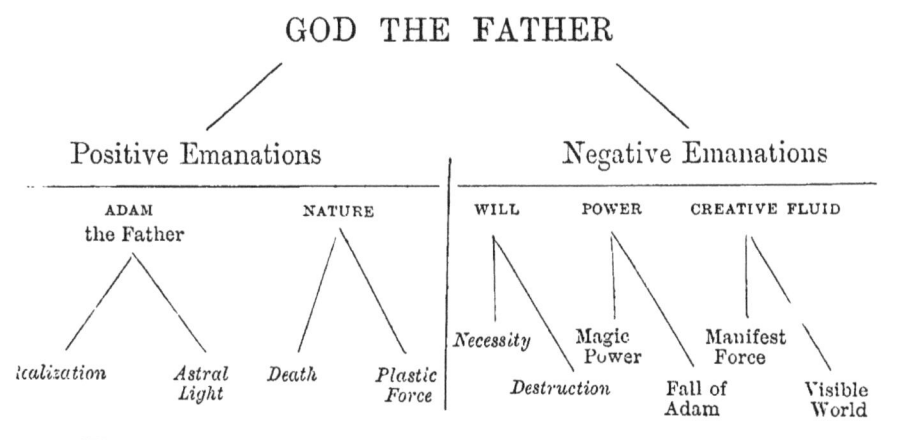

GOD THE FATHER

Positive Emanations | Negative Emanations

ADAM the Father | NATURE | WILL | POWER | CREATIVE FLUID

Realization | Astral Light | Death | Plastic Force | Necessity | Magic Power | Manifest Force | Destruction | Fall of Adam | Visible World

The two following figures arranged upon the same plan as this one, give the emanations of the two other principles of the first ternary.

GOD THE SON

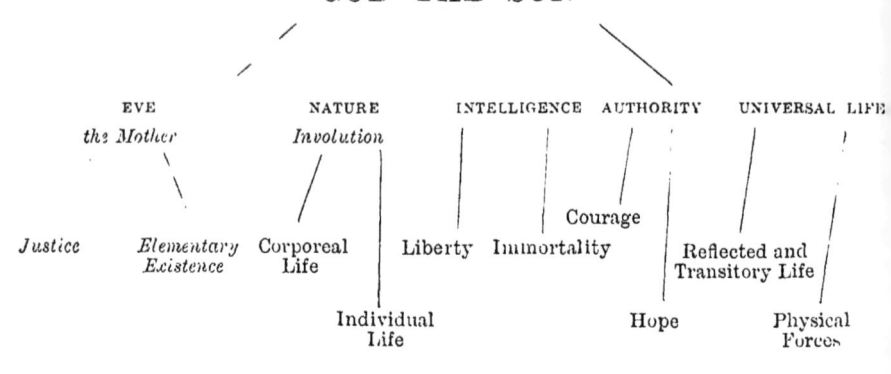

EVE	NATURE	INTELLIGENCE	AUTHORITY	UNIVERSAL LIFE
the Mother	*Involution*			

| Justice | Elementary Existence | Corporeal Life | Liberty | Immortality | Courage | Reflected and Transitory Life |

Individual Life — Hope — Physical Forces

GOD THE HOLY SPIRIT

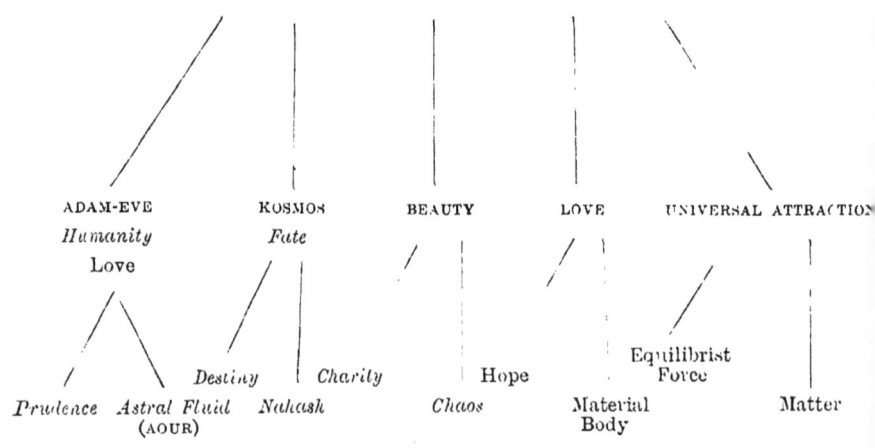

ADAM-EVE	KOSMOS	BEAUTY	LOVE	UNIVERSAL ATTRACTION
Humanity	*Fate*			
Love				

Prudence — Astral Fluid (AOUR) — Destiny — Charity — Nahash — Hope — Chaos — Equilibrist Force — Material Body — Matter

In our Introduction to the study of symbolism we have given a numbered figure which enables us to determine immediately the meaning of any card in the Tarot.

If we now apply all that we have said upon the symbolism of each of our cards to this subject, we can condense the whole *symbolism of the major arcana in one figure*.

The new tableau thus formed will give us the sense of all our principles, whatever their number may be, and this is how we obtain this meaning—

GENERAL SUMMARY OF SYMBOLICAL TAROT.

USE OF THE TABLEAU.

1. Seek in the *horizontal* column, to the left of the principle under consideration, the sense written there.

2. Having ascertained this meaning, return to your principle and search in the *vertical column* at the bottom the great principle (God, Man, or the Universe) which is written there.

3. Combine the meaning first obtained with the name placed in the vertical column, adding to it the word (itself or manifest) written in the vertical column which contains the principle of which you are seeking the meaning.

An example will explain this better.

Let us ascertain the meaning of the MOTHER—

The first term of the 8th arcanum.

1. I look in the *horizontal* column containing the word MOTHER and I find at the end, to the left, the *following meaning*—

Active preserving Principle.

The Mother is the Active preserving Principle. Of what?

2. In order to know, I seek in the *vertical* column containing the word *Mother*, and at the bottom I find Man or Humanity.

The Mother is the Active preserving Principle of Humanity.

3. I add to the word Humanity the word placed in the small vertical column which contains the word Mother. This word is *Himself* if relating to man, or *itself* if we take the sense of Humanity. We should say—

The Mother is the Active preserving Principle of Man himself or of Humanity itself.

This example clearly indicates how this tableau should be used.

T A

Recapitulating the Symbolism of all the Ma
Arcana to be immediately

CREATIVE PRINCIPLE (י) Active י	God the Father 1	Will 4	The Father
CREATIVE PRINCIPLE Passive ה	Adam	Power	Realization
CREATIVE PRINCIPLE Equilibrist ו	Natura naturans	Universal Creative Fluid	Astral Light
PRESERVING PRINCIPLE (ה) Active י	God the Son 2	Intelligence 5	The Mother
PRESERVING PRINCIPLE Passive (ה)	Eve	Authority	Justice
PRESERVING PRINCIPLE Equilibrist ו	Natura naturata	Universal Life	Elementary Existence
REALIZING PRINCIPLE (ו) Active י	God the Holy Spirit 3	Beauty 6	Love
REALIZING PRINCIPLE Passive ה	Adam-Eve, Humanity	Love	Prudence (Be silent)
REALIZING PRINCIPLE Equilibrist ו	Kosmos	Universal Attraction	Astral Fluid (AOUR)
	Himself (י) +	Manifested —	Himself (ה) +
	GOD	(21)	M
			HUM

E A U

cana, enabling the definition of any one of these
mined. (*See its use on page* 219.)

Necessity 10 Magic Power Force potential in its manifest- ation	Universal transforming Principle 13 Death Universal Plastic Force	Destruction 16 The Fall of Adam The Visible World	The Elements 19 Nutrition The Mineral Kingdom
Liberty 11 ourage (TO DARE) Reflected and transitory Life	Involution 14 Corporeal Life Individual Life	Immortality 17 Hope The Physical Forces	Innate Motion 20 Respiration The Vegetable Kingdom
Charity 12 Hope (WISDOM) quilibrist Force	Fate 15 Destiny Nahash Astral Light in circulation	Chaos 18 The Material Body Matter	The Motion of Relative Duration 0 Innervation The Animal Kingdom
Manifested — (21) ITY	Itself (ו) + UNIVERSE	Manifested — (21)	Return (ה) to the Unity

THE TAROT.

Tableau indicating the revolutions yod-he-vau-he *in numbers* (*positive arcana*): (*yod* = 1, *he* = 2, *vau* = 3, *2nd he* = 4).

(Key to the preceding Tableau.)

	1	2	3	4
I. 1	$\left.\begin{array}{c}1\\2\\3\\4\end{array}\right\}$ of 1 in VII. 1	$\left.\begin{array}{c}2\\3\\4\\1\end{array}\right\}$ of 1 in XIII. 2	$\left.\begin{array}{c}3\\4\\1\\2\end{array}\right\}$ of 1 in XIX. 3	$\left.\begin{array}{c}4\\1\\2\\3\end{array}\right\}$ of 1 in 4
II. 2	$\left.\begin{array}{c}1\\2\\3\\4\end{array}\right\}$ of 2 in VIII. 1	$\left.\begin{array}{c}2\\3\\4\\1\end{array}\right\}$ of 2 in XIV. 2	$\left.\begin{array}{c}3\\4\\1\\2\end{array}\right\}$ of 2 in XX. 3	$\left.\begin{array}{c}4\\1\\2\\3\end{array}\right\}$ of 2 in 4
III. 3	$\left.\begin{array}{c}1\\2\\3\\4\end{array}\right\}$ of 3 in IX. 1	$\left.\begin{array}{c}2\\3\\4\\1\end{array}\right\}$ of 3 in XV. 2	$\left.\begin{array}{c}3\\4\\1\\2\end{array}\right\}$ of 3 in XXI. 3	$\left.\begin{array}{c}4\\1\\2\\3\end{array}\right\}$ of 3 in 4
IV. 4	$\left.\begin{array}{c}1\\2\\3\\4\end{array}\right\}$ of 4 in X. 1	$\left.\begin{array}{c}2\\3\\4\\1\end{array}\right\}$ of 4 in XVI. 2	$\left.\begin{array}{c}3\\4\\1\\2\end{array}\right\}$ of 4 in XXII. 3	$\left.\begin{array}{c}4\\1\\2\\3\end{array}\right\}$ of 4 in 4

PART III.

APPLICATIONS OF THE TAROT.

CHAPTER XV.

GENERAL KEY TO THE APPLICATIONS OF THE TAROT.

The Principle and the Forms—The Twenty-first Card of the Tarot is a Figure-principle—The Tarot—The Year—The Month—The Day—The Human Life.

GENERAL KEY TO THE APPLICATIONS OF THE TAROT.

WE have already stated that the twenty-first card gives the key to the construction of the Tarot. The utility of this arcanum does not end here; we shall now see that it is the *key to every application* of the Tarot.

Some explanation may be necessary as to the manner in which a symbolical figure can be applied to conceptions of very different orders, without undergoing the least transformation.

Let us take one very simple example, chosen in the realm of experimental science, by applying the analogical method to its study. Let us represent the well-known phenomenon of the decomposition of the white light by the prism.

We place the prism, indicated by a triangular figure, in the centre; the white light, represented by parallel lines, enters it on one side: from the other the colours issue.

Q

They are represented by the refracted and more or less oblique lines.

The words *Prism, White Light,* and *Colours,* indicate all the phases of the phenomenon.

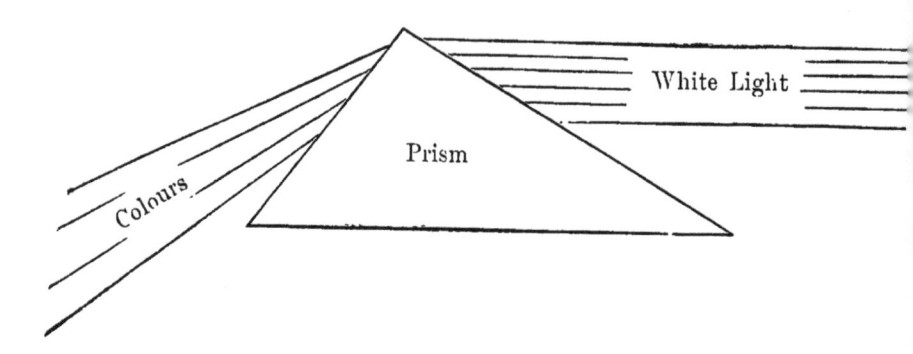

If, however, we reflect that after all it is only a general force (the white light) which undergoes various changes, according to the quantity of matter with which it comes in contact (the different thicknesses of the prism),[1] we shall easily grasp another aspect of the figure.

In fact the work of Louis Lucas, unconsciously continued by contemporary scientific men, proves by evidence the unity of force in action throughout Nature. The different physical forces, heat, light, or electricity, are only representations of this unique force differently modified, according to the quantity of matter with which it comes in contact.

Thus the white light in contact with the large amount of matter at the base of the prism becomes *violet:* in the same way the unique force coming in contact with much matter becomes *heat,* or placed in contact with little matter becomes *light* or *electricity.*

We can therefore represent this new phenomenon without

[1] See Louis Lucas, *Chimie Nouvelle*, chapter upon "Angulaison."

changing the form of our figure in any way; only the words need vary—

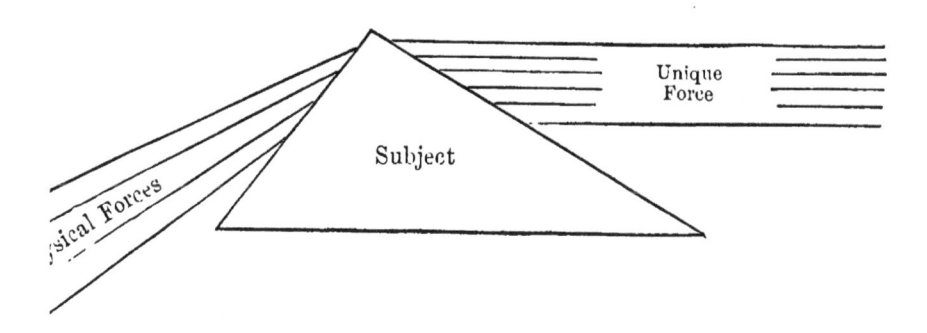

[Figure: a prism diagram labeled "Subject" with "Unique Force" entering as parallel lines on the right and "Physical Forces" exiting as refracted lines on the left.]

Here the *different quantities of matter* are represented by the different thicknesses of the prism, the *unique force* corresponding with the white light by the parallel lines, the *various physical forces* responding to the various colours by the refracted lines.

If any one should consider that these two examples belong to the realm of physics, and are therefore insufficient to generalize a phenomenon to this point, we can answer by another instance quoted from physiology.

Physiology teaches us that all the organs in man act under the influence of the blood. Thus the latter, acting upon the salivary glands, produces the saliva, acting upon the stomach the gastric juice is secreted, upon the liver in certain cases it produces bile, etc., etc.

In short, this physiological phenomenon reduces itself to *one unique agent* (the blood), acting upon the different organs (the salivary glands, stomach, liver), and producing secretions of equally different natures (saliva, gastric juices, bile).

Can we not therefore represent the different organs by the different thickness of the prism, the different transformations of the unique force by the refracted rays, and the unique force itself by the parallel lines?

The correspondence is exact on all points, and the same figure can be used once more—

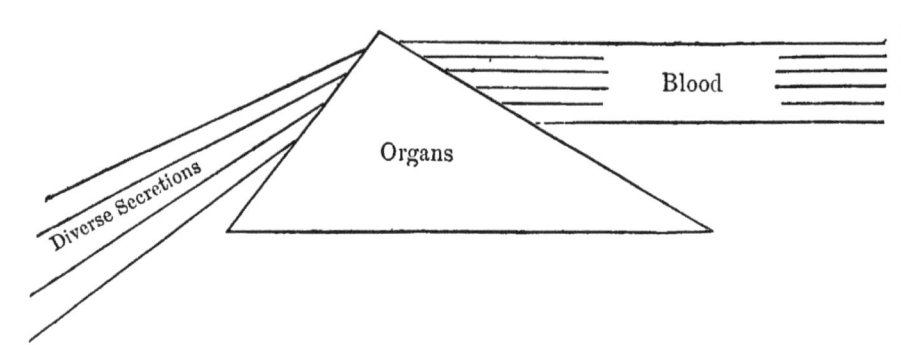

Diverse Secretions — Organs — Blood

Thus the figure has never changed: only the words applied to its different parts have varied. The basis of all occult science and of the analogical method resembles this example: one fixed and invariable figure, which is always the same (Ex.: the figure), to which various orders of phenomena can be successively applied.

The twenty-first card of the Tarot is a *figure-principle* of the same nature as the prism which we have just studied, and a few examples of the various methods in which it can be applied will fully enlighten us upon this point.

We have seen that the four figures in the corners of the twenty-first card represent the four animals of the Evangelist. In the centre stands a woman, the image of Humanity, and between the two symbols is a crown of elliptic form.

This shows us that there will always be four *fixed* principles in every application of this card (since the symbols placed at the four corners of the square do not move), and a certain number of *mobile* principles repre-

GENERAL KEY TO APPLICATIONS OF TAROT. 229

sented by the wheel, *rota*, which occupies the centre of the symbols.

This figure can never change, since it is a *figure-principle*: the words alone that may be applied to it can vary.

Thus we have seen the four following symbols—

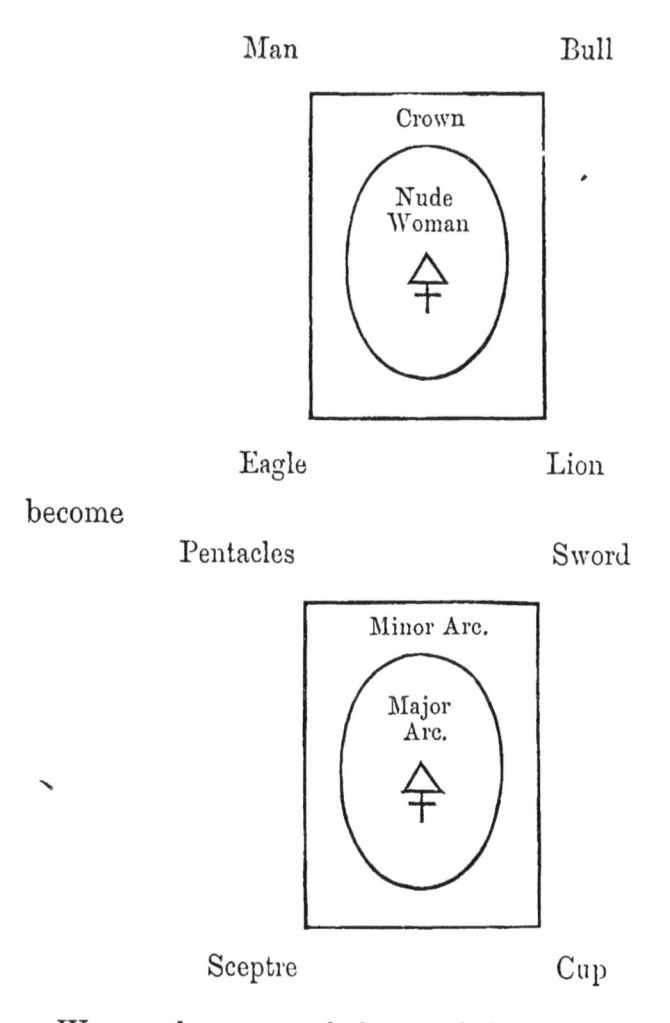

Man	Bull
Eagle	Lion

```
┌─────────────┐
│    Crown    │
│  ╭───────╮  │
│  │ Nude  │  │
│  │ Woman │  │
│  │  △    │  │
│  │  ⟊    │  │
│  ╰───────╯  │
└─────────────┘
```

become

Pentacles	Sword
Sceptre	Cup

```
┌─────────────┐
│  Minor Arc. │
│  ╭───────╮  │
│  │ Major │  │
│  │  Arc. │  │
│  │  △    │  │
│  │  ⟊    │  │
│  ╰───────╯  │
└─────────────┘
```

We see that none of the symbols have changed, but the words only.

The same rule applies to every application of the Tarot. Thus if we take astronomy, the four figures will be the four seasons, the crown is the zodiac, and the nude figure (Eve) the animating system of the zodiac, the planets; thus—

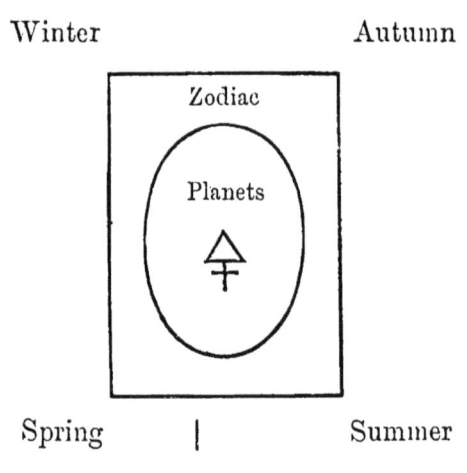

```
    Winter                          Autumn

              ┌─────────────────┐
              │     Zodiac      │
              │   ╱───────╲     │
              │  │ Planets │    │
              │  │   ⚨     │    │
              │   ╲───────╱     │
              └─────────────────┘

    Spring           |           Summer
```

This shows us the progress of the *sun*, as it gives birth to the *year*. If we wish to know *that of the moon* as it produces the *month*, the four seasons would become the four lunar phases, the zodiac would be the twenty-eight houses of the moon, and the centre the sun, which animates the moon; thus—

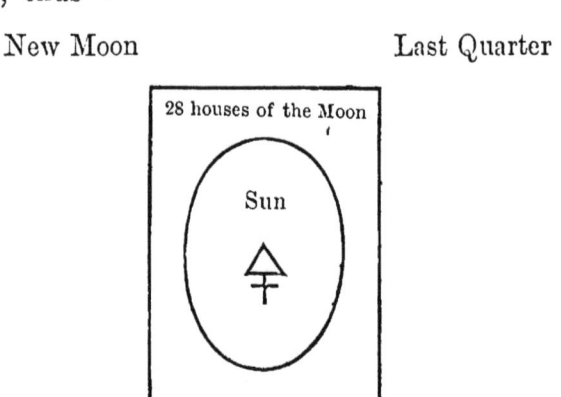

```
    New Moon                        Last Quarter

              ┌─────────────────────┐
              │ 28 houses of the Moon│
              │   ╱───────╲         │
              │  │   Sun   │        │
              │  │   ⚨     │        │
              │   ╲───────╱         │
              └─────────────────────┘

    First Quarter                   Full Moon
```

If we wish for the horoscope of a *single day* we find it in the following figure—

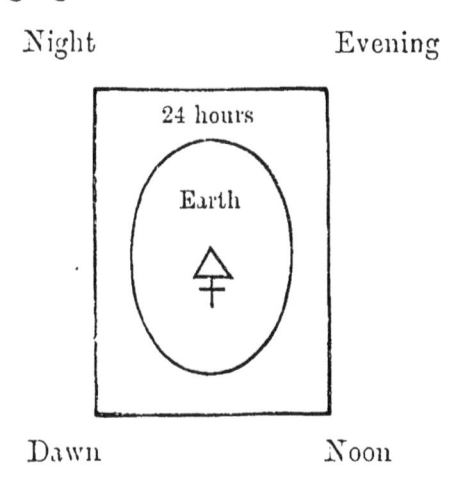

Night   Evening

```
     24 hours
      Earth
        ⚱
```

Dawn   Noon

Here the *earth* occupies the position of the moon in the month and of the sun in the year.

If these astronomical data weary us, we can study the circle of the *Human Life*, and the figure will assume a new aspect.

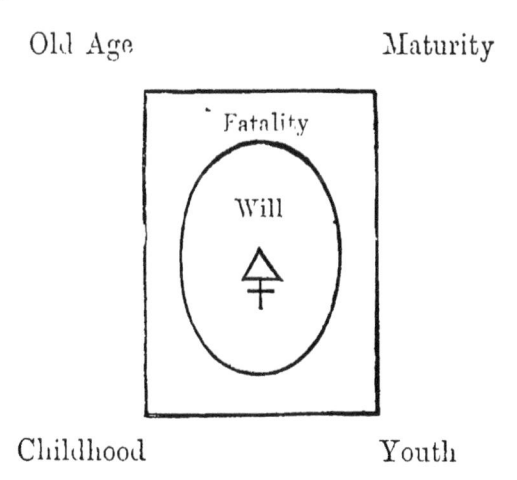

Old Age   Maturity

```
     Fatality
       Will
        ⚱
```

Childhood   Youth

A profound symbol, which indicates that the *Human Will* creates the *fatality* in which man moves, under the influence of the *providential* cycle of the four ages of the human life. If we know that Providence (the outer circle) acts upon the *Future*, Fatality (the intermediate circle) upon the *Past*, and the Human Will (centre circle) upon the *Present*, we shall see the basis of the *divining Tarot*.

We think that these examples are sufficiently clear to enable us to proceed, and we shall now study some applications of the Tarot, leaving to the student the work of discovering a larger number.

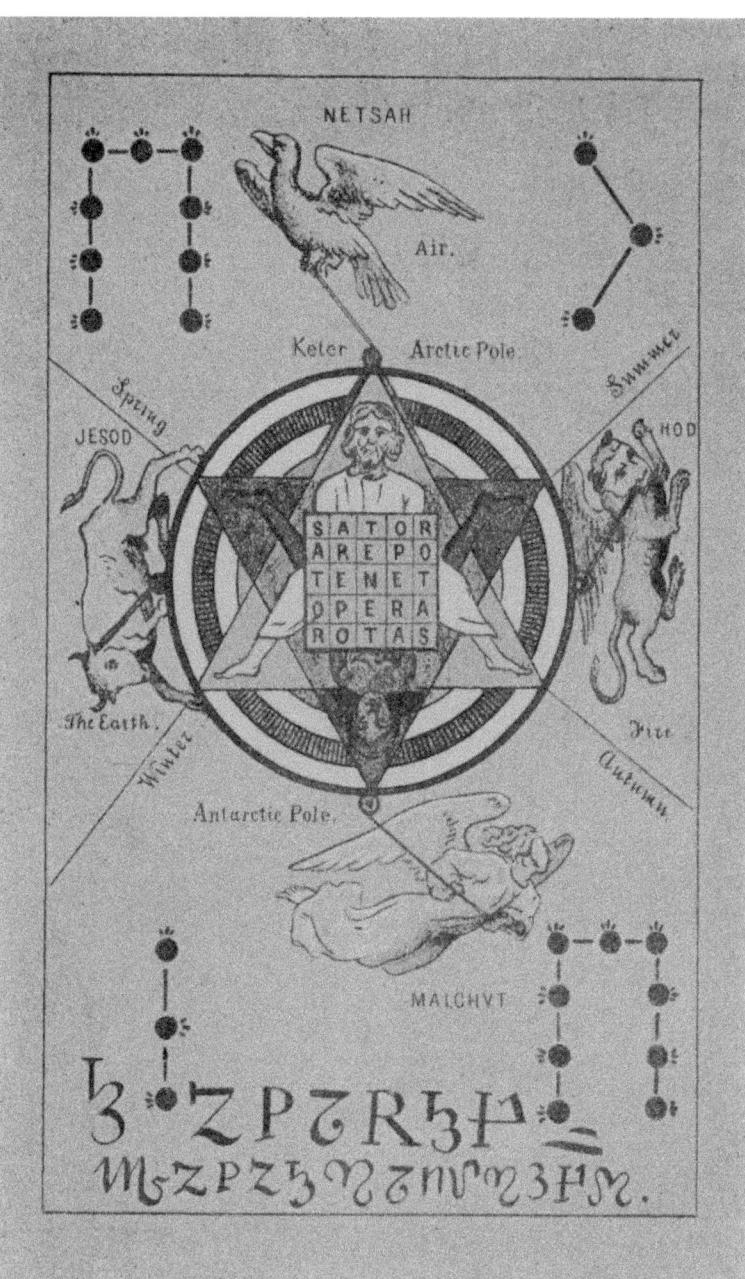

The key to the great arcanum.

CHAPTER XVI.

THE ASTRONOMICAL TAROT.

Egyptian Astronomy—The Four Seasons—The Twelve Months—The Thirty-six Decani—The Planets—Absolute Analogy with the Tarot—Figure containing the Application of the Tarot to Astronomy—Key to the Astrological Works of Christian—Oswald Wirth's Astronomical Tarot.

THE ASTRONOMICAL TAROT.

IN order to demonstrate the accuracy of the principles upon which the construction of the Tarot is based, we will take the constitution of the Universe itself, as shown by Astronomy, for our example of the first application of its system.

It is known that the Egyptians divided the year into four seasons, each composed of three months. Each month contained three decani or periods of ten days, which gave three hundred and sixty days in each year. They added to complete it a period of five days, or *Epagomenes*, placed after the 30th degree of the Lion (August).

We must therefore find in our Tarot—

1. The four seasons;
2. The twelve months, or, better still, the twelve signs of the zodiac;

3. The thirty-six decani.

Moreover each month, or, still better, each zodiacal sign, and each of the decani is ruled by a planet.

1. *The Four Seasons.*

The four figures of the Tarot correspond absolutely with the four seasons of the year.

If we then look at the twenty-first card of the Tarot, the origin, as we have seen, of all its applications, we shall see that the four figures in the corners represent the four colours of the Tarot, and in this case the four seasons of the year.

The elliptic space between these four figures and the centre correspond to the *zodiac* and its divisions.

Finally, the central portion corresponds to the *planets*, which influence the whole system.

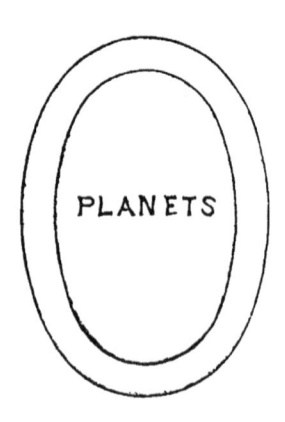

2. *The 12 Signs of the Zodiac.*

Each colour represents one season. Each season is composed of three months. How, then, will the months be represented in our colour?

THE ASTRONOMICAL TAROT.

The months will be represented by the *figures*, and the correspondence is established in this way—

    KING.   1st Month or *Active Month* in the Season. *Creative Month. Yod.*

    QUEEN.   2nd Month or Passive Month in each Season. *Preserving Month. He.*

    KNIGHT. 3rd Month or *Realizing Month, Equilibrist* of the Season. *Vau.*

    KNAVE.   Transition from the preceding Season to the one following. *Epagomene.*[1]

(Consult, for further details, the first part of our study upon the Tarot.)

We therefore find twelve figures, which respond to the twelve signs of the Zodiac, as follows—

SCEPTRES	King of Sceptres Queen Knight	The Ram The Bull The Twins	} SPRING
	Knave *Transition*	*Epagomene*	
CUPS	King of Cups Queen Knight	Cancer The Lion The Virgin	} SUMMER
	Knave *Transition*	*Epagomene*	
SWORDS	King of Swords Queen Knight	The Balance The Scorpion Sagittarius	} AUTUMN
	Knave *Transition*	*Epagomene*	
PENTACLES	King of Pentacles Queen Knight	Capricornus Aquarius The Fishes	} WINTER
	Knave *Transition*	*Epagomene*	

---

[1] Thus the Tarot places one *epagomene*, or complementary day, after each season.

3. *The* 36 *Decani.*

Each season is divided into three months, but each month is divided into three decani, or periods of ten days each.

We need only recall the analogy existing between the *figures* and the *numbers* in the minor arcana, to ascertain which cards of the Tarot represent these new divisions.

If we take one of the figures—the King, for instance—we know that this king governs certain cards: the Ace, two, three, and the first ternary.

We then obtain the following analogies—

KING OF SCEPTRES: zodiacal sign, the Ram.

ACE.	1st Decan or *Active Decan* of the Month. *Creative Decan.* Yod.
TWO.	2nd Decan or *Passive Decan* of the Month. *Forming or Preserving Decan.* He.
THREE.	3rd Decan or *Equilibrist Decan.* Vau.
FOUR.	Transition between the third Decan of the actual series, to the first Decan of the following series, which it forms.

The thirty-six decani are therefore represented in the Tarot in the following series—

King	Ace of Sceptres — 2 — 3 —	1st Decan — 2nd — 3rd —	of the Ram
Queen	4 — 5 — 6 —	1st Decan — 2nd — 3rd —	of the Bull
Knight	7 — 8 — 9 —	1st Decan — 2nd — 3rd —	of the Twins
Knave	10 · *Transition*	*Epagomene*	

THE ASTRONOMICAL TAROT. 237

King $\begin{cases} \text{Ace of Cups} \\ 2 \quad — \\ 3 \quad — \end{cases}$ $\begin{rcases} \text{1st Decan} \\ \text{2nd} \quad — \\ \text{3rd} \quad — \end{rcases}$ of Cancer

Queen $\begin{cases} 4 \quad — \\ 5 \quad — \\ 6 \quad — \end{cases}$ $\begin{rcases} \text{1st Decan} \\ \text{2nd} \quad — \\ \text{3rd} \quad — \end{rcases}$ of the Lion

Knight $\begin{cases} 7 \quad — \\ 8 \quad — \\ 9 \quad — \end{cases}$ $\begin{rcases} \text{1st Decan} \\ \text{2nd} \quad — \\ \text{3rd} \quad — \end{rcases}$ of the Virgin

Knave 10 *Transition* *Epagomene*

King $\begin{cases} \text{Ace of Swords} \\ 2 \quad — \\ 3 \quad — \end{cases}$ $\begin{rcases} \text{1st Decan} \\ \text{2nd} \quad — \\ \text{3rd} \quad — \end{rcases}$ of the Balance

Queen $\begin{cases} 4 \quad — \\ 5 \quad — \\ 6 \quad — \end{cases}$ $\begin{rcases} \text{1st Decan} \\ \text{2nd} \quad — \\ \text{3rd} \quad — \end{rcases}$ of the Scorpion

Knight $\begin{cases} 7 \quad — \\ 8 \quad — \\ 9 \quad — \end{cases}$ $\begin{rcases} \text{1st Decan} \\ \text{2nd} \quad — \\ \text{3rd} \quad — \end{rcases}$ of Sagittarius

Knave 10 *Transition* *Epagomene*

King $\begin{cases} \text{Ace of Pentacles} \\ 2 \quad — \\ 3 \quad — \end{cases}$ $\begin{rcases} \text{1st Decan} \\ \text{2nd} \quad — \\ \text{3rd} \quad — \end{rcases}$ of Capricornus

Queen $\begin{cases} 4 \quad — \\ 5 \quad — \\ 6 \quad — \end{cases}$ $\begin{rcases} \text{1st Decan} \\ \text{2nd} \quad — \\ \text{3rd} \quad — \end{rcases}$ of Aquarius

Knight $\begin{cases} 7 \quad — \\ 8 \quad — \\ 9 \quad — \end{cases}$ $\begin{rcases} \text{1st Decan} \\ \text{2nd} \quad — \\ \text{3rd} \quad — \end{rcases}$ of the Fishes

Knave 10 *Transition* *Epagomene*

' Each decan, governing ten degrees of the zodiacal circle,

corresponds to a certain number of days in the month. Consequently each card in the minor arcana, corresponding to a decan, represents a certain fraction of the year—

> Ace of Sceptres   21st to 30th of March.
> 2   —   31st of March to 9th of April.
> 3   —   10th to 19th of April, etc.

We need only consult the figure at the end of this study of the astronomical Tarot to see which days correspond to each decan.

This is the basis of the *astrological Tarot*, and by its cards a horoscope can be drawn out; but since this application lies beyond the purely scientific field to which we have limited ourselves, we must not dwell upon it here.

In short, our minor arcana are fully represented in the astronomical Tarot, and they exactly determine the limits in which move the planets, that we have still to consider.

The Planets.

The major arcana are represented in this application of the Tarot by the septenary of the planets acting upon the three worlds ($3 \times 7 = 21$).

Each zodiacal sign and each decan is governed by a planet, and the connection between the planets and these different signs is indicated upon the tableau which follows.

This tableau enables us to comprehend all the work that Christian[1] and Ely Star[2] accomplished upon Astrology. Moreover it indicates the astronomical correspondence of

---

[1] Christian, *Histoire de la Magie*, Paris, 1854. 8vo.
[2] Ely Star, *Les Mystères de l'Horoscope*, Paris, Dentu, 1888. 18mo. (3 fr. 50.)

every card in the Tarot. Here is an explanation of its construction—

Here the four figures of the twenty-first card of the Tarot represent the four seasons of the year and the four colours of the Tarot.

The centre of the twenty-first card responds to the seven planets, which animate the yearly system.

Lastly, the ZODIACAL ELLIPSE revolves between these two terms, and it contains the key to the influence exercised by the major arcana (the planets) over the minor arcana (the signs and decani).

This tableau is therefore both a proof of the accuracy of our system of explaining the Tarot, and also a magnificent key to the Tarot itself.

(Consult the tableau.)

We shall now quote two extracts from La Vaillant (Les Rômes, *Histoire des Bohémiens*), which demonstrate the harmony which exists between our deductions and the traditional explanations given by the gypsies.

SOME OF THE GYPSY TRADITIONS

UPON THE ASTRONOMICAL TAROT.

The 21st card, entitled the Universe or Time, is, in fact, the time of the temple and the temple of time.

It represents an *oval* crown of flowers, divided into four by four lotus flowers, and supported by the four symbolical heads, which St. John borrowed from Ezekiel, and the latter from the cherubim and seraphim of Assyria and Egypt.

The four heads are those—

Of the Eagle. The symbol of the East, of the morning, of the equinox of spring.

Of the Lion. — of the South, and of the solstice of summer.

Of the Bull. — of the Evening, the West, and of the equinox of autumn.

Of the Man. — of the Night, the North, and of the solstice of winter.

In the midst of this crown, the symbol of the egg of the world, stands a nude woman, the symbol of *Eve;* one of her feet is raised, symbolizing the flight of time; and she holds two wands of equal length, symbols of the balance and equilibrium of time, of the justice and equity of men, of the equality of day and night, of man and woman.

This *Eve* is the great Mother (*Ava* or *Ebe*) who pours out to the stars the men-gods of heaven, and to men the star-gods of earth, the nectar and ambrosia of immortality, the shadow and light of eternity (*Aon*), of which the crown which surrounds her is the sea or the ocean, the enclosure or the vase, the ark or the vessel.

This symbol is not new. It was throughout antiquity used to express the nature of the Universe, the synthesis of the arcs of the circle, the union of the arches of the sphere, which the Hebrews made into the ark of the covenant, the modification of the ancient coins of Crete, which took this *arch* of the world, the covenant of the rainbows, for the *principle* of *justice* which gives it its name. And, in fact, the name of *Kudas*, of that *Ebee of Crete*, clearly expresses justice, *saduk*, which makes of this Melchi sedek, the spirit of the Lord, and of this spirit (*Eon*) of the sun, the law of the times of the stars, of the life of man; consequently *Noah*, who is himself the spirit

(*Eon*) of eternity (*Aon*) of centuries (*Aion*), has been qualified as *præco justitiæ*, revealer of justice.

***

The Tarot is a deduction of the sideral book of *Henoch*, who is Henochia; it is modelled from the astral wheel of *Athor*, which is *As-taroth*, resembling the Indian *ot-tara*, the polar bear or *arc-tura* of the north; it is the major force (*tarie*) upon which is based the solidity (*ferrale*) of the world and the *sideral* firmament of the *carth*; consequently, like the polar bear, called the chariot of the sun, the chariot of David and of ARTHUR, it is the Greek luck (*tuché*), the Chinese destiny (*tiko*), the Egyptian chance (*tiki*), the fate (*tika*) of the Romanies; and the stars, as they incessantly revolve round the polar bear, reveal to the earth ostentation and misery, light and shade, heat and cold; whilst from them flow the good and evil, the love and hatred, which form the happiness (*ev-tuchié*) and the misfortune (*dis-tuchié*) of men.

***

In truth *Sephora* is one of the harmonies in that triad s. f. r., which united form the light (*Sapher*), the number (*Sipher*), and the word (*Sephora*) of the Hebrews, from the *Sphere* of the Universe. From this sphere,

of which the light is the truth,

the zodiac the book which contains it, the stars the numbers and letters which explain it, the *Anaks* have drawn their *Tara*, the Gypsies their *Tarot*, the Phœnicians their *As-tharot*, the Egyptians their *Athor*, and the Hebrews their *Thora*.

R

But we cannot end this study upon the astronomical Tarot without some allusion to the work of Oswald Wirth upon this subject. In some respects his conclusions differ from our own; but we are anxious on that account to copy his essay upon it, in order that each reader may judge between us for himself.

ESSAY UPON THE ASTRONOMICAL TAROT BY OSWALD WIRTH.

According to Christian the twenty-two major arcana of the Tarot represent the hieroglyphic paintings which are found in the spaces between the columns of a gallery, which the neophyte was obliged to cross in the Egyptian initiations. There were twelve columns to the North and the same number to the South, that is, eleven symbolical pictures on each side. These pictures were explained to the candidate for initiation in regular order, and they contained the rules and principles for the Initiate.

The arcana corresponding to the twenty-two letters of the Hebrew alphabet must have been arranged upon the walls of the secret crypts in the temples of Osiris in the following order. (See p. 243.)

This opinion is confirmed by the correspondence which exists between the arcana when they are thus arranged.

It is at once evident that the arcana 2, 3, 4 and 5 form a complete group; this group corresponds to another formed by the arcana 21, 20, 19 and 18. Now in the interpretation of the symbols each arcanum should be studied in its relations with the neighbouring arcana, and particularly with those which are pendant to it in the grouping that we have pointed out. For instance, the 2nd

THE ASTRONOMICAL TAROT. 243

NORTH	נ	11	Strength	ל	12	The Hanged Man
	י	10	The Wheel of Fortune	מ	13	Death
	ט	9	Hermit	נ	14	Temperance
	ח	8	Justice	ס	15	Devil
	ז	7	Chariot	ע	16	The Lightning-struck Tower
	ו	6	Lovers	פ	17	Stars
	ה	5	Pope	צ	18	Moon
	ד	4	Emperor	ק	19	Sun
	ג	3	Empress	ר	20	Judgment
	ב	2	The High Priestess	ש	21	Universe
	א	1	Juggler	ת	0	Foolish Man

EAST — WEST — NORTH — SOUTH

arcanum (ב), the High Priestess, should not only be compared with the 1st arcanum (א), the Juggler, the 3rd, and 4th (ד), the Empress; but also with the 5th arcanum (ה), the Pope, with the 21st (ת), the Universe, and even with the 18th (צ), the Moon. By studying each of the twenty-two arcana in this way, we shall discover that the whole are closely linked together, and we shall acquire unexpected light upon the most ancient of all the sacred books which we possess.

It should be noticed that the 7th, 8th, 9th, and 10th arcana represent a quaternary, to which a last group corresponds, formed of the 16th, 15th, 14th, and 13th arcana. We therefore have sixteen pentacles divided into four quaternaries, which give a definite general meaning. Six other pentacles are placed in pairs at the commencement, the centre, and the end of the double series of the arcana of the Tarot. These six arcana appear to frame the others, and this fact gives them great importance. Their signification is easily discovered by their mutual comparison, and the judicious application of the laws of analogy supplied by the keys of the Book of Thoth, as well as by those of the Eternal Book that Nature, symbolized under the form of Isis, holds half-opened in the 2nd arcanum (ב), the High Priestess.

But it is necessary to proceed methodically in these researches, by means of a progressive analysis starting from the whole, before we can grasp each arcanum separately, for each one must be carefully examined under the numerous aspects which it presents. When this work of dissection is once accomplished, the student must retrace his steps, and synthetically recompose the whole by reverse operation.

In applying these principles here, we must first repeat

THE ASTRONOMICAL TAROT.

that the Tarot considered as a whole is pre-eminently the Sacred Book of occult initiation. Now we attain this initiation by two different paths, by one of which we develop the powers which we innately possess to their utmost extent; by the other we subdue ourselves, and thus attain a state of being which renders us susceptible to the action of the cosmic forces which surround us. Although these two methods differ completely, we can accomplish this great work by following either of them. This is the meaning of the Hermetic precept, "that the philosopher's stone can be prepared by the dry path or by the moist, by the red dye or by the white." Initiation, androgynous as a whole, is therefore subdivided into male and female. It is masculine from the 1st (א) to the 11th (כ) arcana, and becomes feminine in the arcana 21 (ת) to 12 (ל). With regard to the arcanum 0 (ש), which is unnumbered in the Tarot, although it is eminently passive in itself, it must not be included in the feminine series, for reasons easily discerned in the study of the exact signification of each arcanum taken separately.

Let us then content ourselves for the moment with asserting that masculine or Dorian initiation starts from א to end in כ, whilst feminine or Ionian initiation starts from ש to end in ל. The two unite and complete each other in the androgynous initiation, which can start from א to end in ש, or start from ש to return to it again, after traversing the whole series of the arcana, taking their numbers in the inverse order.

But initiation can be regarded not only under the double aspect of activity and passivity represented by the North and South, but it can be also contemplated as light and life, that is to say, as the intellectual instruction as well as the moral education of the Initiate. In this respect the Tarot is divided by the 6th arcanum (ו), the Lovers, and the 17th (פ), the Stars, into two parts, which represent the West and the East.

This double division produces the four quaternaries of which we have already spoken. Each represents one especial section, its general sense being indicated by its orientation; the North-West thus corresponds with intellectual activity; the North-East with moral activity; the South-West with intellectual passivity, and the South-East with moral passivity. These four sections are also united in the arcana 1 (א) the Juggler; 11 (כ) Strength; 12 (ל) the Hanged Man; and 0 (ש) the Foolish Man.

The 6th arcanum, the Lovers, indicates the passage of intellectual activity to its moral application, the 17th פ. The stars form the transition between passive intellectuality and its practical employment in the exercise of the occult powers.

We think that enough has been now said to enable each student to discover for himself the complex signification of every arcanum in the Tarot. We will therefore end this sketch by some classifications, intended to prove that the order in which we arrange the arcana of the Tarot does not form a purely arbitrary system.

It will, in fact, be easily seen that connection in their opposition links the arcana when they are grouped in four quaternaries of different formation from the four first, which we have already examined. (See p. 247.)

The analogy of these significations is particularly striking between the arcana 7 and 16, 10 and 13, which yet present an antagonistic meaning, as soon as 7 is compared with 16, and 10 with 13. It is the same with the other quaternaries represented here, although the fact may be less visible at the first glance. But we will now

THE ASTRONOMICAL TAROT.

leave a free field to individual investigation on this point, and pass on to the study of the Tarot from another point of view.

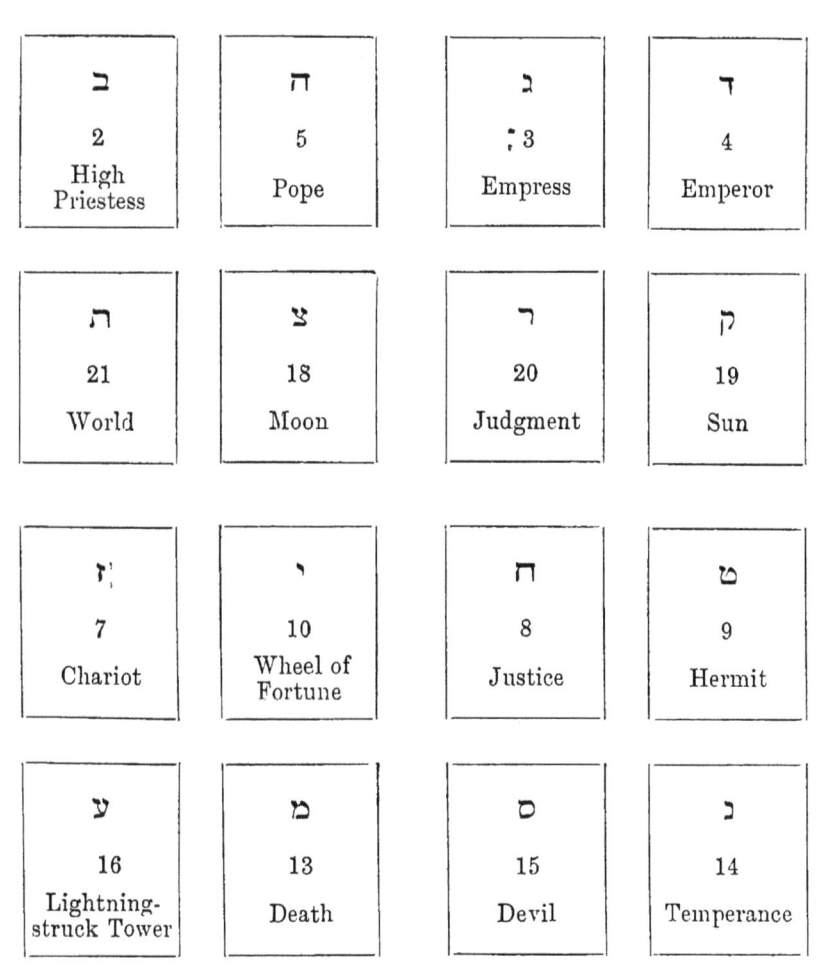

ב 2 High Priestess	ה 5 Pope	ג 3 Empress	ד 4 Emperor
ת 21 World	צ 18 Moon	ר 20 Judgment	ק 19 Sun
ז 7 Chariot	י 10 Wheel of Fortune	ח 8 Justice	ט 9 Hermit
ע 16 Lightning-struck Tower	מ 13 Death	ס 15 Devil	נ 14 Temperance

The 22 major arcana of the Tarot compared to the figures representing the constellations upon the celestial sphere, according to the Greek and Egyptian planispheres.

The Tarot which we possess represents a series of symbolical images adapted to the ideology of the fourteenth century, and fixed by the invention of xylography. It is impossible for us to retrace through the darkness of the middle ages the origin of the twenty-two significative figures known as *atouts*, in the pack of seventy-eight cards by which the Gypsies claim to reveal the secrets of fate.

Still it has been proved that the major arcana of the Tarot are disfigured reproductions of a primitive model dating from the earliest ages. It would be difficult to refind this model in its original purity; and if it were possible to do so it could only be through judicious study of every manifestation of symbolism throughout the history of Oriental mythologies. They have bequeathed to us an hieroglyphic monument of immense importance in the representative figures of the signs of the Zodiac, and of the constellations of the celestial Sphere. But it would be most interesting if we could prove that these allegorical figures absolutely reproduce the 22 major arcana of the Tarot. From this affinity we might obtain great light upon the genesis of human knowledge. For the same identity of origin which manifestly unites the plates of the Book of Thoth to the subdivisions of the Greek and Egyptian planispheres, leads to the conclusion that in both cases we possess a special adaptation, made from documents which we have not yet found, but which may still give us complete information respecting primitive India.

In any case the arcana of the Tarot explain many of the anomalies in Greek mythology. We cannot now enter into any minute details upon this subject, for it would lead us beyond the limits of this book. We must content ourselves with giving the reader a tableau indicating the constellations which appear to correspond with the 22 major arcana of the Tarot, and therefore with the 22 letters of the Hebrew alphabet, although their correspondence

THE ASTRONOMICAL TAROT.   249

with the latter is much less clearly defined. We will then trace a planisphere grouping the arcana of the Tarot according to the order of the constellations, and we will end by a pentacle in the form of a double hexagram, in which the Hebrew letters will represent the signs of the zodiac, and the circumpolar constellations to which they correspond, according to our first tableau.

OSWALD WIRTH'S TABLEAU.

No. of the Arcana of the Tarot.	Corresponding Hebrew Letters.	DENOMINATION OF THE ARCANA.	CONSTELLATIONS.
1	א	The Juggler	Orion—The Bull
2	ב	The High Priestess	Cassiopeia
3	ג	The Empress	The Virgin
4	ד	The Emperor	Hercules, Lyra and Boreal Crown
5	ה	The Pope	The Ram
6	ו	The Lovers	Eagle, Antinoüs, and Sagittarius
7	ז	The Chariot	Great Bear
8	ח	Justice	The Balance
9	ט	The Hermit	The Ox-Driver
10	י	The Wheel of Fortune	Capricornus (opposed to Sirius)
11	כ	Strength	Lion (and Virgin)
12	ל	The Hanged Man	Perseus
13	מ	Death	Dragon of the Pole
14	נ	Temperance	Aquarius
15	ס	The Devil	Goat and Coachman
16	ע	The Lightning-struck Tower	Scorpion, Ophiuchus
17	פ	The Stars	Andromeda, the Fishes
18	צ	The Moon	Cancer, Sirius, and Procion
19	ק	The Sun	The Twins
20	ר	The Judgment	The Swan
21	ת	The Universe	Lesser Bear and Pole Star
22	ש	The Foolish Man	Cepheus

PLANISPHERE,

ACCORDING TO THE DATA OF THE PRECEDING TABLEAU, BY

OSWALD WIRTH.

	14 Temperance — Aquarius	10 Wheel of Fortune — Capricornus	6 The Lovers — Sagittarius	
17 Stars — The Fishes	2 The High Priestess — Cassiopeia	0 The Foolish Man — Cepheus	20 The Judgment — The Swan	16 The Lightning-struck Tower — Scorpion

5 The Pope — The Ram	12 The Hanged Man — Perseus	21 The Universe — Pole Star	13 Death — Dragon	4 The Emperor — Hercules	8 Justice — The Balance

	1 Juggler — Bull	15 Devil — The Coachman	7 The Chariot — Great Bear	9 The Hermit — The Ox-Driver	3 The Empress — Virgin

		19 Sun — Twins	18 Moon — Cancer	11 Strength — Lion	

THE ASTRONOMICAL TAROT. 251

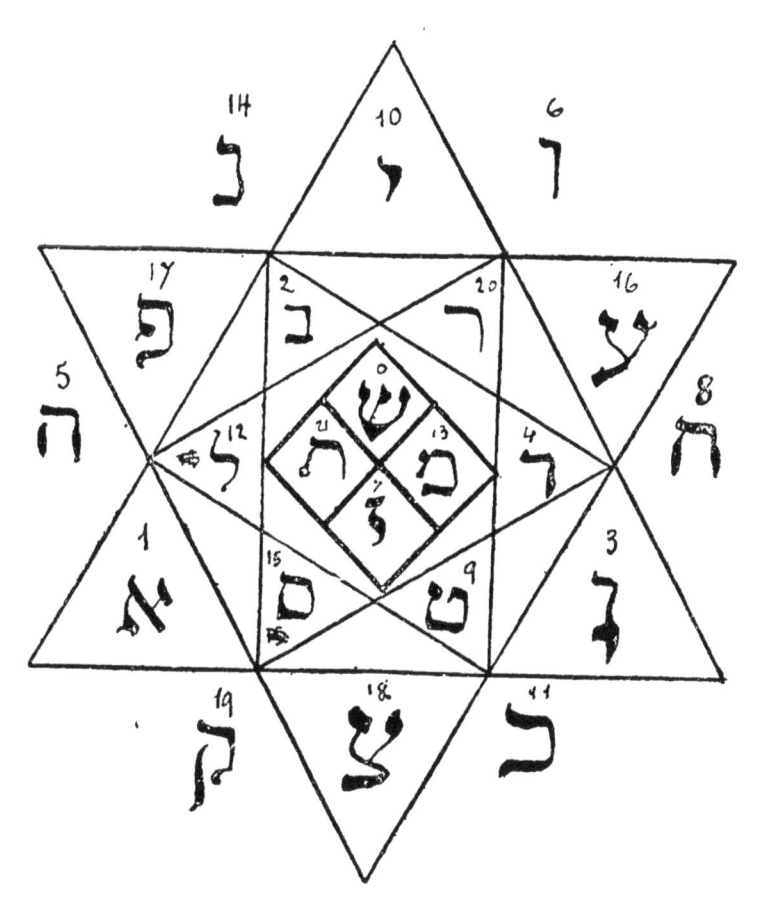

PENTACLE OF OSWALD WIRTH.
Signs of the Zodiac and Circumpolar Constellations.
Affinities with the Tarot.

To face page 252.

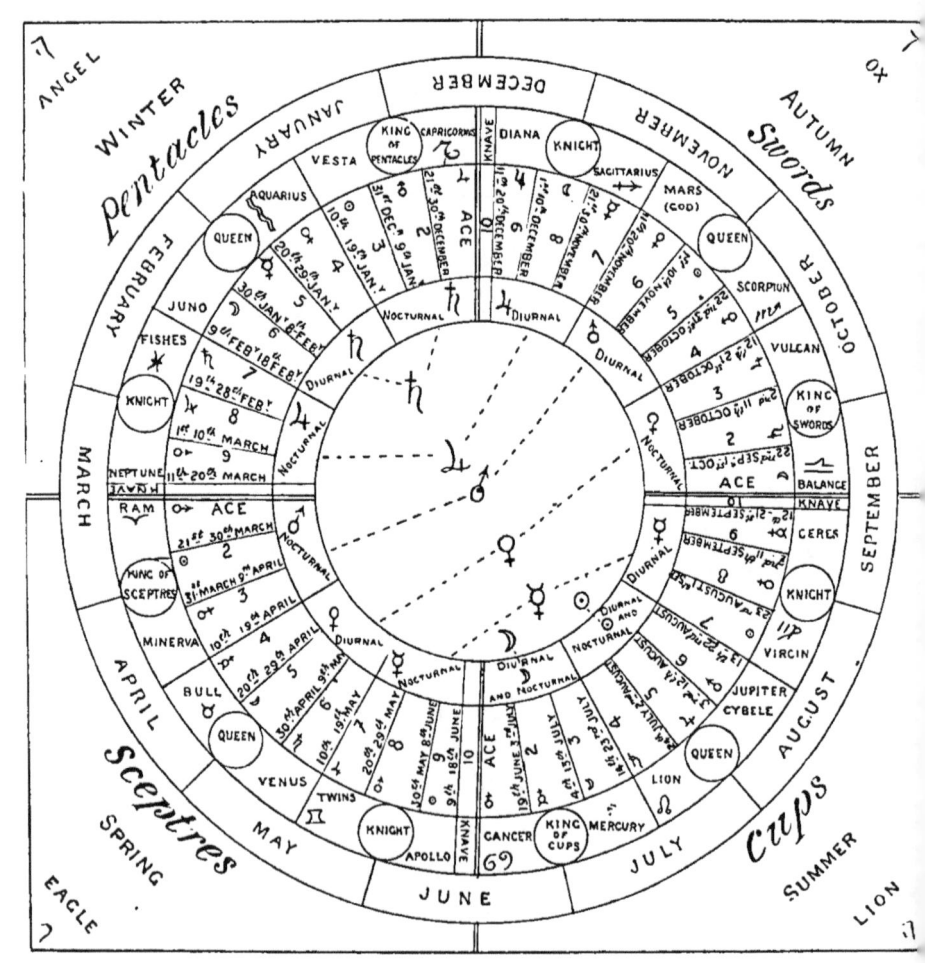

CHAPTER XVII.

THE INITIATIVE TAROT.

Ch. Barlet's Essay on this Subject—Involution and Evolution—The Hours of Apollonius of Tyana—The Phases of Initiation represented by the Tarot.

THE INITIATIVE TAROT.

APPLICATION OF THE TAROT TO THE THEORETICAL AND PRACTICAL DOCTRINES OF INITIATION.

OUR friend F. Ch. Barlet has written a very interesting article upon this subject, which we will quote *in extenso*. Our readers will then see the exactitude with which his conclusions harmonize with our own.

INITIATION.

Amongst the ancients the scientific men were also the sages, such as Pythagoras, Plato, Aristotle; in modern times, on the contrary, science and wisdom are unsuccessfully seeking for each other, or struggling in mortal conflict over the religious question. That such a separation is against nature is easily seen by the study of those Positivist philosophers whose extensive learning and admirable efforts to build up a synthesis of scientific wisdom merit high rank in the modern intellectual world. Whilst their fundamental aphorism is that nothing is attainable by man beyond the world of phenomena, their works display an increasing though unintentional tendency to cross the limits which they seek to impose upon themselves, for they are led by that nature which they love, and which in its final manifestations they know better than any one else. We may compare them to insects imprisoned behind a window; in despair they beat themselves against the glass, clearly seeing the sunbeam which should lead them to the source of all light, yet unable to follow it beyond the invisible wall of their prison. On the other hand, the Spiritualists are outside, free, and as it were lost in the luminous ocean, wandering without a compass, unable to find the guiding sunbeam which is the despair of the Positivists.

However, one school exists which promises to guide the one, to free the other, and to direct each student towards the centre of Truth so ardently desired; an unknown school, little frequented, like every transcendent degree, although its masters have always given proofs of considerable learning—the school of *Theosophy*, a positive spiritualism preserved for ages in the ancient mysteries, transmitted with more or less purity by the Kabbalists, Mystics, Templars, Rosicrucians, and Freemasons, often degenerate, like every other doctrine prematurely divulged, yet hidden at the root of every religion, and carefully perpetuated in a few unknown sanctuaries, chiefly situated in India.

The secret of Theosophy, in the reconciliation between science and metaphysics, lies in a certain practical development of those human faculties which are best fitted to

THE INITIATIVE TAROT.

extend the limits of reliable knowledge. Let us first try to understand this possibility.

An attentive examination of any scientific method, however positive it may be, proves that there is no evidence or certainty save in axioms, and that the fragile and changeable scaffolding of our sciences, built upon this immovable basis, is entirely due to *intuition*, of which observation and experience are only instruments.

But the field of direct perception in which intuition exerts itself is capable of extension; this fact is now demonstrated by the phenomena of hypnotism and magnetism, the torments of our modern sciences; for by them the limits of opaque matter, of space and time, are suppressed in variable but incontestable degrees.

But still, in this realm of transcendental faculties the perception is not always so reliable as the unvarying certainty which characterizes an axiom; for amongst the hypnotizable or magnetizable subjects, the material lucidity presents a number of gradations which are reproduced in the intellectual order, and which vary between the fancies of a disordered imagination and the sublime revelations of healthily inspired genius.

We do not therefore exceed the possibilities given by the reliable evidence of observation and experience, when we assert that the physical or intellectual perception of the human being is capable of extending beyond the limits of ordinary judgments and sensations; and that in the transcendental regions which it can attain it is susceptible of more or less certitude in its impressions. This assertion opens new fields for human knowledge, an hierarchy of new immediate causes, and the prospect of an indefinite progress in science.

Now Theosophy inspires man with the enthusiasm

which enables him to draw near to these transcendent regions of perception, whilst it guards him from illusion, through the forces and the new beings which he will meet there: it is this instruction which constitutes *Initiation*.

The slight sketch which will now follow will at least give some idea of the principles by which Religion and Philosophy, Wisdom and Science, are united in Theosophy. Any defects which the reader may find in it must be attributed to want of skill on the part of the student who has undertaken it.

* * *

Initiation comprises two different but united sections. The *Theory* of the resources and necessities of his enterprise, which the neophyte always receives as an inheritance which leaves him absolute liberty of thought—and the *Practice* in which he exercises, under the direction of his masters, the physical, intellectual, and moral self-control which will render him an *Initiate*.

The *Theory*, the primary instruction of Theosophy, is a preliminary definition, consisting almost exclusively of the contents of the Theosophical publications; but a student should not fancy himself one of the Initiate because he possesses these public works; the knowledge of them is an excellent preparation, but nothing more.

This theory is found scattered throughout a number of more or less well-known and accessible books; but there are very few of them which explain it as a whole, simply and methodically enough to satisfy a beginner. This first difficulty, chiefly due to the actual state of many minds, which will not admit regular instruction, also corresponds to the numerous varieties of intelligence which examine them. Some, previously opened to theosophical doctrines, approach every detail with equal profit to themselves; others, on the contrary, who cannot at first accept them as a whole, willingly examine them by means of a secondary door which especially suits them, but which often forces them to make enormous digressions through our sciences and philosophies. The first steps are consequently very varied, and they require guidance, from some more advanced brother, who is capable of discerning the intellectual and moral state of the neophyte.

This is why no work on the subject can be especially recommended here. An excellent bibliography of theosophic works will be found in the *Traité Élémentaire de Science Occulte*, by Papus. We now add to it an excellent list of a series of studies, long but reliable, which will form a gradual transition from Positivism to Theosophy:

For facts. Study: Richet, d'Assier, Liebault, Philipps, Dupotet, Reichenbach, Mesmer, &c.

Hypothesis of the whole: Comte, Stuart Mill, Bain, Ribot, Spencer, Taine, &c.

Philosophers: Du Prel, Hartmann, Schopenhauer, Hegel. Great profit can then be derived from older works: Spinoza, Leibnitz, and even from the ancients: Aristotle, Plato, the Neoplatonists, the Pythagorists; then the modern mystic scientists: Wronski, Fabre d'Olivet, Lucas, &c.

The student will then fully understand Theosophy.

This series will, however, require further modifications, according to the character and the scientific aptitudes of the student. We must also point out some features of the theory, which are necessary for the comprehension of our principal subject; the reader must only remember that this explanation is entirely due to the author of this article, and he must not impute any of its errors to Theosophy itself.

* * *

Our positive sciences give the last formula of the visible world in the following words—

There is no matter without force : no force without matter.

An indisputable but incomplete formula, unless the following commentary be added to it—

1. The combination of what we call *Force* and *Matter* presents itself in various proportions, from that which is called materialized *Force* (rocks, minerals, simple chemical bodies), to *subtilized Matter* or *Matter-Force* (a grain of pollen, spermatozoid, the electric atom). *Matter* and *Force*, although we cannot isolate them, therefore present themselves as the extreme and opposing mathematical limits (or contrary signs) of a series of which we see only a few medium terms, abstract but indubitable.

2. The terms of this series, that is to say, the substances of nature, are never stable; *Force*, which is characterized by infinite mobility, sways essentially inert matter from one pole to the other, as though it were drawn by a continual current, while it retorts by a counter-current, which leads it back to its inert condition. For instance, an atom of phosphorus borrowed by a vegetable from the mineral phosphates, becomes the element of a human *cerebral cellule* (subtilized matter), then through disintegration falls back into the inert mineral kingdom.

3. The movement resulting from this unstable equili-

brium is not disorganized; it presents a series of chained harmonies which we call *Laws*, and which are synthetized in our eyes in the supreme law of *Evolution*.

One conclusion is forced upon us: This harmonious synthesis of phenomena is the eminent manifestation of what we call a *will*.

Therefore, according to positive science, the visible world is the expression of a will which manifests itself by the unstable but progressive equilibrium of Force and Matter.

It is represented by this quaternary—

I. WILL (simple origin).
III. FORCE (Elements of this polarized Will).   II. MATTER.
IV. THE VISIBLE WORLD
(The result of their unstable, dynamic equilibrium).

The positive method will not allow us to pause there, we must analyze the *Will* in its turn. We will abridge this analysis here, for the reader will easily master it with the aid of the treatises on psychology; it leads through the two opposing terms of *affirmation* and *negation* to a new superior, apparently simple cause, the *Idea*, which analysis again decomposes into *consciousness* and *unconsciousness*, gradually remounting to its furthest limit, the absolute term, the *One*, both conscious and unconscious, affirmative and negative, force and matter, nameless, incomprehensible to man.

Let us designate this supreme term by A, and the material atom by Ω, we shall then have, according to our analysis, the following series of hierarchized quaternaries as a representation of the Universe—

	+	(1) A	−	*Divine World*
(3) *Consciousness*		(2) *Unconsciousness*		(The Transcendent)
		(4) IDEA		
(6) *Affirmation*		(5) *Negation*		*Intelligible World*
		(7) WILL		(Logic)
(9) *Force*		(8) *Matter*		
		(10) KOSMOS		*Visible World*
		Ω		(Positive Science)

The extreme terms, *a* and ω, Spirit and Matter, equally incomprehensible to human intelligence in their infinite grandeur and infinite littleness,[1] are not only linked together by invariable intermediate chains, but they also make an incessantly descending movement from one to the other, in which the Spirit becomes Matter by the successive disintegrations which express the Idea, the Will, and Kosmos. This constitutes the *creation*.

But since, as our sciences prove to us, the Kosmos itself is in a state of evolutive movement, and since according to their teachings this movement clearly inclines towards a progressive synthesis, which spiritualizes the living being by entering more and more into its composition, the preceding scheme expresses but one half of the Universe, the *one which* descends. We must now add to it a second half, which restores the atom, ω, to its opposing principle *a*, through the progressive synthesis of individual lives. This is *Progress*, the sequence of Creation.

Thus the Universe appears to us like a circular current, in which the flow is necessarily inverse in the two opposing arcs: from the positive pole *a* to the negative pole ω the

[1] The first *a*, *One* and infinitely great; integration of Ω. The second ω, a multiple composed of an *infinite number* of infinitely tiny elements; analysis of *a*.

current descends—this is *Involution*, the descent of the Spirit into Matter; from the negative pole ω to the positive pole a the current re-ascends—this is *Evolution*, the spiritualization of Matter. We shall describe it presently.

***

Let us then infer for man—

The evidence of our sciences shows him to be upon the ascending arc, already far from the negative pole, since he is at the head of the three kingdoms of the terrestrial world. He thus belongs to the *visible world* of the Universe; the imposing monument of science is a proof of the position which he also occupies in the *intellectual world;* but at the same time his errors, his doubts, the enormous deficiencies in his knowledge, and his passions, sufficiently prove that he is no longer master in this sphere, as he is in the inferior world. As to the *divine world*, he conceives it, presses towards it; but if he attain it, it will be by faith rather than by science.

Man is then a being who in his re-ascension has reached the middle region, and even the centre of that region; his place is in the centre of the ascending arc, between the superior and the inferior beings of creation, ruling the one, ruled by the others, midway between the Angel and the Beast. A situation inevitably painful through the equality of the two opposing forces, which retard his ascension; he has come to a dead stop, which must be overcome by a special effort.

At the present time Initiation is the instrument which facilitates the development of the human butterfly. We shall soon understand of what it consists.

***

The Ancients, with the usual force of their synthetic genius, have symbolized the whole of Involution and Evolution by a sequence of twenty-two figures, full of hidden significations, which the occultists name the *Twenty-two Great Arcana*.

Taking the ten first as a description of Involution, we find in the others the successive phases of Initiation, such as they are depicted in the *twelve hours* (or sentences) which form the *Nuctemeron* attributed to Apollonius of Tyana. These we shall now enumerate.

To be perfectly clear we must first return to Evolution for one moment.

In fact its analysis is not completed by the ten terms which have led us to the Kosmos, the dynamic equilibrium of Force and Matter. This Kosmos can be analyzed in its turn as two principles which, according to all the sciences, are conflicting in every movement of matter: the *Active* and *Passive* (male and female of organizations, acid and basis of chemistry, the opposing poles of electricity, &c.). Completely inert matter is only found in their absolute equilibrium in the unsiezable pole exactly opposed to the a—the ω of the Universe.

The occultists have represented this 4th tetractys, of which the Kosmos is the first term (the tetractys of the inferior world, *infera, hell*), by the 11th, 12th, and 13th arcana, the Kosmos being its first term. The arcanum which bears the generally dreaded number 13 requires further notice. It is called DEATH and RESURRECTION, and it represents absolute Inertia, only found in Death; but here Involution stops and Evolution commences, for the equilibrium of the two principles, active and passive, is never prolonged.

This would seem to contradict the preceding remark,

THE INITIATIVE TAROT.

that the description of Initiation, that is to say, of the re-ascension, opens with the 10th arcanum, and not with the 14th. This however is not so, because in Involution the being should retrace in an inverse sense, to complete the synthesis, every stage by which the a has been disintegrated in the course of its Involution. Man is the actual result of a work of this kind anterior to his present state, but of this work which has raised him from the ω to the stage of Will he is quite unconscious; at first he was subjected to it under the fatal pressure of pure Force only, then of instinct, desires, and passions; his previous evolution is therefore *unknown* to him, and yet how can he master any of these worlds without knowing them all? His first work in Initiation must therefore be to re-descend to his first steps in Evolution, to become acquainted with all the degrees, all the forces, and all the beings that he has passed through, to penetrate the roots of life to *death* itself, and to learn to dominate them all.

We shall see presently that this is not a figurative assertion; the Neophyte cannot attain any reliable voluntary exercise of the transcendental faculties without first obtaining the mastery over the forces which would produce illusion, which would threaten his life itself; without reaching *Inertia* and conquering it. Like the Christ, the model of regenerate man, he must expire upon the cross and rise again the *third* day; that is to say, after descending the three last steps represented by the 11th, 12th, and 13th arcana, into the depths of hell, there to discover *Death* and to overcome him.

This fully understood, we will describe the twelve hours or phases of *Initiation*.

*_**

The 10th arcanum, the first hour of the series, corresponds with the stage which man has reached at the present time. The symbol of this arcanum is the *Sphinx*, which guarded the entrance to the Egyptian world; the Neophyte descended between its paws into the tunnel which led to the sanctuary, through a series of tests, the image and noviciate of the descent which we have just mentioned.

This is then the hour of preparation; it separates the common life from the transcendental life; in it the student learns the work that he must undertake, and prepares himself for it. Let us see in what way.

The human head of the Sphinx, the centre of the intelligence, says to the Neophyte: "First acquire the *Knowledge* which shows the goal, and lights the way to it." This is the theoretic instruction mentioned above.

Its bull's thighs, the image of the rough, persevering labour of the agriculturist, say to him: "Be strong and patient in thy work."

Its lion's paws say to him: "Thou must *brave* all, and defend thyself against every inferior force."

Its eagle's wings say to him: "Thou must will to raise thyself towards the transcendent regions, which thy soul already approaches."

The riddle attributed to the Greek Sphinx, and the answer required for it, are an equally expressive image of *man*, and his aim. He is the animal that in the *morning* (that is to say, in the infancy of humanity) goes on four feet (4 being the number of realization, expresses matter and its instincts, the visible world); at *noon* (that is to say, in the maturity of his humanity) he walks upon two feet (2, the number of opposition, the image of science, of its contradictions, its doubts, and of the intelligible world); and in the *evening* (when the day is nearly over) walks upon three feet (3, the number of the divine world, in which the Trinity gives the solution of all the oppositions, of all the antinomies, by the superior term, the harmonious synthesis of the two adverse terms).

Apollonius describes the same hour in these words: " Here the Neophyte praises God, utters no injurious words, inflicts no more pain," which means that his theoretic knowledge of the Creation is increased, and that he practises self-control. We will now pause and examine the consistency of these various prescriptions.

We have seen that man, having reached the ascending arc, has become the object of dispute between the inferior forces of inertia, which he has traversed under the impulse of instinct, and those active forces which draw him upwards; we have noticed that the struggle must now be decided by the intervention of the *Will*, sufficiently developed by Evolution, and sufficiently free to exert its influence on one side or on the other: man can therefore decide either for the inferior forces of disintegration, or for the superior ones of synthesis, under the names of *Good* and *Evil*. And truly evil for him if he redescend, for he will meet the terrors of decomposition, of Death. Good, on the other hand, if he ascend, for he will enjoy the realization of his natural aspirations, the knowledge of the Creation and dominion over it.

Now where is the index of the forces of inertia in the human organization?—In instinct, in the *passions*. Where, on the other hand, is the index of the active forces?—In moral energy, in *Virtue*.

Where is the index of the forces of disintegration, which lead to inertia in the human organization?—In the tendency to isolation, in *egoism*. Where, on the other hand, is the index of the integrant forces?—In the tendency to joint responsibility, to altruism, in *Fraternity*.

The transcendent world is therefore open to whoever has sufficient *Will* (or even artificial impulsion) to triumph over the forces which guard it; but woe to that man who approaches it with a passionate and selfish heart; with lowered head he will fall back into the current of decomposition, where he will be dissolved. Nature destroys all *Evil;* it is the law of selection!

Only the man whose heart is full of charity can raise himself to the true destination of the human being in the region of Principles.

This is why the Sphinx prescribes, with the persevering will of the Bull, the courage of the Lion against the forces of the passions; and why Apollonius commands reserve and fraternity, with the Gospels which place self-control at the foundation of all Law.

Such then, with the aid of knowledge, is the preparation for Initiation; we shall soon see the importance of these precepts.

* * *

The Neophyte, sufficiently exercised in these preliminaries of the first hour, then descends the three lower steps as follows—

Arcanum XI.: *Strength.*

Second hour of Apollonius: "*The abyss of fire—the virtues of the stars close as a crown through the dragons and the fire*" (*the magnetic chain*).

The Neophyte learns to distinguish universal Force and its double current, positive and negative, in his own organization. The application of this knowledge will be found in the two following hours—

ARCANUM XII.: *The Great Work.*

Third hour of Apollonius: "*The serpents, the dogs, and fire.*"

The first manifestation of force applied externally to inert matter for affecting transmutations; this is *Alchemy*. The Neophyte having attained this step in practice must be ready morally to make a complete sacrifice of his personality; in the language of the alchemists, he must have destroyed his fixed nature by fire so as to volatilize it.

ARCANUM XIII.: *Death.*

Fourth hour of Apollonius: "*The Neophyte wanders in the sepulchres, and it will injure him; he will experience horror and fear of visions; he should devote himself to magic and to géotie.*"[1]

This is Necromancy, the application of Force to the domination of inferior living beings: *Elemental*, or organisms ready to synthetize themselves, and *Elementary*, remains of the dead, on the way to disorganization.

Morally, the Neophyte should die to ordinary life, to enter the spiritual life; the celestial man will be born from the corpse of the terrestrial man.

The foundations of the Universe are now reached; the Neophyte touches the extremity of the terrestrial aura, the sublunar atmosphere which surrounds every planet, like the reservoir of the elements of its life; he has now reached a terrible moment, when he must lose the earth

[1] The magic which evokes the evil genii who injure man—A.P.M.

to launch out into the ocean of space; a formidable crisis, to which two periods are consecrated.

The first is transitory.

ARCANUM XIV.: *The two Urns* (the terrestrial and celestial fluids).

Fifth hour of Apollonius: "*The waters above the heavens.*"

Here the Neophyte learns the flow of the astral currents in the planetary aura, just as in the second hour he acquired a preliminary knowledge of Force, before exposing himself to it in the following hour.

ARCANUM XV.: *Typhon* (the electric whirlwind).

Sixth hour of Apollonius: "*Here one must remain quiet, immovable through fear.*"

Unprotected the Neophyte exposes himself to the double and formidable fluid-current of celestial space, by which the ignorant or imprudent is carried away without mercy, but which raises the strong man who has purified himself. Silence, prudence, courage!

According to your deserts you will be enraptured like St. Paul, or you will expose yourself either to madness, to the spiritualization of evil, or to sorcery. This is the *Sabbat* or the Ecstasy!

The reader cannot pay too much attention to this solemn monument of practical occultism, so well described in Lytton's novel *Zanoni* under the name of the *Dragon of the Threshold;* it is the formidable danger which necessitates so many secrets. This threshold is reached by many artificial paths: the hachich, narcotics, hypnotics of every kind, the practices of spiritual mediums;

but woe to him who attempts to pass it before he has triumphed in the long and laborious preliminary preparation! His fate is foretold in the next arcanum.

ARCANUM XVI.: *The Lightning-struck Tower.*

Seventh hour of Apollonius: "*Fire comforts every living creature, and if some priest, himself a pure man, purloin and use it, if he blend it with holy oil, consecrate it, and then anoint some ailing limb with it, the malady will be cured.*"

The irresistible current has touched the man who exposed himself to its vortex on the terrestrial heights; if he be impure he is threatened with disorganization more or less complete, according to his intellectual or moral unworthiness, and his energy (incoherent mysticism, folly, death, or complete disintegration, represented by the genius of evil, the Devil)!

If, on the contrary, he be worthy of the higher regions, this baptism of fire renders him one of the Magi; the sources of terrestrial life are at his disposition; he becomes a Therapeut.

Having reached this point, he will then learn to know the celestial spheres progressively as he knows the terrestrial one, and to dominate them; three hours are consecrated to this exploration—

ARCANUM XVII.: *The Star of the Magi.*

Eighth hour of Apollonius: "*The astral virtues of the elements, of seed of every kind.*"

This is the region of the principles of the solar system; in it life becomes clear; its distribution from the solar centre to all the planets, and their reciprocal influences, are understood in all their details, in what the occultists name the *Correspondences*. The Initiate is then master of *Astrology* in every branch of the science, in the widest meaning of its acceptation.

ARCANUM XVIII.: *The Twilight.*

Ninth hour of Apollonius: "*Nothing is finished here.*"

The Initiate now extends his perceptions beyond our solar system, "beyond the Zodiac"; he is in sight of the Infinite; he touches the limits of the *intelligible world;* the divine light commences to show itself, the object of new terror and danger.

ARCANUM XIX.: *The Resplendent Light.*

Tenth hour of Apollonius: "*The gates of heaven are open, and man is born again, docile in the lethargic sleep.*"

The *Idea* appears to the regenerate soul of the Initiate, or, in the language of the Occultist, the *spiritual sun* will rise for him; he will by a new regeneration enter the *Divine World*, in which man dies no more.

Two steps remain before the highest human destinies can be accomplished—

ARCANUM XX.: *The Awakening of the Dead.*

Eleventh hour of Apollonius: "*The Angels, the Cherubim, and the Seraphim fly with rustling wings; there is joy in heaven, the earth rises, and the Sun, which issues from Adam.*"

This is the hierarchy of the Divine world, which appears upon new earths and new heavens. The Initiate will not pass through death again; henceforth he will live eternally.

ARCANUM XXII.: *The Crown of the Magi.*

Twelfth hour of Apollonius: "*The cohorts of fire rest.*"

Nirvana! Complete return to a.

Let us recapitulate these twelve hours of the initiation.

0.—Preliminary studies and tests.	Arcanum X.	1st hour
I.—Transcendent study of the *Visible World*. Inferior Manifestations:		
1. Preliminary study of Force. (*Magnetism*)	Arcanum XI.	2nd hour
2. Application to the inert world. (*Alchemy*)	Arcanum XII.	3rd hour
3. Application to the animate elementary world. (*Necromancy*) (*Magic*)	Arcanum XIII. (DEATH)	4th hour
Transitory phase:		
1. View of the superior forces.	Arcanum XIV.	5th hour
2. Entrance into the ultra-terrestrial world. (*Ecstasy*)	Arcanum XV. (TYPHON)	6th hour
THE DRAGON OF THE THRESHOLD!		
Higher regions:		
1. Application of the higher forces to the terrestial life. (*Therapeutics*)	Arcanum XVI.	7th hour
2. The forces in the solar system. (*Astrology*)	Arcanum XVII.	8th hour
3. The forces of the whole Universe.	Arcanum XVIII.	9th hour
II.—Study of the *Intelligible World*. On the borders of the Infinite.	Arcanum XIX.	10th hour
III.—Study of the *Divine World*. Divine hierarchies	Arcanum XX.	11th hour
Nirvana!	Arcanum XXII.	12th hour

Need we add how much effort and time (years, lives, often centuries) are required for each of these *hours*, how few there are who pass even the first steps!

And what can we expect from their knowledge? The hope of indefinite progress towards the realization of our most radiant hopes, the desire to attain at least those first realizations, so that we may derive from them the assurance of the others; confidence in the instruction of those whom we recognize for masters already far advanced; lastly, the certainty that in these fruitful doctrines we shall find the salvation of our suffering societies, as well as the most longed-for individual happiness. And these desires, this confidence, are felt after the first preliminary studies.

To succeed, we need undertake but one work at first, that which the Sphinx depicts to us: moral and intellectual preparations. But only the man who seriously undertakes them can know what immense and persevering efforts they exact! May this rough glimpse of them inspire the reader with the desire and the courage to devote himself to them with all the ardour of Hope!

F. Ch. Barlet.

THE DIVINE NAME IN THE TAROT.

By Ch. Barlet.

The totality of the symbols which form the Tarot is distributed through a series of 78 plates or cards, instead of being presented in a single figure; the reason for this is, that the signification of this totality is very multiple; for it is at the same time theologic, cosmologic, psychologic, and divining, and this variety is the result of the different combinations which can be produced by the arrangement and comparison of these 78 cards. This variety is not one of the lesser beauties of this unique masterpiece, in the sense that it adds movement and consequently life to the usual immobility of every written representation, without counting the diversity of its appliances, which include numbers, words, form, and colour.

The Tarot can therefore be *made to speak* when one of its innumerable combinations has been found; that is to say, when the student knows how to arrange the whole or part of his cards upon the table, in the order necessary to discover the answer which he seeks.

We ask him: What is the Creation from man's point of view, that is to say, what is the life of the Great All, and how can or should man participate in it? The whole Tarot, with its 22 great arcana and 56 minor arcana, will answer us, as we shall show by quoting only a few of the profound interpretations which it provides.

To obtain this information we must remember that the three first cards which express the Trinity form at the same time the key to the 22 great arcana, which, when the 0 is abstracted, are only seven repetitions of this Trinity. We must also notice that the card IV., the fourth term of the divine tetractys, is both the realization of the Trinity restored to the unity, and the first term of the following Trinity. The four first cards thus represent the divine name of 4 letters, IEVE (יהוה), so that if we repeat the Trinity seven times, to obtain the sequence of the 21 great arcana, the numbers will correspond to the four letters as follows—

Numbers 1. 2. 3 — 4. 5. 6. — 7. 8. 9 — etc.

Letters... $\begin{cases} \text{י ה ו} - \text{ה י ה} - \text{ו ה י} - \text{etc.} \\ \text{I E V} - \text{E I E} - \text{V E I} - \text{etc.} \end{cases}$

We will assume that these letters are thus attached to the corresponding arcana, and this remark will be the first key to the arrangement which we are looking for.

To find a second key, we must redeal our cards in a given space; at first only their place in the plane will appear; then it will be clearly defined. We know that the Kosmos is conceived as the final expansion of the mathematical point, that is to say, of the Absolute, which before this expansion included all force or potentiality in its nothingness. Let us draw this sphere (see Fig. 1). The centre of it will be represented by one of the cards, 0, the *Foolish Man* or *Crocodile*, which is the pivot of the whole pack, at the same time that it participates in all the other cards, for they include all the properties of our universe. From some point of the sphere, a point which becomes our north pole, the movement will start, by which the creation will appear on its surface.

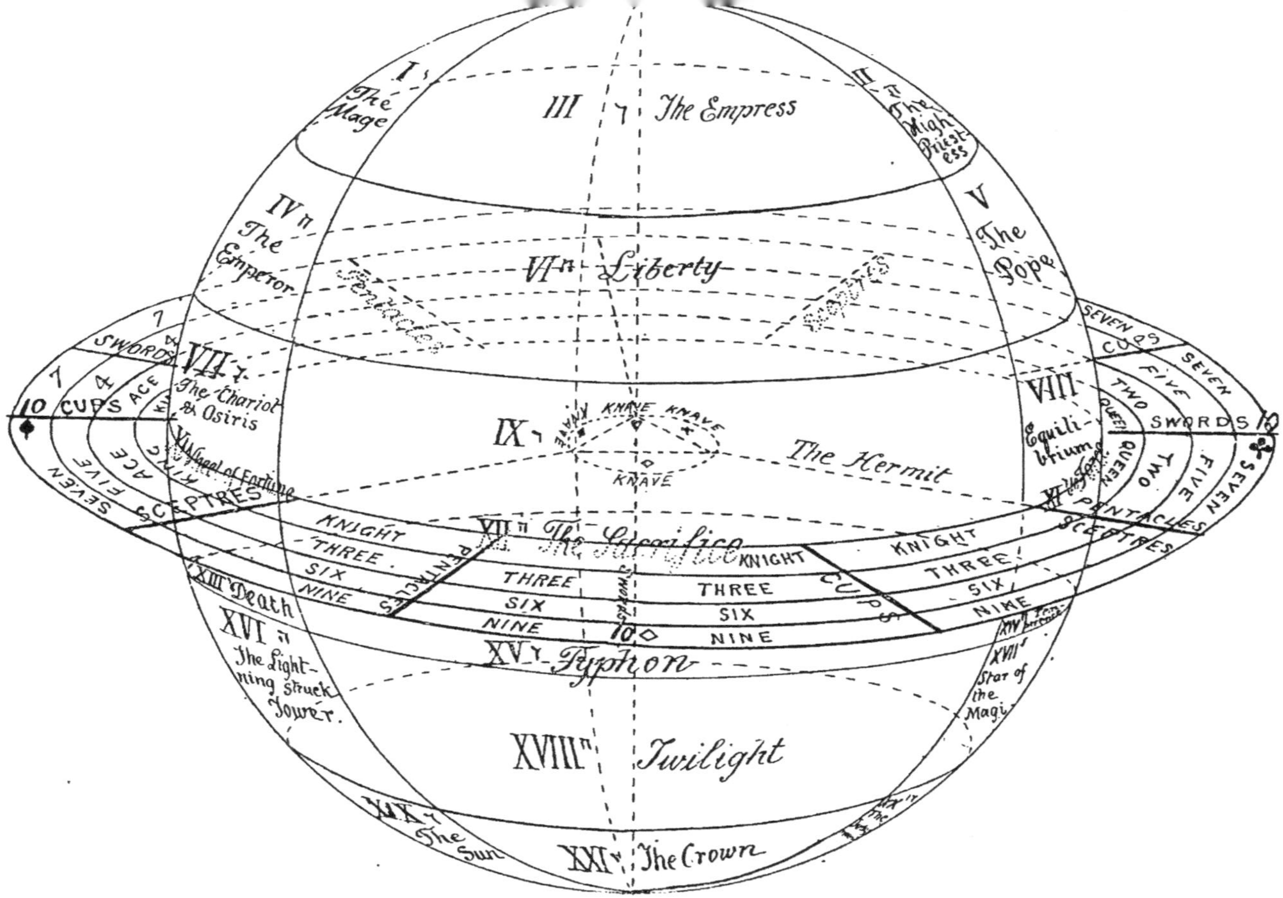
I The Mage
II The High Priestess
III The Empress
IV The Emperor
V The Pope
VI Liberty
VII The Chariot & Osiris
VIII Equilibrium
IX The Hermit
X Wheel of Fortune
XI
XII The Sacrifice
XIII Death
XIV
XV Typhon
XVI The Lightning Struck Tower
XVII Star of the Magi
XVIII Twilight
XIX The Sun
XX
XXI The Crown
Pentacles
Swords
KNAVE
KNAVE
KNAVE
KNAVE
SWORDS
CUPS
SCEPTRES
PENTACLES
KNIGHT
THREE
SIX
NINE
ACE
FIVE
SEVEN
TWO
QUEEN
KING
10

Around this point upon the sphere, the reflex of the centre, we will place the cards of our 3 first arcana: I. (the Mage, the Spirit, י); II. (Knowledge, Substance, ה); III. (Love, the fertile Power, the Being, ו); and in order that this Trinity may be repeated in the whole septenary of our distribution we will make it the root of 3 great divisions, representing the 3 terms of the Trinity, which will divide the surface of our sphere by 3 meridians.

We can then continue the distribution of our cards upon this surface in the following way. The head of each partial Trinity will be in division 1; each second term will be in division 2; each third term in division 3. Consequently our IV. card (the Emperor, ה) will be in the I.; the V. card (the Pope, ו) will be in II.; the VI. card (Liberty, ה) will be in III., and this second sequence will form a new zone upon the sphere. A third, a little inferior, will be formed by cards VII., VIII. and IX., cards XI., X. and XII. will occupy the Equator, and the 9 cards from XIII. to XXI. will be distributed like the 9 first, in 3 bands placed upon the lower hemisphere as shown in Fig. 1.

Now our 22 great arcana are placed; let us pause and look at their significations. Above the Equator we see an ever-increasing expansion of the North Pole, represented by the 3 upper triangles, then by the 6 trapezes which follow, each larger than the one before. Here are the three planes of the Creation: The Divine, metaphysic (I., II., III.), the Intelligible, moral (IV., V., VI.), and the physical, that of the generative attributes or elements (VII., VIII., and IX.).

The creation is realized upon the equatorial line (X., XI., XII.), in which the first term, with the preceding cards, represents the 10 sephiroth of the Kabbalah.

Below the Equator, in the world of material realization,

which is quitted by *Death* (XIII.), this expansion is retracted and synthetized by an inverse and symmetrical movement of the above. The arcana which follow represent Initiation carried to its extreme limits, the path by which the creature (X.) returns from its multiplicity to the unity of the spirit, goes back to the point—the southern pole—a new reflex of the Absolute, towards which it reascends by the vertical axis of the sphere.[1]

The Neophyte, after his preparation (positive science, magnetism and alchemy, X., XI., XII.), travels through the sublunar world (XIII., XIV., XV.), then through the solar system (XVI., XVII. and XVIII.), and escapes by the sun in the abyss of the Infinite (XIX., XX., XXI.).

We may now end this short explanation of the practical distribution of our 22 arcana upon a plane (the reader will do well to imitate it upon a table with a pack of Tarot cards). The student should imagine that our sphere is seen from a considerable distance, vertical upon its axis; for instance, at the distance of the earth from the sun, the upper hemisphere only will appear, the other being seen but *transparently;* and it will look like a circle, with the Equator for its circumference. The limits of the 3 superposed zones appear like 3 concentric circles; the meridional planes, seen by their dividing lines, only look like 3 equally divided radii, making of the 3 sectors 3 equal arcs. This representation, which geometricians name *projection* upon the plane of the Equator, gives the second figure (the 4 circles of the centre only); to it, for the sake of clearness in the symbols, has been added an equilateral triangle inscribed in the inner circle, with the points posed upon the 3 meridians. The Roman figures inscribed

[1] The details which justify this assertion will be found in the first part of this chapter.

in the circles represent the numbers of the cards placed as we have said, and, consequently, also indicate their place upon the table. The arcana of the lower hemisphere are indicated upon the figure in dotted letters, in the same circles as the preceding; since the lower zones, seen only transparently, might be confused with the upper, through their mutual symmetry.

Here, in its great features, is already an answer to our questions: the Spirit descends by three trinities from the Absolute into Matter (upper hemisphere). It is realized by the trinity X. (Malchut), XI. and XII. (the Equator), and it returns to the Absolute by a trinity of growing synthesis, which constitutes human progress (lower hemisphere).

We will presently explain some of the philosophic interpretations which this distribution furnishes; let us first complete it by our 55 minor arcana. They especially represent our solar world.

Since we are now in the world of realization, 4 is its number, its fundamental basis; it is the Trinity realized; the divine name of 4 letters IEVE (יהוה). Our cards will be divided into 4 sections: the 4 colours of the pack, spades, hearts, clubs, and diamonds, with their hieroglyphic and far more significant names: the *Sceptres, Cups, Swords,* and *Pentacles.*

Everything is dual in this world, where the equilibrium is unstable, unable to find any rest, except in the return to the Trinity, from which it proceeds. Thus these 4 fundamental divisions will divide into 2 duads: the one spiritual, the other material, each composed of a masculine and feminine principle, namely—

Spiritual duad, the *Sceptre* (spades, a full triangle, masculine); the *Cup* (heart, an open triangle, feminine); religious attributes;

THE INITIATIVE TAROT. 279

Material duad: the *Sword* (club, a lobed triangle), and the *Pentacle* (diamond, double triangle); the attributes of the warrior and of the artisan.

Four other divisions correspond to these 4 colours, those of the figures which also form 4 duads, namely—

King and Queen;

Knight or Warrior, and Knave.

As to the numbers which follow these figures, they lead us to another consideration, which is also essential to the distribution of our cards—

If 4 is the fundamental number of these minor arcana, the symbols of our world, we must not forget that it is also connected with the Trinity, from which it emanates; that it realizes it, and returns to it. We must then also find the ternary element in it: after the colours and the figures, which have provided the basis of our world, the numbers, which are, as it were, the essence of it, will reflect the sephiroth in it, and by them the act of creation. They pause, in fact, at 10, including 3 trinities besides the tenth, Malchut, which unites them.

Our distribution must also take the two numbers 3 and 4 into account, by combining them so as to utilize all the elements which we have just enumerated. This is how we can do this (follow Fig. 1 upon the plane of the Equator, represented as a ring outside the sphere)—

We will first separate some of the cards: the *Knave* of each of the 4 colours (ה), which, as the realization of the Trinity, King (י), Queen (ה), Knight (ו), serves as the transition from the quaternary to the ternary; and the 10 of each colour, the unity of complete realization, the multiple unity 1 and 0—Malchut.

The Knaves, by their participation in the quaternary and ternary, and their return to the Unity by the Trinity, have a universality which connects them with the un-numbered card 0 of the great arcana; we will therefore place them round this card, as a cross, in the centre of our equatorial circle. In this way the centre will express: By the card 0, the original unity, the source and aim of creation; by its triangle, the primitive Trinity; by its 4 colours, the quaternary in which it is realized; by the character of the 4 Knaves, the return of this quaternary to the ternary; in short, the whole creation assembled in one point, in potentiality, which is the characteristic of the Spirit.

On the other hand the four 10 will be placed at the extremities of the cross formed by the Knaves, outside all our circles, as the expression of the Unity multiple, in its last term of differentiation.

As to the other cards, they include first 3 kinds of figures, which correspond with the 3 terms of the Trinity; it is quite simple to distribute them in the 3 parts of our external equatorial plane, corresponding with the 3 divisions of the sphere—

The Kings opposite to division I (י);
The Queens opposite to division E (ה);
The Knights opposite to division V (ו);

and, since there are 4 colours for each of them, 4 sub-divisions are naturally produced in each of our 3 principal divisions; these 4 subdivisions, corresponding to the Sceptre (י), the Cup (ה), the Sword (ו), and the Pentacle (ה), also repeat the Divine name of 4 letters (IEVE) (יהוה), and form the passage from the ternary to the quaternary.

Now only the numbers remain to be placed; and we have only to make them correspond with the terms of the Trinity—

THE INITIATIVE TAROT.

> The four 1 behind the Kings;
> The four 2 behind the Queens;
> The four 3 behind the Knights.

Then, in a still more external circle—

> The four 4 outside the Kings and the 1;
> The four 5 outside the Queens and the 2;
> The four 6 outside the Knights and the 3.

Finally, an outlying circle will include the four 7, 8 and 9 in the same order. As to the four 10, they are placed quite outside, as we have already said.

We thus obtain the distribution represented by the figures 1 and 2.

Let us now consider their signification.

The living atom descended upon the sphere has reached the point represented by arcanum X., *the wheel of Ezekiel, which raises man and lowers the elemental.* From this, the atom falls, so to speak, through the material world, which he has just entered. He first descends through the spiritual decade (Sceptre and Cup) (see the figure), traversing numbers of increasing complexity : King, 1, 4, 7, then 10. By this 10, the multiple unity, limit of materialization, which unites the two portions of the decade Sceptre-Cup, he resumes in an inverse sense, as though by a reascending arc, the road which will lead him back to plate X., remounting the 4, 7, 10, and King of Cups and Swords, the substantial duad.

This is only one-third of the voyage which the living atom must accomplish in the real world; and, in this first excursion through matter, he has still retained the spiritual character which he received from Yod (׳), the characteristic of plate X.; he must now lose this character for that of the following E (ה). To this end, he passes from plate X., which he has just re-entered, to plate XI. (ה), the *Hermit*, the *veiled Lamp*, to pass in the same way as he has already done through the dual series of the Sceptre-Cup, through the Queens, the 2, 5, and 8, passing by the 10 of Cups, and remounting by it through the second series, Sword-Pentacles, to the arcanum XI., the starting-point of this second excursion.

Finally, from this last arcanum he passes to number XII. (ו), *the Sacrifice*, descends the neuter series of the *Knight*, 3, 6, 9 of Sceptres and Cups, crosses the 10 of Swords and the 10 of Pentacles, and remounts by the dual Swords and Pentacles to the intelligible world.

His journey across the material world is completed; he has travelled over the Zodiac; he will now *die;* the arcanum XIII. is ready for him, and will give him access to the spiritual world, to the Redemption.

We will now explain some other features of this distribution.

It divides the external circle of the Equator into 3 arcs, subdivided into 4 portions; in all 12 divisions of different characters. These are the 12 signs of the Zodiac. The first is naturally ranked with the first card of the minor arcana in the spiritual sector, *i. e.* the King of Sceptres (Spades); the second corresponds with the King of Cups, and so on to the twelfth.

One observation will suffice to justify the connection between the zodiac and our cards. We must note the 12 divisions of the circle into the triple repetition of the 4 letters of the Sacred Name; an operation legitimized by the remark already made, that these 4 colours correspond with these letters (see Fig. 2, in the intermediate circle, where the signs of the Zodiac are written). We at once recognize the 4 trigons of the Zodiac, corresponding

THE INITIATIVE TAROT. 283

with the elements which the 4 colours also represent, and these trigons are characterized as well as designated.

The *fiery* trigon (♈, ♌, ♐), corresponding with the *Sceptre* and the letters ייי, is swayed by the spiritual element.

The *earthy* trigon (♉, ♍, ♑), corresponding to the *Cup* and to the letters ההה, namely, two E's of the name of 3 letters, and the final E of the name of 4 letters— an essentially feminine character, substantial, but of superior order.

The *airy* trigon (♊, ♎, ♒), corresponding to the *Sword* and the letters ווו, swayed by the masculine element of the second order.

The *watery* trigon (♋, ♏, ♓), corresponding to the *Pentacle* and to the letters ההה, comprising, this time, the final E of the name of 4 letters twice repeated, and the E of the name of 3 letters—the dominant character, the inferior feminine.

But we must leave the minor arcana to the investigations of the reader—they would lead us too far—and return to some further notice of the great arcana.

Let us first notice how the three chief sectors preserve and reproduce their innate characters in all their divisions.

We find, in the first, that of the letter Yod (י), the Spirit, the *numbers* of the unity, I., IV., VII., X. (repeated in the minor arcana); as *figure*, the Kings; as *colour*, the Sceptre; in the *Zodiac*, the lines of the ascension of the sun above the Equator from the spring to the solstice.

In the second sector (ה) the substantial principle is the feminine numbers II., V., VIII., XI. (repeated in the minor arcana); as *figure*, the Queens; as *colour*, the Cup; in the *Zodiac*, the four signs of the descent of the sun towards the Equator; the season of harvests and vintages, fecundity in all its forms.

FIG. 2.

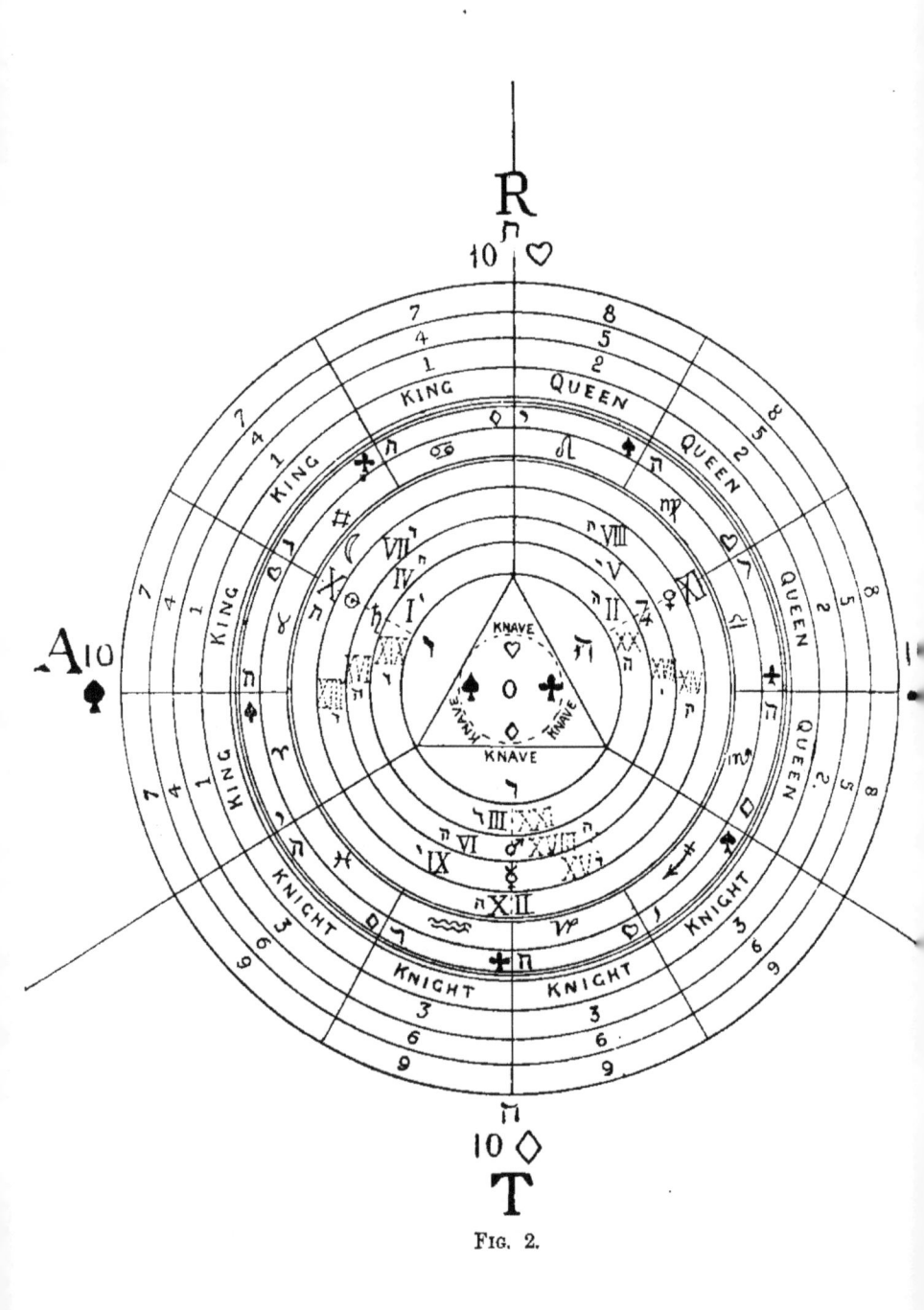

In the third sector (ו), the Son, the Element, are the sacred numbers which participate in the two preceding orders, III., VI., IX.; as *figure*, the Knight; as *colour*, the Pentacle of the practical world, and the Sword also, which close the preceding sector; in the *Zodiac*, the signs through which the sun passes in the southern hemisphere; our winter, the season for the consumption of the produce of the earth, of renovation for the cycle which follows: *Christmas* is in the centre; the new birth in the winter of death; the time when the Son was born into an inferior world to reanimate it.

The divine Name יהוה is not only written in the series of concentric circles, it is also found upon the lines belonging to those circles, either in descending or in remounting.

The first sector gives it without transposition, as we see in Fig. 2.

In the second sector the divine Name is preceded by the feminine letter E, the Mother, and finally pauses at it: E, IEVE, IE. (See the figure.)

In the third, it commences by the letter of the Son and ends by that of the Father, to which he returns: VE, IEVE, I.

We shall now inquire from the symbols of the cards the *different ways of pronouncing the divine Name*, and also the *various manifestations* in the Kosmos *of each of these four letters*. Let us question even the spirit of these symbols, instead of their number, colour, or form, which have chiefly occupied us at present.

By first following the regular order of our arrangement we shall find—

In the divine world: the arcana I., II., III., IV., the divine Tetractys, comprising: (1) the *Absolute Being;* (2) the *Consciousness* of the Absolute; (3) *Love* or the power of fecundity; (4) the *realization* of the virtualities of the *Absolute*.

In the world of laws: arcanum V., the laws of the relation of the Created with the Uncreate (the *Initiator, Fear also*).[1] VI. (*Liberty, Beauty*); knowledge of good and evil; knowledge of the Law. VII. (Glory); rule of the Spirit over Matter, the fertile power of the Law; and VIII. (*absolute Justice, Victory*), realization of the Law.

In the physical world: arcana IX. (the *veiled Lamp*), the light extinguished in the darkness of the substance, the spirit imprisoned in the material world, *Yesod.* X. (*Wheel of Fortune*), which raises the fallen spirit to lead it back, with the nature which it has spiritualized, to all its power, by *Strength* (arcana XI.), and by *Sacrifice* (arcana XII.).

The phases of spiritualization then follow. XIII.: First phase: (*Death*) to the physical world. XIV. (*the two Urns*) combination of the movements of life. XV. (Typhon) Magic. XVI. (the *Lightning-struck Tower*); the interplanetary force.

Second phase: XVII. (the *flaming Star*), the internal light. XVIII. (the *Twilight*), the aurora of the divine sun. XIX. (the *Sun*), central; and XX. (the *Judgment*), after which the supreme realization is obtained, the *Crown of the Magi*.

We have said that the divine Name is again enunciated in following the three sectors.

In the first are the arcana I., IV., VII., X. The absolute, the realization of its virtualities, the dominion of Spirit over Matter, and the animating principle of beings. Then, in return, XIII., XVI., XIX. and I. Death (Inertia)

[1] Consult for the generation and signification of numbers the *Traité Élémentaire de Science Occulte*, by Papus, a learned author whose good counsels have produced the best part of this article.

THE INITIATIVE TAROT.

the astral light, the central sun, and the Unspeakable himself.

This is the account, by the principles, of the differentiation and integration of the Absolute.

In the second sector, the one which corresponds to the consciousness of the Absolute or faith, we have the series, V., VIII., XI., XIV.: the Hierophant, or religion; Justice, Force, and the combination of the movements of life; the image of the Saints; the *Mystics* of all religions, who by absolute Faith and Justice, receptive, feminine virtues, acquire, without seeking for it, the power of working prodigies.

Lastly, in the third Sector, that of Love or power of fecundity, we have the series: IX., Wisdom and Prudence; XII., the Sacrifice; XV., self-abandonment to the astral forces; and XVIII., the attainment of the Infinite. The essence of this series of efforts, both active and passive, constitutes Initiation, the Redemption.

Let us once more seek for the divine Name, through the three divisions at once. We shall find, for instance, the arcana I., II., III., VI., which demonstrate the divine Trinity, manifesting itself by Beauty and Liberty in the Intellectual world: it is the passage of the Father (י) to the Son (ו).

Or again, I., VI., IX., X.: The descent of the Father (י) into the physical world (X.) by the Son (VI.) and by Yesod (IX.); the Word made flesh. This is the Redemption, the series which in the *Sepher Yetzirah* represents the *Column* of the Sephiroth (Kether—Tiphereth—Yesod and Malchut).[1]

---

[1] The signification of the cards is borrowed from Fabre d'Olivet, Wronski, E. Levi, Christian, and the *Sepher Yetzirah* (translation by Papus).

But we must limit these examples, which the reader will easily multiply for himself. Let us only add a few more words upon our second problem: the different manifestations of each of the three persons of the divine Trinity.

The Yod is found in the arcana I., V., IX., XII. and XIII.; in Keter, in the Hierophant, in the Wise Old Man; then it presides over *death*, which will bring the world from the depths of gloomy Inertia to the resplendent crown of the Magi, by the internal light.

It will be noticed, at the same time, that the Yod is the only one of the four letters which, by its various positions, forms a complete spiral round the sphere, from the north to the south poles; a symbol which may appear very remarkable to any one acquainted with the mysteries of the life of a planet.

The first E, the celestial Mother (arcana II.), is found in the arcana VI., X., XIV. and XVIII., that is to say, Beauty, Form, the Angel of Temperance, which balances the movements of life, and the aurora of the divine Sun; Diana the Moon.

The V, the Son, is characterized upon the various planes by the arcana III., VII., XI., XV. and XIX.; Love, the fertile power; the Ruler over Matter, Force; then Typhon, the mysterious Baphomet of the Templars, which collects the superior forces to spread them over the Earth; and lastly, the central Sun. In a word, the *Christ* of the Gospel, the Spirit of Love, the Master of the Elements, the Word made flesh to spiritualize the flesh; the divine reflex of the Universal Sun.

Lastly, the second E; the terrestrial Mother is seen in the arcana IV., VIII., XII., XVI. and XX. The realization of the divine virtualities, and also Mercy, absolute Justice, Sacrifice, the overwhelmed and suffering Spirit, and finally Resurrection; the head of the Serpent crushed beneath the woman's heel, by the force of abnegation and resigned faith.

We need only follow these various arcana upon the sphere, to see once more that the Yod has 3 superior arcana (northern hemisphere), and 2 inferior;

That the V (ו) has only 2 superior and 1 medium (upon the Equator);

And that the E has 4 superior, 2 inferior, and 2 medium.

Let us close these remarks, already too lengthy, by a simple observation upon the general effect of our arrangement.

The three worlds, Divine, Intelligible, and Physical, are found not only in the three zones of the sphere, but they are again reproduced in the whole arrangement; the Divine is in the centre, through the Foolish Man of the Tarot, and the cross of four colours; this we have already pointed out.

The Intelligible and its developments are provided by the sphere (Fig. 1), or the circular distribution of the 21 great arcana (Fig. 2).

The physical is seen in the external plane of the Equator (Fig. 1), with the distribution of the 56 minor arcana, representing the Zodiac and the various degrees of the multiplicity of Force through substance to the extreme pole, the negative unity 10.

Moreover, the whole (Fig. 1) reproduces the form of the planet Saturn, with its ring, a form which in itself, according to the theories of our positive sciences, is the clearest manifestation, the demonstration of the great laws of the formation of the Universe; namely, the concentration of the substance in a radiant state around a point of attraction, producing with a progressive condensation a rotatory movement, particularly accentuated at the Equator, and giving birth to the stars, planets, and satellites, thus descending from the ethereal *nébuleuse* to the atom, to the solid ultimate; from living nothingness to inert nothingness, from the unit to an infinite multiplicity.

Thus the Tarot, the secular fruit of the genius of our ancestors, can represent not only the creation in its actual state, but its history even in details, and its future with that of the human creature, even to their principles; yet avoiding, by the combination of its analogical symbols, borrowed from natural life, the rock upon which all philosophy breaks—namely, the definition of *words*, the clear, full expression of the *Word* in the sublunar world.

CHAPTER XVIII.

THE KABBALISTIC TAROT.

Deductions by Etteila upon the Book of Thoth—Example of the Application of the Tarot to the Kabbalah, the Hierogram of Adam by Stanislas de Guaita.

DEDUCTIONS BY ETTEILA UPON THE BOOK OF THOTH.

WE will now recapitulate some of the conclusions which Etteila attained in the course of his work upon the *Book of Thoth* (the Tarot).

The *Book of Thoth Hermes* indicates by its name alone that our author had discovered its Egyptian origin. It is composed of 78 leaflets, forming 4 volumes.

The 1st volume contains 12 leaves
The 2nd — 5 —
The 3rd — 5 —
The 4th — 56 —

Thus the 22 major arcana form 3 volumes, and the 56 minor arcana form the last.

The 56 leaves of the last volume divide in the following way, according to the operation indicated in the first reading of the cards—

$$26 + 17 + 11 + 2 = 56.$$

The 4 divisions of the 56 leaflets (the 4 colours) respectively represent—

    1. Agriculture.
    2. Priesthood.
    3. Nobility, { Magistrates. Soldiers.
    4. People, { Art. Commerce.

The *Book of Thoth* contains three parts, viz.:

22 Major Atouts.
16 Minor Atouts (the figures).
40 Small cards.

It is formed like a living being, for—

    78 is its body;
    3 its spirit or mediator;
    1 its soul.

If we add the 12 first leaflets of the book together, we shall discover the number of its total—

$$1 + 2 + 3 + 4 + 5 + 6 + 7 + 8 + 9 + 10 + 11 + 12 = 78.$$

If we now look back at the first operation in reading the cards according to our author, new deductions will arise.

Number 78 will be found to represent Salt, or the incorruptible Spirit.

The number 1 (a book) represents the Unity, the Divinity; lastly, the number 26, which divides the Tarot into three parts, is exactly that of Jehovah (יהוה).

    Yod = 10
    He   =   5
    Vau =   6
    He   =   5
    Total 26

In the first operation[1] upon the packets of 26 cards nothing remains, — 0.

In the second operation upon the packets of 17 cards 1 remains, which represents the point in the centre of the circle zero.

Lastly, in the third operation upon the packets of 11 cards 2 remain, which represent Man.

To sum up—

    0—The Circumference of the Universe.
    1—The point of the Centre-God.
    2—The Male and the Female. Man.

God, Man, and the Universe, obtained by the mystic system of Etteila!

We shall never end if we try to follow our author in all the deductions he makes from the above; let us content ourselves, in closing, with demonstrating the meaning which he gives to the numbers of the packets which have been successively placed on one side.

    26—*The Soul.*
    17—*The Spirit.*
    11—*The Body.*

Finally, the remainder of the cards $11 + 11 + 2 = 24$ is *Life.*

These few pages will suffice to give the student a glimpse of Etteila's method of proceeding. We have rendered his deductions as clearly, and presented them as methodically, as possible. The curious had better consult his work on the subject—

---

[1] See, for an explanation of these packets and the method of obtaining them, Chapter XX. (6th lesson).

COLLECTION SUR LES HAUTES SCIENCES, or a theoretical and practical treatise upon the wisdom magic of the ancients, absolutely complete in twelve books, which contain all that Etteila has written upon the Hermetic philosophy, the art of fortune-telling by cards . . . and particularly the sublime *Book of Thoth*. 2 vols. 8vo., bound, 1780.

EXAMPLE OF THE APPLICATION OF THE TAROT TO THE KABBALAH.

THE HIEROGRAM OF ADAM, BY

STANISLAS DE GUAITA.

In asserting that the hierogram of Adam conceals the most profound arcana of the living Universe, we shall not astonish those who have made a serious study of the *Sepher Bereschit*. By comparing the admirable translation of Fabre d'Olivet with the pentacular revelations of the *Book of Thoth*, it is not impossible to strike out the supreme light of truth. Here are a few data which will aid us to reach it.

Adam אדם is written in Hebrew, *Aleph, Daleth, Mem.*

א (1st key of the Tarot: The Juggler). God and man; the Principle and the end; the Equilibrant Unity.

ד (4th key of the Tarot: The Emperor). The Power and the Kingdom; the verbal Quaternary; the Multiplication of the cube.

מ (13th key of the Tarot: Death). Destruction and Restoration; Night and Day, moral and physical; Eternity and the Ephemeral; feminine Passivity; at once the gulf of the Past, the matrix of the Future.

The ternary analysis of the fathomless principle that Yod manifests in its inaccessible and synthetic unity, *Adam*

THE KABBALISTIC TAROT.

is, in fact, very analogous to the hierogram *Aum*, which is so famous in the sanctuaries of India.

In אדם, *Aleph* corresponds to the Father, the source of the Trinity; *Daleth* to the Son (whom the Kabbalah also names the King); and *Mem* to the Holy Spirit, whose ethereal body, devouring yet fertilizing transitory forms, causes life (inexhaustible and unalterable in its essence) to blossom upon the changing hot-bed of *Growth*.

I have said that אדם is the cyclic analysis of the principle, of which י (Yod) is the inaccessible synthesis.

A simple calculation of the numerical Kabbalah confirms my assertion. Let us translate the letters into numbers (Tarotic method).

$$\aleph\ 1 \quad \daleth\ 4 \quad \mem\ 13.$$
$$1 + 4 + 13 = 18. \quad \text{In } 18, 1 + 8 = 9.$$

In Kabbalistic absolute numericals the analytical number of Adam is then 9. Now we obtain 10 by adding to 9 the specific unity which leads the cycle back to its starting-point, and closes analysis in synthesis, and 10 is the number which corresponds to the letter *Yod*: this we were anxious to prove.

The hierogrammatic vocable אדם (Adam) then represents the ninth evolution of the cycle, which emanated from י (Yod), and which closes in 10 by returning to its starting-point. Principle and end of all, the eternal Yod, revealed in its expanded form *tertriune*.

Let us go further still.

We have then the right (noting, however, that Adam differs from Yod, or from Wodh, as the totality of the sub-multiples differ from the Unity),—we have the right to say, pursuing our analogies,

If Adam be equal to 1,

Adam-ah = I-ah; and *Adam Eve = I-eve.* He (ה) represents Universal Life, *natura naturans;* יה then represents Yod united to Life, and אדמה (Adamah), Adam united to Life. This is the union of the Spirit and of the Universal Soul at two different degrees (always remembering the distinction noticed above).

Lastly, in יהוה (IEVE), as in אדמ-הוה (Adam-Eve), Vau (ו) represents the fecundity of this union, and the last He (ה) symbolizes *natura naturata* (issued from *natura naturans,* increased by the mixed principle).

These four letters, יהוה (IEVE), symbolize the quaternary of *Mercavah,* the six letters of Adam-Eve, אדמ-הוה, the senary of *Bereschith.*

(Fragment of the Serpent of Genesis published in the *Lotus* of March 1888, p. 327, and 328 *note.*)

CHAPTER XIX.

LIST OF THE AUTHORS WHO HAVE INTERESTED THEMSELVES IN THE TAROT.

Raymond Lulle—Cardan—Postel—The Rosicrucians—Court de Gébelin—Etteila—Claude de Saint-Martin—J. A. Vaillant—Christian—Eliphas Levi—Stanislas de Guaita—Joséphin Péladan—*The Platonist*—Theosophical Publications—F. Ch. Barlet—Oswald Wirth—Poirel—Ely Star—H. P. Blavatsky—Ch. de Sivry—Mathers.

SOME ACCOUNT

OF THE AUTHORS WHO HAVE SPECIALLY INTERESTED THEMSELVES IN THE TAROT.

RAYMOND LULLE (1235—1315), an eminently learned man, the founder of a system of philosophy, but chiefly of logic, entirely based upon the application of the Tarot; this is the *Ars Magna*.

CARDAN (JÉRÔME). Born in Paris in 1501, died in 1576. Professor of Mathematics and Medicine at Milan and Boulogne. Travelled through Scotland, England, and France, working miraculous cures. His treatise *On Subtility* (1550) is entirely based on the keys of the Tarot.

POSTEL (GUILLAUME). Born at Dolerie (diocese of Avranches)

in 1510. Sent to the East by Francis I., he brought back some valuable manuscripts, and was appointed Professor of Mathematics and Oriental Languages in the College of France. Died in the Convent of Saint-Martin des Champs in 1581.

One of the greatest Initiates of the sixteenth century. He discovered the key to the Tarot, but did not disclose the secret, in spite of the promise given in the title to his work, *The Key to the Hidden Mysteries* (1580). A list of his works will be found in the index.

THE MYSTERIOUS FRATERNITY OF THE ROSICRUCIANS (1604). *La Fama Fraternitatis Rosæ Crucis* (1613) shows the Initiate that the Rosicrucians possessed the Tarot, which is described thus—

They possess a book from which they can learn everything that is in the books already written and to be written.

We must not forget that the Rosicrucians are the Initiators of *Leibnitz*, and the founders of actual Freemasonry through *Asmhole*.

COURT DE GÉBELIN. Born at Nîmes in 1725, died at Paris in 1784. An illustrious scholar, who discovered the Egyptian origin of the Tarot. Consult his *Primitive World* (1773—1783).

ETTEILA (1783). We have given a summary of his work upon Fortune-telling with the Tarot, and upon the application of this work to the Kabbalah.

CLAUDE DE SAINT-MARTIN. The unknown philosopher. Born in 1743 at Amboise, died in 1803. The disciple of Martinez Pasqualis and Jacob Bœhm, the founder of the so-called Martinist order. His book, the *Tableau Naturel des Rapports qui existent entre Dieu, l'Homme et l'Univers*, is based upon the Tarot.

J. A. VAILLANT. Lived many years with the Gypsies, and received a great many of their traditions orally: these are contained in his works—

LIST OF AUTHORS.

Les Rômes, Histoire vraie des vrais Bohémiens (towards 1853).
La Bible des Bohémiens (1860).
Clef Magique de la Fiction et du Fait (1863).

CHRISTIAN. Librarian of the Arsenal. Has published an occult manuscript upon the Tarot, blending with it his personal reflections upon astrology in—
L'Homme Rouge des Tuileries (1854).

ELIPHAS LEVI. Amongst contemporary Masters of Occultism, he had the greatest knowledge of the Tarot. His work *Dogme et Rituel de la Haute Magie* (1861, 2 vols., 8vo.) is based upon the keys of the Tarot. Eliphas Levi had a most romantic life, and died in 1870, leaving a son (I believe).

STANISLAS DE GUAITA. Contemporary Kabbalistic scholar. He made several applications of the Tarot to the Kabbalah. We have given one extract of them already. Consult also, *Au Seuil du Mystère* (1886), and *Le Serpent de la Genèse*.

JOSÉPHIN PÉLADAN. A clever novelist and eminent Kabbalist. He often wrote upon the Tarot in his works (1885—1889).

"THE PLATONIST" (1888). Review of American Occultism. It contained a poor study upon the application of the Tarot to horoscopy. This essay has been reproduced in the
Theosophical Publications. Small pamphlets called "Siftings," No. 14 (London 1888) (7, Duke Street).

F. CH. BARLET. One of the most learned and most highly-esteemed authorities amongst French Occultists. The summary of one of his works on the *Tarot Initiatique* (1889) is quoted *in extenso*, page 253.

OSWALD WIRTH has studied the astronomical Tarot (see Chapter XVI.), and has carefully reproduced the twenty-two symbolical figures, according to the most recent information obtainable upon Symbolism (1889).

E. Poirel. Occultist. Editor of the *Tarot d'Oswald Wirth* (1889).

Ely Star. An author known by his interesting work upon Astrology, the *Mystères de l'Horoscope* (Dentu, 1888). It contains a chapter upon the Tarot.

H. P. Blavatsky. This author, rendered eminent by her works upon Theosophy, mentions the Tarot in her books (*Isis Unveiled and the Secret Doctrine*), but very superficially and without any synthetic basis.

Ch. de Sivry. A very talented occultist, chiefly known by his works upon music. To his kindness we owe the summary of a *Tarot Bohémien* entitled—

Extract from the sacred book of the Opâchti tribe, the primitive family, which adored Otchâvâtri, representing the only God Otchawatra. This tribe lived at the foot of the Himalaya.

This book describes the symbolism of the twenty-two arcana, according to the Gypsies, with interesting details upon esoterism.

Mathers, an English author, has recently published a short account of the Tarot, which contains nothing very original: it is rather a summary of the principal authors who have studied the question. It is chiefly written as an aid to *fortune-telling by cards*.

This closes the list of authors whose books we have heard of, and who have *alluded to the Tarot or used its keys*. We may have omitted some of them, if so we must beg them to excuse us.

CHAPTER XX.

THE DIVINING TAROT IN SEVEN LESSONS.

Introduction: To our Lady Readers—Astronomy and Astrology—Intuition—Fortune-telling by the Tarot in Seven Lessons.

1st Lesson: Simplification of the Rules of Fortune-telling by the Tarot.

2nd Lesson: Minor Arcana—Significations—A good Memory unnecessary for their retention—Key to the Divining Tarot—Sceptres—Cups—Swords—Pentacles.

3rd Lesson: Major Arcana—Significations from a Divining Point of View.

4th Lesson: Basis of the Application of this Knowledge—Arrangement of the Cards.

5th Lesson: Reading the Tarot—Rapid Process—Elaborate Process.

6th Lesson: Etteila's original and unpublished Method of reading the Tarot (from one of his rarest works): 1st deal—2nd deal—3rd deal—4th deal.

7th Lesson: Conclusion—Bibliography.

THE DIVINING TAROT.

INTRODUCTION.

To our Lady Readers—Astronomy and Astrology—Intuition —Fortune-telling by the Tarot in Seven Lessons.

THE first part of our study of the Tarot, full of numbers, of Hebrew letters, and abstract deductions, is not calculated to attract the attention of ladies. But if women enjoy mystery and idealism, prefer and excuse the flights of a vivid imagination, men exact precision and method in studies of this kind, and I have therefore built this arsenal of technical arguments for them, confining imagination in the narrow limits of deduction; so that, if she has sometimes escaped and scattered the brilliant gems of illusion over the course of my work, the escape was only made with great trouble, and in spite of my efforts to retain her. It is, however, traditional that the future can be read through the Tarot, and our feminine readers will never forgive me if I ignore their natural curiosity on this point.

I have therefore decided to approach this delicate question, and I hope that the pleasure gained by the fair inquirers will balance the scepticism of sterner intellects. It is true that I can quote the opinion of all the writers of antiquity, who assert that the Egyptians used the Tarot as a means of predicting the future, and that the Jews also employed it to confirm their prophecies. But in my opinion an important distinction should be made on this subject.

Unquestionably the Egyptians predicted the future through the Tarot; but they used its astronomical applications only. Nothing was left to chance. Thus, knowing that most of the important events which take place upon the earth are determined by the magnetic currents produced by the position of the earth at the moment that the event takes place, these learned men first defined the relations existing between the position of the stars in the heavens, and the circumstances they created upon the earth. Since the stars accomplish fixed revolutions, that is to say, that they return to the same position at the end of a certain number of years, which are mathematically

THE DIVINING TAROT.

determinable, the Egyptians thought that the same events would be also reproduced at fixed intervals. It would therefore suffice to know the movements of the stars, to predict the coming events. This is why *astronomy* was only the commencement of *astrology*.

As the Tarot reproduced the movements of the stars upon a table, we can easily guess how the ancients proceeded when they read prophecy by its aid. They drew up the *Horoscope* of the coming year, according to the position which the stars would occupy during its course, and could then at once predict two-thirds of the events likely to occur. Fabre d'Olivet in his works shows that one-third of the events are *Determined*, another third depend upon the *Human Will*, and the last third is subject to *Providence*. As the determining Fatality and the human Will usually unite, almost unconsciously, we see that the astrological Horoscope can predict two-thirds of the events.

Later on reliable data were lost, and men commenced to read fortunes by chance, without using any scientific method. The astrological systems, called *onomantic*, that is to say, which use the numbers formed by the letters of the name and pronoun of the individual, are generally false, and produce no practical results. For this reason the astrological system described by Christian can be regarded only as a deceitful, lying dream. The truth of the predictions, then, depends upon the *intuition* of the prophet, and this leads us to consider the differences which may be noticed between the predictions of fortune-tellers.

Intuition plays the most important part when the more exact methods disappear, and therefore woman's nature, which is essentially intuitive, is well qualified to read these divinations.

The discussion of the *wherefore* of all this would lead us much too far from our subject. We cannot either teach *astrology* by the Tarot in a few pages—a whole volume is necessary for this purpose—nor have we the time to handle these difficult subjects. Perhaps we may decide to undertake them some day.

However, we see that chance and intuition are the chief instruments in divination by the Tarot, as it is usually practised at the present time. We must therefore aid our readers to undertake it for themselves, and will now explain the most simple principles of the art, dividing them into seven lessons, so as to render them as clear as possible.

We will arrange them so that they may be complete, and therefore it will be unnecessary to read all the preceding abstract studies before using the Tarot from this point of view. Lastly, we will explain the principal methods used by masters in the art of fortune-telling, so as to enable our readers to become adepts in the prediction of the future. But we must remind them that science has little empire over the subject, and that imagination and intuition reign over this charming domain.

FIRST LESSON.

SIMPLIFICATION OF THE RULES OF FORTUNE-TELLING BY THE TAROT.

THE great difficulty encountered by a beginner in the study of divination by the Tarot, is the number of meanings to be remembered in reading the cards.

Open any treatise upon this subject, and you will see that you must first learn the different significations of the 78 cards of the Tarot. Then you must learn the significations of these 78 cards *reversed*, without counting the *meetings* and other complications, which bring them to about 200 different meanings, which must be retained in the memory before any one can become a good fortune-teller by cards. Habit only will enable the student to remember all these details, and in this case *intuition* becomes an important aid to the memory.

Now this complication always points to an imperfect system. Nature is synthetic in its manifestations, and simplicity is always found at the bottom of the most outwardly complicated phenomena. Whilst admitting that our work upon the Tarot may be erroneous, no one can deny the absolute simplicity of the constituent principles. We will therefore apply the same method to the divining Tarot, and endeavour to establish a system which will enable us to dispense with memory almost entirely, or at least to considerably reduce its work. We shall thus allow a certain scope for scientific data, although we are unwilling to create any prejudice by this influence, considering the subject we are dealing with.

The first point to retain from the commencement of this study is the necessity for clear, simple rules, by which the divining Tarot may be read. We will explain them in the following lessons.

SECOND LESSON.

MINOR ARCANA.
SIGNIFICATION FROM THE DIVINING POINT OF VIEW.

THE Tarot pack is composed of 78 cards or plates; 22 of them bear symbolical names (the Juggler, Sun, Moon, Hanged Man, etc.), and they should be separated from the 56 others, which are divided into four great series: Sceptres, Cups, Swords, and Pentacles.

These four series each contain 14 cards (King, Queen, Knight, Knave, Ace, 2, 3, 4, 5, 6, 7, 8, 9 and 10), corresponding with the four series of common playing cards (clubs, hearts, spades, diamonds), but called Sceptres, Cups, Swords, Pentacles. These are the *Minor Arcana.*

The 22 symbolical cards are the *Major Arcana* or Great Arcana.

1. MINOR ARCANA, formed of four sequences of 14 cards each, or 56 cards in all.

2. MAJOR ARCANA, formed of 22 cards.

These are the two great divisions which must first be remembered.

We have already said that the minor arcana were divided into four sequences: Sceptres, Cups, Swords, Pentacles. Each of these series represents one of the four great principles, as follows—

The Sceptres represent *Enterprise and Glory.*
The Cups — *Love and Happiness.*
The Swords — *Hatred and Misfortune.*
The Pentacles — *Money and Interest.*

ENTERPRISE, LOVE, HATRED, FORTUNE, are the four great principles which must be remembered.

If you now take one of these packets of 14 cards, you will see that it is formed of four figures, and of 10 other cards, which bear numbers formed by the symbols.

We will first look at the 4 figures—

The King represents *Man.*
The Queen — *Woman.*
The Knight — *A Young Man.*
The Knave — *A Child.*

The Man represents the creator, the one who undertakes the *enterprises;* the woman characterizes *love;* the young man, conflict, struggle, rivalry, *hatred;* the child symbolizes the absolute neuter, the second He, which varies according to circumstances, *money,* which addresses itself to all, and applies itself to all, *universal transition.* Man, Woman, Young Man, Child, are therefore the same symbols applied to the family as the four great principles applied to humanity, and to know them in one case is to know them in the other.

To sum up all this, we may say that the first element represents the *positive,* the second the *negative,* the third the *opposition* between the two; finally, the last the *absolute neuter;* and these elements are symbolized by the four figures of each of the minor arcana.

But even as the cards are divided into two colours, red and black, so humanity is divided into *dark* and *fair.*

The eight figures of the Sceptres and Swords therefore

represent *dark people*, the eight figures of the Cups and Pentacles, *fair people*.

The figures of the Sceptres and Cups are *good;* of the Swords and Pentacles, *bad.*

We shall presently repeat this in connection with each colour, and will now recapitulate the meanings of the four figures of the Sceptres.

King of Sceptres : Dark man ; good ; a friend.
Queen of Sceptres : Dark woman ; good.
Knight of Sceptres : Dark young man ; good.
Knave of Sceptres : Dark child or messenger ; good.

Besides our four figures we have to consider the 10 cards bearing numbers. How can we discover the meaning of these 10 cards, and above all how can we recall it?

We have nothing new to learn, but need only apply all that we already know. We divide our 10 cards into four packets: three packets of 3 cards each, and one packet formed of a single card, the 10th. When this is done we say—

The first packet of 3 cards, formed of the ace, 2, and 3, will have the same meaning as the *Man*, enterprise, commencement, the creation of some undertaking (enterprise, love, hatred, or money).

The second packet, composed of the 4, 5, and 6, represents *Woman*, and all the ideas of negation, of reflection, associated with her; that is to say, the opposite of man, antagonism, opposition in any matter.

The third packet signifies the equilibrium which results from the action of the two opposites upon each other, represented by the *Young Man.*

Lastly, the *Child*, the absolute neuter, will be represented by the 10th card.

Each of the 3 cards in these packets have the same meaning.

The first card of these 3 packets will indicate the commencement; the second, opposition, antagonism; the third, equilibrium, which gives us the following general sequence in our 10 cards.

KEY TO THE DIVINING TAROT.

1. Commencement
2. Opposition   } *of Commencement.*
3. Equilibrium

4. Commencement
5. Opposition   } *of Opposition.*
6. Equilibrium

7. Commencement
8. Opposition   } *of Equilibrium.*
9. Equilibrium

10. Undetermined : The card which follows will explain it.

Thus the three words, Commencement, Opposition, Equilibrium, the synonyms of *Thesis, Antithesis, Synthesis,* or of *Brahma, Siva, Vishnu,* etc., suffice for the explanation of all the minor arcana of the Tarot. We need only add the words love, hatred, enterprise or fortune to each of the series, and we can define the meaning of every card without wearying the memory. This we will now do.

SIGNIFICATION OF THE FOUR SERIES OF THE MINOR ARCANA IN THE DIVINING TAROT.

SCEPTRES.

Creation. Enterprise. Agriculture.

KING.	The King of Sceptres symbolizes a dark man, a friend. He generally represents a married man, the father of a family.
QUEEN.	A dark woman, a friend. Represents a serious woman, a very good counsellor, often the mother of a family.
KNIGHT.	A dark young man, a friend.
KNAVE.	A dark child, a friend. Also represents a message from a near relation.
ACE OF SCEPTRES.	*Commencement of an Enterprise.*
TWO.	*Opposition to the commencement of the Enterprise.*
	The Enterprise is commenced when an unexpected obstacle suddenly prevents its execution.
THREE.	*Realization of the commencement of the Enterprise.*
	The basis of the work is now definitely established, and the undertaking can be fearlessly continued.
FOUR.	*Obstacles to the Enterprise.*
	Nothing can be accomplished without obstacles. We therefore now find them appearing, and must prepare ourselves to overcome them.
FIVE.	*Opposition to the obstacles. Victory after surmounting them.*

Six.	*Realization of the opposition.* At last the obstacles succeed. *Failure of the Enterprise* in the midst of its execution.
Seven.	*Certain success to the Enterprise.*
Eight.	*Opposition to its success.* The Enterprise will only partially succeed.
Nine.	*Realization of success.* Success is continued.
Ten.	Uncertainty in the management of the Enterprise.

CUPS.

Preservation. Love. Instruction.

Knowing the meaning of one series, we know *à priori* the significations of the three others. We shall however give them in order to facilitate the work.

King of Cups.	*A fair man, a friend.* This card also represents a barrister, judge, or ecclesiastic. It symbolizes a Bachelor.
Queen of Cups.	*A fair woman, a friend.* The woman loved. The Mistress.
Knight of Cups.	*A young fair man, a friend.* The young man loved. The Lover.
Knave of Cups.	*A fair child.* A messenger. *Birth.*
Ace of Cups.	*Commencement of a love affair.*
Two.	*Opposition to this commencement.* Unimportant obstacles raised by one of the lovers.
Three.	*Realization of this commencement.* The love is mutual.
Four.	*Serious obstacles to the love.* They arise from other persons, not from the lovers.
Five.	*Opposition to the obstacles.* Victory over the obstacles after a struggle.

Six.	*The obstacles triumph.* Love destroyed in the midst of happiness. *Widowhood.*
Seven.	*Success assured to the lovers.*
Eight.	*Partial failure of love.* Love only partially succeeds.
Nine.	Motherhood.
Ten.	Uncertainty in the management of the love affair.

SWORDS.

Transformation. Hatred. War.

King of Swords.	*A dark, bad man.* He is a soldier, a powerful enemy, who must be distrusted.
Queen of Swords.	*A dark wicked woman.* The card also indicates her actions, *gossip and calumnies.*
Knight.	*A young, dark man, an enemy.* He is also a *spy.*
Knave.	*A child, an enemy.* Bad news. *Delay.*

The figures generally indicate opposition raised outside the house.

Ace of Swords.	*Commencement of enmity.*
Two.	*Opposition to this commencement.* The enmity does not last.
Three.	Realization of the enmity. *Hatred.*
Four.	Opposition to the hatred. *Success against the enemy.*
Five.	*Opposition to this opposition.* The enemy triumphs at the moment one fancies the victory is secured.
Six.	*Equilibrium of the opposition.* The enemy is rendered powerless at last.
Seven.	*Success assured to the enemy.*

314   THE TAROT.

Eight.   *Partial opposition to this success.* The enemy only partially triumphs.
Nine.   *Certain duration of the hatred.*
Ten.   Uncertainty in the enmity.

PENTACLES.

Development. Money. Trade.

King of Pentacles.   A *fair man*, inimical or indifferent.
Queen of Pentacles. A *fair woman, indifferent,* or inimical.
Knight.   A *young, fair man.* A stranger. *An arrival.*
Knave.   A *fair child.* A messenger. *A letter.*

The figures of the Pentacles are inverse to those of the Sceptres and Cups, and indicate all that comes from outside, from the country or abroad.

Ace of Pentacles. *Commencement of fortune.* Inheritance. Gifts. Economy, etc., etc.
Two.   *Opposition to this commencement.* Difficulty in well establishing the first landmarks of good fortune.
Three.   *Realization of this commencement of fortune.* A small sum.
Four.   Opposition of fortune. *Loss of money.*
Five.   Opposition to this opposition. *A success coming which will balance the loss.*
Six.   Realization of the opposition. *Ruin.*
Seven.   Success assured. *A large fortune.*
Eight.   *Partial success.* Great loss of money at the moment apparently of definitely securing the fortune.

Nine.   Equilibrium of Equilibrium. *A durable fortune.*

Ten.   *Uncertainty in the fortune.* Great success and great reverses.

As a whole, we see the same series always repeating themselves. It therefore requires little time to thoroughly learn the meaning of the minor arcana, even without much memory. We advise those readers who fear they may forget them, to simply write the meaning on the cards themselves. However, professional card readers are careful not to do this, for intuition often leads them to an interpretation which differs from the exact meaning of the card.

THIRD LESSON.

MAJOR ARCANA.
SIGNIFICATION FROM THE DIVINING POINT OF VIEW.

We now know the signification of the minor arcana, and need only study the major arcana.

As we have already stated, the major arcana consist of 22 symbolical cards, which we have not yet examined as a means of predicting the future.

Their meaning is very easy to remember, if any one will take the trouble to consider them carefully one by one, as their signification is described.

One general rule will also aid the memory in this matter, that is, that the seven first cards chiefly refer to the *intellectual side* of man, the seven next to his *moral side*, and the seven last to the *various events of his material life*.

We will now give the signification of these 22 cards of our Tarot—

1. *The Juggler*   signifies MALE INQUIRER.
2. *The High Priestess*   —   FEMALE INQUIRER.
3. *The Empress*   —   ACTION. INITIATIVE.
4. *The Emperor*   —   WILL.
5. *The Pope*   —   INSPIRATION.
6. *The Lovers*   —   LOVE.

THE DIVINING TAROT.

7. *The Chariot* — TRIUMPH. PROVIDENTIAL PROTECTION.
8. *Justice* — JUSTICE.
9. *The Hermit* — PRUDENCE.
10. *The Wheel of Fortune* — FORTUNE. DESTINY.
11. *Strength* — STRENGTH. FORTITUDE.
12. *The Hanged Man* — TRIALS. SACRIFICE.
13. *Death* — DEATH.
14. *Temperance* — TEMPERANCE. ECONOMY.
15. *The Devil* — IMMENSE FORCE. ILLNESS.
16. *The Lightning-struck Tower* — RUIN. DECEPTION.
17. *The Stars* — HOPE.
18. *The Moon* — HIDDEN ENEMIES. DANGER.
19. *The Sun* — MATERIAL HAPPINESS. LUCKY MARRIAGE.
20. *The Judgment* — CHANGE OF POSITION.
21. *The Foolish Man* — INCONSIDERATE ACTIONS. MADNESS.
22. *The Universe* — ASSURED SUCCESS.

FOURTH LESSON.

BASIS OF THE APPLICATION OF THESE DATA.
ARRANGEMENT OF THE CARDS.

We are now in a position to handle the Tarot as a means of divination.

But before we attempt to read it, we must settle how to arrange the cards upon the table.

To know the meaning of the cards is only the first step in the art of cartomancy; to know how to arrange them is still more important. As a fact, the astronomical data should not be lost sight of, and the Tarot ought only to be used to represent the revolutions of the stars, the source of future events; but that is the realm of Astrology, and we must confine ourselves to that of telling fortunes by the Tarot cards, and their combinations depend a little upon chance.

We shall, however, give as many reliable elements in this study as possible. We need only look back to the commencement of the third part (Key to the Applications of the Tarot), to see that the human life passes through the four great periods of—

>   Childhood.
>   Youth.
>   Maturity.
>   Old Age.

THE DIVINING TAROT.

If the student is not interested in Human Life, and simply wishes to see the evolution of an *event*, it will also pass through four great evolutions—

>Commencement.
>Apogee.
>Decline.
>Fall.

We must then first determine, in our arrangement of the cards, four points facing each other in pairs, upon which we can afterwards place the cards which are to reveal the future to us.

This, therefore, is our first point: the *determination of the four places which the cards will occupy*.

```
                    4
                  Apogee
                  Youth
       1                            3
 Commencement                    Decline
   Childhood                     Maturity
                    2
                   Fall
                 Old Age
```

We must notice that the disposition of the points goes from *left* to *right*. This is seen by the order of the numbers, whilst the symbols are read from *right* to *left*.

The Human Life or the Event moves in three very distinct periods—

>The Past.
>The Present.
>The Future.

Which gives us a new figure as follows—

```
        4
     Future
1 ──────────── 3
  \    Past Present  /
   \              /
    \            /
     \          /
      \        /
       \      /
        \    /
         \  /
          \/
          2
```

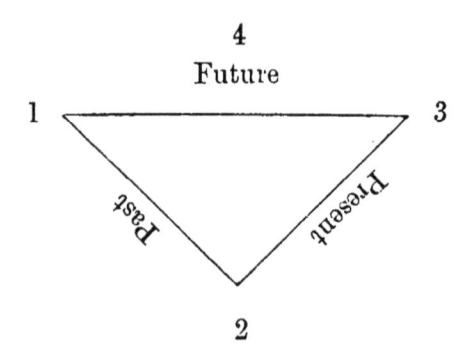

The Inquirer is found in the Centre. The arrangement of the triangle follows that of the figures and not of the symbols.

However, since four points are not enough to reproduce the movement of the sun exactly, we take, for important readings of the Tarot, twelve points which correspond with the twelve months of the year. The figure already obtained will, at any rate, serve as a means of consulting the Tarot upon small events. But we can also get the following figure, which we must remember for the arrangement of our cards when we wish to inquire about great events or the course of a lifetime.

THE DIVINING TAROT.

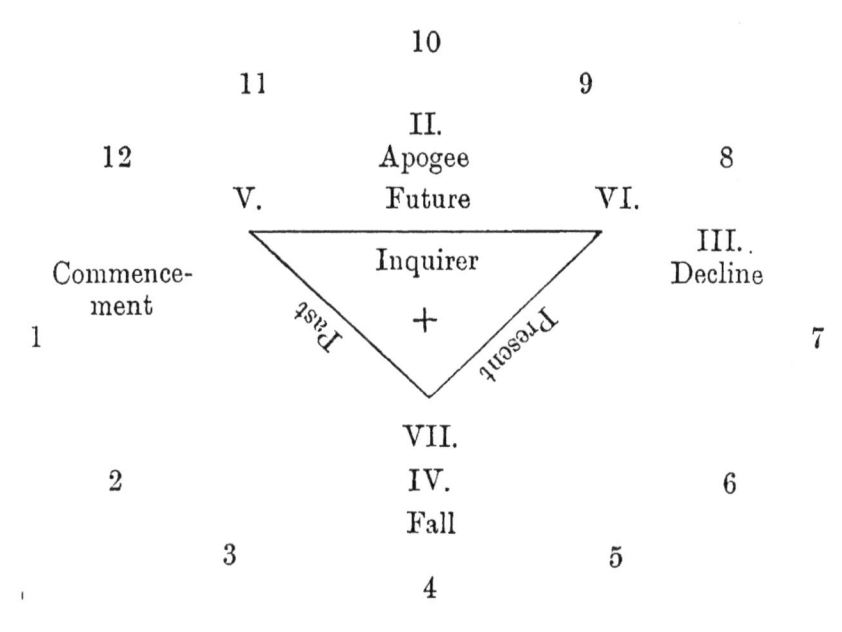

```
              10
       11            9
             II.
  12        Apogee        8
       V.   Future   VI.
              ╲ Inquirer ╱      III.
Commence-      ╲   +   ╱        Decline
  ment       Past ╲ ╱ Present
1                  V                    7
                 VII.
  2              IV.              6
                Fall
         3               5
                 4
```

This figure, which is very important and should be carefully studied, is composed of three circles.

1. An outside circle, formed of *twelve houses*, filled by the minor arcana. The houses are arranged from *left* to *right;* this is shown by the numbers.

2. A second intermediate circle, composed of four houses, arranged from *right* to *left*.

3. A central circle, formed by the triangle, and containing a house at each point, giving three houses in the circle.

The last three houses and the four preceding ones will be filled by the *major arcana*.

The Inquirer will be in the centre of the figure.

Y

FIFTH LESSON.

FORTUNE-TELLING BY THE TAROT.

I.—Rapid Process:

What must we do if we wish to draw out the horoscope of any matter?

1. You should take the minor arcana and separate the suit of cards that refers to the kind of consultation you require.

If it is some *business you are about to undertake*, you must take the Sceptres or Diamonds.

If it is a *love affair*, take the Cups or Hearts.

For a *law-suit*, or any struggle, take Swords or Spades.

In a *money matter*, the Pentacles or Clubs.

2. Shuffle the cards selected, then ask the Inquirer to cut them.

3. Take the four first cards from the top of the pack, and without looking at them place them in a cross in the following way, from left to right, as shown by the numbers.

```
        4
   1        3
        2
```

4. Then take your major arcana (which should always be separated from the minor arcana), shuffle them, and let them be cut for you.

5. You then ask the Inquirer to draw out *seven cards* from the major arcana by chance, and to give them to you without looking at them.

6. Shuffle these seven cards, and when the Inquirer has cut them, take the three top cards, and without looking at them arrange them in a triangle, in the following order—

I.   II.
III.

You thus obtain the following figure—

4
Major Arcana
I.   .   II.
1   3
III.
Minor Arc.
2

7. Take up the cards so that you can see them and read the oracles, noticing that the card placed at number 1 indicates the *commencement*.

The card placed at number 2 indicates the *apogee*, at number 3 the *obstacles*, lastly, at number 4 the *fall*.

The major arcanum placed at I. indicates the influences that have weighed in the affair during the *Past*.

The major arcanum in II. indicates the influence exerted over the *Present*.

The arcanum at number III. shows the influence which will affect and determine the *Future*.

These cards can be very rapidly deciphered when the habit is once acquired. But one important point should be noted, that when the rapid process is used for fortune-telling, the figures do not exclusively represent persons of especial complexion. The King represents a man, without any other distinction, the Queen a woman, the Knight a young man, and the Knave a child.

II.—A more elaborate Process:

1. Shuffle all the minor arcana together and let them be cut for you.

2. Take the twelve first cards from the pack, and place them in a circle thus—

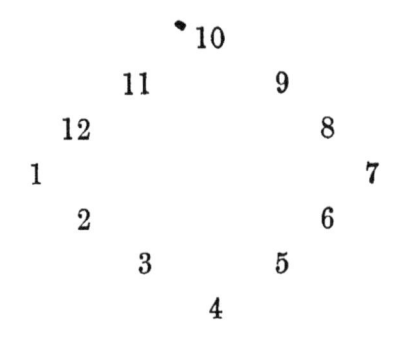

```
            10
        11      9
      12          8
    1               7
      2           6
        3       5
            4
```

3. Shuffle the major arcana, and let them be cut by the Inquirer, who will then choose *seven cards*.

4. Take the four first of these cards from the pack, and arrange them opposite the cards placed at numbers 1, 10, 7, 4, thus—

```
            II.
        I.      III.
            IV.
```

5. Then place the three others in a triangle in the centre of the figure, thus—

```
        V.      VI.
            VII.
```

THE DIVINING TAROT.

You thus obtain the following general figure, which we have already given.

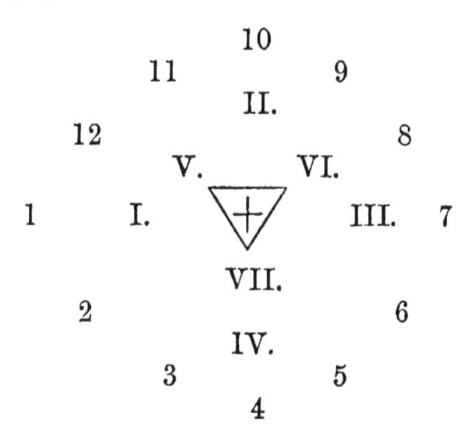

```
                    10
              11          9
                   II.
        12                     8
              V.        VI.
    1     I.   \+/    III.   7
                  VII.
        2                     6
                   IV.
              3           5
                    4
```

Place the Inquirer in the centre of the figure, unless it has been drawn amongst the other cards. If the Inquirer has been drawn you must place it in the centre, and replace it by another major arcanum chosen by the person whose fate is being studied.

The 12 minor arcana indicate the different phases through which the individual life will pass, or the evolution of the event during the four great periods: *Commencement*, indicated by the major arcanum I., which displays its character; *Apogee* (arc. II.); *Decline* or *Obstacle* (arc. III.); *Fall* (arc. IV.).

Lastly, the 3 major arcana placed in the centre indicate the especial character of the horoscope in the *Past* (V.), in the *Present* (VI.), and in the *Future* (VII.).

The future is indicated in the minor arcana by the cards placed from 7 to 12;

The past by those placed from 1 to 4; and the present by those placed from 4 to 7.

These numbers only indicate the numbers of the *places* occupied by the arcana, and never the numbers of the arcana themselves. It is important to avoid the idea that the arcanum VII. must always return to the place numbered VII. But our readers are sufficiently intelligent to make any further insistence upon this point quite unnecessary.

The explanation of the meaning of the arcana will be perfectly easy, when the lessons 2 and 3 have been once read.

Practice will teach all these details far better than all the theories in the world.

SIXTH LESSON.

Etteila's original and unpublished Method of Fortune-telling by the Tarot (from one of his rarest works).

WE have explained a method which is original in a great measure, but as we have no intention of monopolizing the art of Cartomancy, we will now say a few words upon the system used by Etteila, the great master in this portion of occultism.

Etteila, whose real name was Aliette, was a hairdresser's apprentice who lived at the time of the French Revolution. Having accidentally found a pack of Tarot cards, he was interested by its eccentricity and began to study it. After thirty years he believed that he had discovered the secret of this Egyptian book. Unfortunately Etteila did not possess any synthetic knowledge, and this ignorance led him to the most erroneous conclusions, whilst many of his intuitive solutions are really marvellous. There is too much inclination to calumniate this ardent worker; but we must recognize the real truths contained in his works without laying too much stress upon the ignorant simplicity which disfigures them.

However this may be, Etteila devoted all his powers to fortune-telling, and if his contemporaries may be believed, he succeeded wonderfully in his aim. He therefore became the great authority for all fortune-tellers by cards.

We will describe his system in some detail, instead of alluding to those used by his female successors, who as a rule misrepresented without understanding his explanations.

*_**

Four deals are required before the Tarot can be clearly read according to this method: we will now enumerate them one by one.

FIRST DEAL: Shuffle all the cards of the Tarot, without making any distinction between the major and minor arcana. Then let them be cut, and divide your pack into three heaps, each containing 26 cards.[1]

  26   26   26

Take the central heap and place it on your right—

  26   26   26 on one side
                  to the right.

You have still two packets of 26 cards. Take them, shuffle the cards, cut them, and divide them into three heaps, each containing 17 cards—

  17   17   17
        1

One card will remain, but you need not trouble about it.

You then take the central packet and put it on your right hand by the side of the one of 26 cards already there—

  17   * 17   17 26 on one side.
      1

[1] Etteila quite realized that the number 26 corresponded with the divine name יהוה, the total being 10 + 5 + 6 + 5 = 26.
       yod he vau he

THE DIVINING TAROT.

You then take the 35 cards which are not on one side, shuffle and cut them, then divide them into three heaps of 11 cards each—

    11   11   11
                 2

Two cards remain, but these are of no consequence; take the central packet as before and place it on your right by the side of those already there—

  11   *   11   11 17 26
        2

This ended, you collect the 24 cards that you have not placed on one side, and you are then ready to explain the oracle.

                    * *

For this purpose you first take the packet of 26 cards from your right and lay it upon the table card by card, going from right to left—

    26..1

Then take the packet of 17 cards, which you place beneath the others, then the 11 cards, which you also spread out beneath the other two. You then obtain the following arrangement.

Soul   26..1
Mind   17..............................1
Body   11....................1
              Waste packet
                  24

You then explain the meaning of the cards, remembering that the lowest line of 11 refers to the *body*, the centre one to the *mind*, and lastly, the upper line of 26 cards to the *soul* of the Inquirer.

From this system of arrangement Etteila deduced his subtle arguments upon the creation of the Universe, the Kabbalah, and the Philosopher's Stone. But we need not linger over it. We will rather pass on to complete this study of fortune-telling by the Tarot.

SECOND DEAL: Reshuffle all your cards (78) and let them be cut for you.

Take the 17 first cards and arrange them thus—

17..........................1

Look quickly at the 18th card (it will be under your hand when you have placed the 17 first) and the 78th, which will be found beneath the pack.

The meaning of these two cards will tell you whether any fluidic sympathetic communication is established between the Inquirer and yourself.

You can then read the oracles spoken by the line of cards, commencing as usual on the right.

When your line is read, you pass the 17th card to your right and the 1st to your left, then move the 16th and the 2nd, etc., and so on until the cards have all changed places except the one in the centre. This card falls on one side.[1]

THIRD DEAL: Take up all your cards, let them be shuffled and cut for you, then arrange them as shown in the following figure, according to the order of the numbers.

You thus obtain Etteila's great figure, which gives the key to the Past, Present, and Future of the person about

[1] Perhaps we have misunderstood Etteila, who is very obscure in his books, and whom we are trying to explain; but this last operation seems perfectly useless.

THE DIVINING TAROT.

whose fate you are inquiring. To use this method successfully you must follow this figure very carefully. The best plan is to draw it with all its numbers upon a table or a large sheet of cardboard, and then to arrange the cards according to the order of the numbers.

For reading the results of this figure you must take up

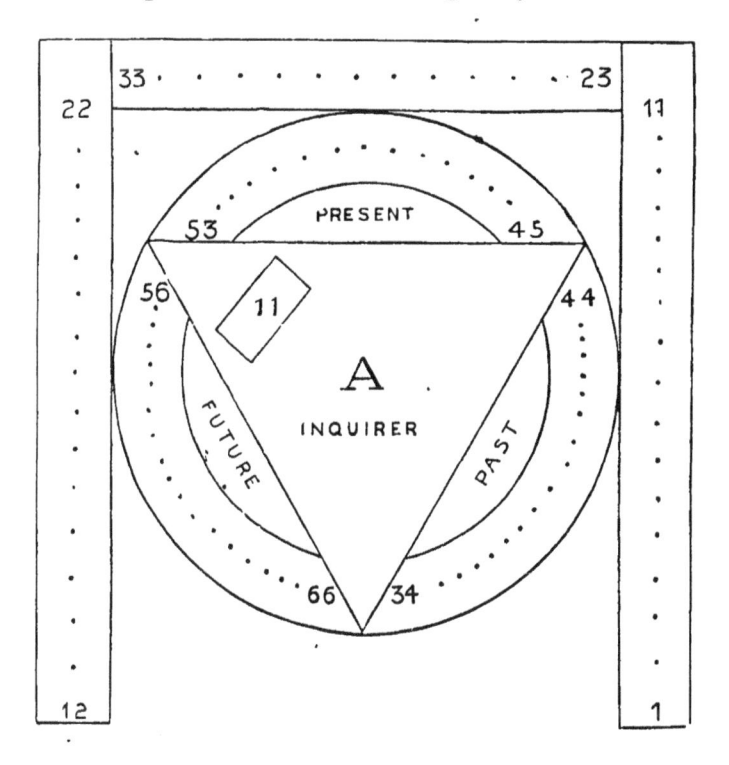

the cards two by two, the 1st with the 34th, the 2nd with the 35th, etc., for the Past.

The 23rd with the 45th, the 24th with the 46th . . . . . the 33rd with the 55th, for the Present.

The 12th with the 66th, the 13th with the 65th . . . . . the 22nd with the 56th, for the Future.

One careful survey of the tableau will render it easily understood.

FOURTH DEAL: The fourth deal is only subsidiary. By it answers can be obtained to any questions asked. Shuffle all the cards, let them be cut, and then deal out the first seven of the pack thus—

$$7\ldots\ldots\ldots\ldots\ldots\ldots\ldots\ldots 1$$

then read the answer.

The above system of fortune-telling is based upon Etteila's original method. We have summed up in these few pages, an—on some points—obscure pamphlet by this author—*The Book of Thoth*. It contains a portrait of Etteila and is very rare, like the other works of this author. We must add that his method has never been seriously elucidated by any of his numerous disciples; and we believe ourselves to be one of the first to explain it upon simple principles.

SEVENTH LESSON.

CONCLUSION.

WE have learnt that intuition and practice are necessities in the art of fortune-telling by cards, now that this art has lost its scientific principles (Astronomy) and launched into empiricism. Having made this reserve in our opinion of its present value, we have studied the best method of applying the Tarot to this curious practice, and with this object we have learnt the meaning of the minor and major arcana, and the best arrangement of the cards for reading them. With this method, which is chiefly the result of our previous studies, we were anxious to give one of the most ancient systems, and chose the one used by Etteila, the founder of Cartomancy.

Our readers are therefore able to choose whichever system they prefer, and whichever they find most successful. We must repeat that intuition is the great secret of all these divining arts, and that fortune-telling by cards, in water, in earth, or coffee, is precisely the same thing.

We wished to speak of the modern divining Tarot to render our work more complete, and our lady readers will thank us for not ignoring them in these abstract digressions.

BIBLIOGRAPHY.

Mademoiselle Lemarchand, *Récréation de la Cartomancie.* Paris, 1867, 12mo. R.

Julia Orsini, *Le Grand Etteila, ou l'Art de Tirer les Cartes.* 1853, 8vo. V.

Madame Clément, *Le Corbeau Sanglant ou l'Avenir Dévoilé.* R.

The works of Etteila we have already quoted.

CHAPTER XXI.

APPLICATION OF THE TAROT TO GAMES.

The Royal Game of Human Life played by the Egyptians.
The Unity of Games in the Tarot.

THE ROYAL GAME OF HUMAN LIFE,

ACCORDING TO THE EGYPTIANS.

1. When the players have chosen their *Magian*, they also choose from amongst the non-players a man and a woman, whom they name *Osiris* and *Isis*.

2. When commencing a game, the Magian having taken the central place, the players settle the amount of the principal fine together (we will suppose it to be one halfpenny), and a basket is placed on the table to receive the money.

3. When all the players are seated, the Magian takes the Book of Thoth, *i. e.* the pack of Tarot cards, and shuffles them, carefully placing their heads alternate ways, but without looking at them, lets them be cut by some player on his left, and then deals the cards to his right, giving as many as he likes, up to seven, to each player and to himself.

4. Each player should notice that the top of the card (when the Magian deals it) is facing his chest; it is therefore in that sense, and according to the order in which the cards are dealt, that the players should read the oracles traced upon it, which they refer to whomever they choose amongst the persons in the house.

5. When one of the players reads an oracle he assumes the character of an *interpreter*, and if the person to whom he refers the oracle will not give him a present, he must pay half the fine.

6. When a person has received three veracious oracles upon the past, the present, or according to probabilities the future, and he refuses to reward the interpreter, the players will hold a council, and judge by a majority of voices whether his refusal is justified or not. In the latter case, the Magian must pronounce the word PAMENES, which warns all the household that there is one person present who does not join in the royal game of the Human Life, and then Osiris and Isis are obliged to pay for him, for when they accepted these titles, they undertook to diffuse peace and abundance over the heroes who are playing.

7. When one of the spectators asks to buy the hand of one of the players, the Magian fixes its price, which is divided into three parts: the first third is paid into the fine-box; the second to the Magian; and the third to the player, who however can avoid parting with his cards by paying the two first thirds of the price fixed by the Magian.

8. When one of the spectators has acquired the hand of one of the players, he takes with it all the player's chances of fines and presents.

9. When one of the players cannot read the oracles, he

places his seven cards on one side and pays one-fourth of the fine.

10. If the player, although able to read the oracle, cannot find any one to whom he can refer it, he must lay his cards upon the table, face upwards, and read the meaning that he sees in them, without paying anything. If, on the other hand, he interprets them badly, according to the judgment of the other players, the Magian condemns him to pay half the fine.

11. When the interpreter has pronounced the oracle, aloud or privately, and has received a present, he can have his seven cards re-shuffled by the Magian, who will return them to him to cut; and finally, if the same cards produce three presents from the same or other persons to whom the oracles have been uttered, all the players, except the Magian, give the interpreter three times the value of the fine. This is the civic crown.

12. The Magian arranges and directs the games as he likes; he awards the fines according to the nature of the faults, such as showing the cards to other players, hiding them from the spectators, any indiscretion in the utterance of the oracles, reading oracles which are not justified by the cards, etc.

13. The spectators can join in the game until the Magian indicates that it will soon end, by saying in a quarter of an hour, or half an hour, the game will close.

14. If the Magian should forget to announce the coming end of the game, all the spectators have a right to share the fines, which are divided equally amongst all the players, when the expenses have been paid.

THE UNITY OF GAMES.

Is it not true that man has displayed more inventive faculties to satisfy his vices, than for anything else? To convince ourselves of this fact we need only look at the innumerable inventions destined to aid him in losing the time which has been so parsimoniously dealt out to us all.

But the human brain acts in accordance with a very small number of laws, and the inventor cannot escape from the effect of this rule. Look at the basis of most games, however they may differ in appearance. Is it not possible to find one single game, from which most of the others are derived?

Follow me in thought, dear reader, over one of the highroads of Spain or Italy, and let us ask some old Gypsy to leave her camp for a moment and tell our fortunes. Look at the strange cards she draws from her greasy bag: the Universe, the Sun, the Stars, Death, Fortune, Love, are only a few of the names of these eccentric figures, which depict the phases of our daily life with so much simplicity. What is this game? The Gypsy Tarot.

It is composed of our cards with four additional figures called Knights, who are placed between the Queen and the Knave. But its originality lies in the twenty-two supplementary and symbolical figures. Each of them represents an image, a number, an idea. Court de Gébelin, a savant of the eighteenth century, has shown us that this game, as possessed by the Gypsies, is of Egyptian origin, that it also existed in China and India from the earliest antiquity, and we shall see that it is the father of most of the games now known.

It is composed of numbers and figures, which mutually react upon and explain each other. But if we separate

APPLICATION OF THE TAROT TO GAMES.

the figures and arrange them upon a paper in the form of a wheel, making the numbers move in the shape of dice, we produce the *Goose game*, with which Ulysses, according to Homer, practised cheating beneath the walls of Troy.

If we fix the numbers upon alternate black and white squares, and allow the lesser figures of our game to move upon them—the King, Queen, Knight, Foolish Man or Knave, Tower or ace—we have the *Game of Chess*. In fact, the primitive chessboards bore numbers, and philosophers used them to solve problems of logic.

If, leaving the figures on one side, we confine ourselves to the use of numbers, the *Game of Dice* appears, and if we weary of throwing the dice, we can mark the characters upon horizontal plates and create the *Game of Dominoes*.

If the symbolical figures are in our way, we replace them by black and white draughts, and by using the numbers upon the dice we invent *Backgammon*, another combination of the Goose game.

Chess degenerates in the same way into the *Game of Draughts*.

Lastly, our *pack of cards*, instead of first appearing under Charles X., according to the common report, is of far older date. Spanish regulations are in existence dated long before this reign, forbidding the nobles to play at cards, and the Tarot itself is of very ancient origin.

The sceptres of the Tarot have become clubs, the cups hearts, the swords spades, and the pentacles or money diamonds. We have also lost the twenty-two symbolical figures and the four knights.

But if all these games are derived from the Tarot, what is its origin and its primitive derivation?

These are grave questions, which for their solution lead the mind into dangerous researches. Let me therefore relate to you a certain confidence upon this subject which I received from a dusty old manuscript, forgotten in a corner of a library. Take it as romance or as history, whichever you like, it does not matter so long as your curiosity is gratified.

Now, let us transport ourselves in imagination three thousand miles away, into the midst of the wonderful and grandiose Egyptian civilization, which archæologists are each day revealing more fully to our century.

Let us enter one of those cities, of which Paris would form but one district, passing through the defensive outworks guarded by a well-equipped body of soldiers, and glide amongst the inhabitants, who are as numerous and as busy as those of our greatest cities.

On all sides immense monuments of strange architecture rise to enormous heights; the terraces of rich houses indicate the first steps of a gigantic staircase, formed by the palaces and temples, and dominated by the silent residence of the supreme head of the Empire.

The great cities are everywhere fortified, the Nile is restrained by moles, and enormous reservoirs are ready to receive its surplus waters, and thus transform terrible inundations into beneficent irrigation.

All this involves science and savants, but where are they?

At this epoch science and religion were blended in a single study, and all the men of science, engineers, doctors, architects, superior officers, scribes, etc., were called *priests* or *Initiates*. We must not confuse the priest of antiquity with the word taken in the modern sense, or we shall fall into many errors, amongst others that of believing that Egypt was given over to clerical despotism in its worst form.

APPLICATION OF THE TAROT TO GAMES.

Instruction of every kind was given in the temples in various degrees, according to methods perfectly established, and, at that epoch, imitated in every country in the world.

The highest instruction which man can acquire was given in the great temple of Egypt, and it was there that the great reformers of the future completed their studies: Orpheus, Lycurgus, Pythagoras, and Moses amongst many others.

Astronomy was one of the sciences which became the object of constant investigation. We now know through Pythagoras, who has perpetuated the knowledge of the wise men of Egypt, that they were acquainted with the movement of the earth round the sun, as well as with the position of the latter in relation to its satellite planets. Many of the mythological stories relate to these mysteries and the wise men of the epoch, that is to say, the priests taught astronomy to their disciples, by means of small cards, which represented the months, seasons, signs of the zodiac, planets, sun, etc., etc. In this way they imprinted upon the imagination of the students the data which later on they verified in nature.

A time followed when Egypt, no longer able to struggle against her invaders, prepared to die honourably. Then the Egyptian savants (at least so my mysterious informant asserts) held a great assembly to arrange how the knowledge, that until that date had been confined to men judged worthy to receive it, should be saved from destruction.

At first they thought of confiding these secrets to virtuous men secretly recruited by the Initiates themselves, who would transmit them from generation to generation. But one priest, observing that virtue is a most fragile thing, and most difficult to find, at all events in a continuous line, proposed to confide the scientific traditions to vice.

The latter, he said, would never fail completely, and through it we are sure of a long and durable preservation of our principles.

This opinion was evidently adopted, and the game chosen as a vice was preferred. The small plates were then engraved with the mysterious figures which formerly taught the most important scientific secrets, and since then the players have transmitted this Tarot from generation to generation, far better than the most virtuous men upon earth would have done.

Such is the story or the history confided to me by this old manuscript, upon the origin of the father of our great games, and I am very glad that it provided me with the means of proving my perhaps paradoxical assertion of their original unity.

CHAPTER XXII.

CONCLUSION.

HAVING reached the end of our journey we must cast one rapid glance over the road we have followed, in order to give some account of the scope of our work.

Seeing that materialistic science was giving way, in spite of the desperate efforts of its partisans, under the irresistible pressure of the new era, the impotence of purely analytical methods forced itself upon us, and we were led to search for the possible basis of a synthesis which each day renders more indispensable.

At this moment, the ancient wisdom revealed itself to our investigations, and we find that it contains this synthetic method as the immutable basis of all its scientific, religious, and social discoveries.

The secret societies entrusted with the transmission of this sacred deposit have lost its key as well as its ritual; the nomad Gypsies and the Jews only have guarded their Bibles intact throughout the centuries: the latter had the Sepher of Moses, the former the Tarot attributed to Thoth Hermes Trismegistus, the triple hierarchic University of ancient Egypt.[1]

[1] Consult Saint-Yves d'Alveydre, *Mission des Juifs*.

The Tarot appeared to us as the Egyptian translation of the book of initiation, starting as the now missing key to Freemasonry and the whole occult science.

How could we decipher this series of hieroglyphics? How discover the mysterious grouping of these plates, now become the accessory of gamblers?

Wronski teaches us that the faculty to conceive implies the faculty to execute. Strong in this truth, we have questioned antiquity. Its Sphinxes, dumb to the profane, have spoken, its old temples have unveiled their mysteries, its Initiates have re-awakened in answer to our call: four mysterious letters have been revealed to us—

י	ה	ו	ה
Yod	*He*	*Vau*	*He*

The sacred word, which shines above every initiation, the object of the veneration and respect of all the sages.

The study of the Tarot has shown us that it only expresses the combinations of IEVE. However, since we must in these questions guard ourselves above all things from leaving too much scope to the imagination, we have chosen as the starting-point for our studies a fixed principle, as basis to these immutable combinations, the sole guarantee against all possible error: the *number*.

We then approached the symbol, and there we again encountered new difficulties. The history of the Tarot has shown us that its figures have often changed in passing through the hands of various peoples, and through different epochs, although its meaning has been preserved in all times and in all places.

It was therefore necessary to find for the symbols a principle as fixed and immutable in its combinations as the number. The study of the origin of the letters used

CONCLUSION.

to inscribe human languages led us back to the determination of the sixteen primitive hieroglyphic signs, the source of the first alphabets. The 22 Hebrew letters immediately derived from these signs furnished us with this indispensable basis to all serious researches, as definitely *fixed* for the *symbol*, as the numbers were for the whole Tarot. We thus had a sure guide, which rendered error still more unlikely.

Thanks to the application of these principles, exact, although very general, information was furnished to us upon *Theogony, Androgony*, and *Cosmogony*, and we could at last recapitulate the symbolism of the Tarot in a very interesting tableau.

We then wished to show that the Tarot was really the *general key* which we had pronounced it to be. A few applications proved the fact. Astronomy is unquestionably the most important amongst them through its fixed principles. Therefore, when we wish to discover how an evolution *can advance*, and we wander in the labyrinth of inexactitude, Astronomy shows us how the evolution of the sun *progresses*, and that knowledge gives us the key to every possible evolution.

The gigantic labours of Dupuis were fruitless, because he did not understand that the *solar Myth* was only a representation of the *general law of evolution*, and not that of the especial evolution of the sun. The method of occult science is neither induction nor deduction, but analogy, an unknown method at the present date which the Tarot reveals to us in all its splendour.

Afterwards we have made other applications of it, and could have made still more; shown the key of Philosophy, of the Holy Kabbalah, of Theosophy, of the Physiology of Man and of the Universe in the Tarot; but we have restricted ourselves to giving the key, and to showing the way to use it by some examples.

We were unwilling to exceed the strict limits of our engagement.

Such as it is, our work still contains some imperfections which we would willingly efface. We are under no illusions on this point, and time alone can remedy it. But we would draw attention to the aim which is visible throughout its pages; the application of the most exact methods possible to occult science.

Through the modern exact sciences we have reached the study of occultism, and starting ourselves from materialism, of which we were one of the most ardent disciples, we felt the necessity of advancing further. But we had retained one trace of our early affections, the taste for method, and it is the absence of this method which spoils occult science. Louis Lucas had clearly seen that physics must advance by the side of metaphysics to serve as its basis: in the same way we have endeavoured to place fixed principles, such as numbers and the Hebrew letters, side by side with the metaphysical data, like the symbols or abstract conceptions.

Occultists as a rule are lost through this lack of precision. We have made every effort to avoid this stumbling-block, without however asserting that we have succeeded. An author is not qualified to judge his own work.

Be this as it may, we have been frequently obliged to speak of occult science without the leisure to enter into these explanatory details—this is the reason we addressed our book

To Initiates.

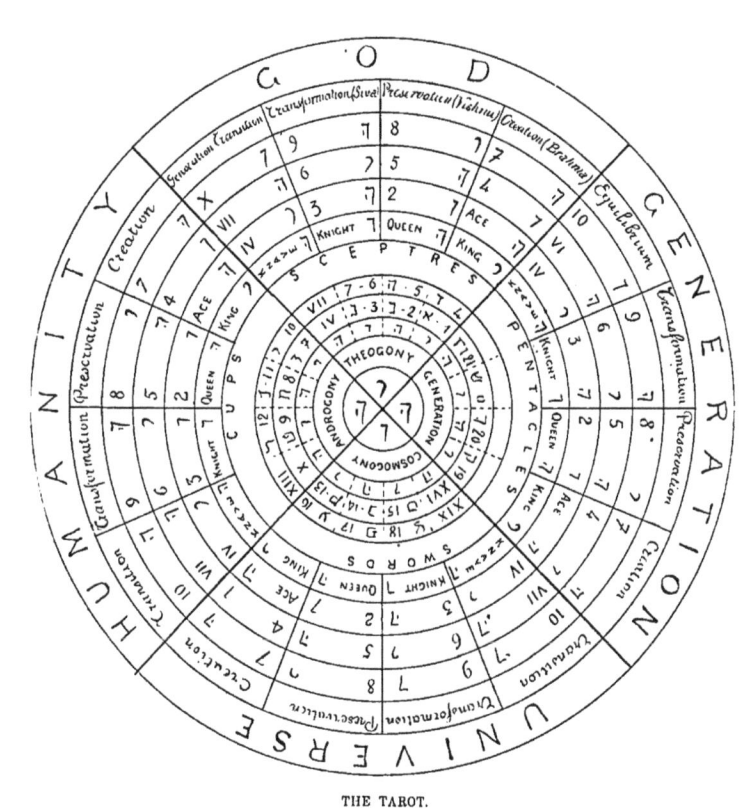

THE TAROT.
CYCLE OF REVOLUTIONS OF IEVE (יהוה).
ABSOLUTE KEY TO OCCULT SCIENCE BY
PAPUS.

To face page 319.

An Initiate is one who possesses the elements of
:ultism, and who is therefore familiar with a whole
:abulary, which may well alarm a man of the world;
s is our excuse for words which may sound pretentious
some minds, and this is why we were anxious to express
r ideas quite clearly.

Still, since it is customary for the Tarot to be used for
tune-telling, we have touched upon this subject, and
idered it as attractive as possible. We have tried
simplify the systems used, so that a woman of even
;le intelligence can easily and with little exercise of
:mory amuse herself with this art.

But since our own system may not please all the
rtisans of Cartomancy, we have summed up the process
the great master *Etteila*, so that, even in this purely
ipiric region, we have tried to introduce as much
entific exactitude as possible.

We hope that this recapitulation of the efforts of
/eral years may prove useful to occultism, and to its
/ival, which becomes daily more pronounced. This is
₃ aim which we have kept in view. May the social
iorders which are preparing give rise to an era of peace
d harmony amongst the now divided nations, and may
₃ knowledge of these mysteries overthrow European
₃sarism in all its forms! This should be your aim,
ibbalists, Theosophists, Martinists, Rosicrucians, and
eemasons! On this point believe the humble disciple
your doctrines, who will be only too happy if his work
s retained one feeble ray of the Eternal and Holy
uth.

INDEX.

ADAM, 111, 294
Addition, theosophic, 27
Air, 189
Alchemists, 5
Aleph, 105
Alphabet, Hebrew, 93—5
Amen, 203
Androgony, 210
Animal, 187
Arabs, 5
Arcana, major, 51—60, 61—67, 316
Arcana, minor, 35—50, 61—67, 307
Astronomical Tarot, 233
Atlantides, 8
Attraction, universal, 131
Authority, 125, 126
Authors who have spoken of the Tarot, 297
Axe, hieroglyphic, 181

Balance, sign of the Zodiac, 152
Barlet, C., 253
Beauty, 131
Beth, 112
Bible, Christian, 7
— Freemason, 7
— Greek, 7
— Hindu, 7
— Jewish, 7
— Roman, 7
Binah, 118, 205
Blood, 228
Body, 180
Body, material, 176, 177
Bologna, Tarot of, 85
Brahma, 75, 146, 195, 204

Cards, fortune-telling by, 305
Chaos, 176
Chariot, the, 135
Charity, 131, 153
China, 103
Chinese Tarot, 87
Chocmah, 114, 205
Clubs, 36
Colours, 44

Conclusion, 343
Cosmogony, 216
Courage, 150
Creator, 74, 109
Creeds, 6
Cross, symbol of the, 34, 44
— episcopal, 44
Cups, 36, 44, 312

Daleth, 119
Day, 231
Death, 158, 159
Decan, 236
Destiny, 101
Devil, 164, 165
Diamonds, 36
Divine world, 41
Divining Tarot, 301

Earth, 189
Elements, the, 180, 181
Element, Being, 101, 102
— Neuter, 101, 102
— Wisdom, 101, 102
Emperor, 120
Empress, 116
En Soph, 205
Epagomene, 235
Esoterism, 26
Etteila, 88, 291, 327
Eve, 114, 240
Existence, elementary, 140, 141
Experience, 153, 154
Eye, 127, 131

Faith, 126
Fall, the, 169, 170
Fatality, 166, 167
Father, 75, 136, 137
Figuration of the sacred word, 23
Figures, 37—41
Fire, 189
Fo-hi, trigram of, 103
Foolish man, the, 185, 186
Force, 153, 154, 160
Forces, the physical, 227

350　INDEX.

Fortune, wheel of, 145
Four, 32, 37
Freemasons, 5
Friday, 118

Game, royal, of human life, 335
Games, unity of, 338
Generation, 116
German Tarot, 89
Gimel, 115
Gnostics, 5
God, 102, 109, 111
Guaita (Stanislas de), the kabbalistic Tarot, 299
Gypsies, 8, 239

Hanged man, 151
He, 21, 38, 66, 123
He, second, 22, 24 *note*, 38
Hearts, 36
Hermit, 142
Hesiod, 104.
Hieroglyphics, 91
Hindu Tarots, 86
Hiram, legend of, 7, 10
— heart of, 11
— tomb of, 10
Holy Spirit, 75, 117, 118
Hope, 173
Horus, 75, 117, 195
Host, 44
Human world, 41, 48, 118

Immortality, 173
Initiates, 4, 6, 124
Initiative Tarot, 253
Innervation, 186, 187
Inri, 10, 11
Instinct, 186, 187
Intellectuality, 41
Intelligence, 125, 126
Inventors, 107
Isis, 75, 113, 114, 195

Jakin, 106
January, 176
Judgment, 184
Juggler, 106
Juno, 195
Jupiter, 120, 121, 195
Justice, 138—141

Kabbalah, 17, 32, 144

Kadosh, 10
Kaph, 148
Karma of the Hindus, 147
Kether, 111, 205
King, 37
Kingdoms (animal, vegetable, mineral), 192
Knave, 37
Knight, 37
Kosmos, 118

Lamed, 151
Liberty, 150
Life, 123—126, 150, 163, 180, 231
Light, astral, 136, 137
Lightning-struck tower, 168
Lingam, 124
Love, 130, 131
Lovers, 128

Macrocosm, 108
Man, 102, 103, 105, 111, 113, 155
Mantegna pack, 84
Materialism (approaching end), 3
Material world, 43, 48
Matter, 215, 227
Mem, 158
Mercury, 171
Microcosm, 105, 108
Mineral kingdom, 180, 181
Monday, 114
Months, 233, 235
Moon, 114, 175
Moses, 7, 8
Mother, 140, 141
Motion, innate, 184
Motion, of relative duration, 186, 187
Mysteries, 4

Nahash, 166, 167
Natura naturans, 111, 206
Natura naturata, 114, 207
Nature balanced, 117
Nizah, 141
Numbers, 26
— law of the evolution of, 29
— signification of, 30
— affinities of, 33
Numbers (of the minor arcana), 38
Nun, 161
Nutrition, 180, 181

INDEX.

Occult science, 4
Operations upon numbers, 18, 20
Osiris, 75, 114, 116, 195, 203

Parabrahm, 204
Pe, 171
Pechad, 126
Pentacles, 36, 47—49, 52, 251, 314
People, the, 8, 107
Planets, 238
Pope, 125
Power, 122
Power, magic, 147
Priestess, High, 112
Prism, 226
Providence, 101
Prudence, 144
Ptah, 203
Pythagoras, tetractys of, 33

Queen, 37

Ra, 203
Reduction, theosophic, 27
Religion, 126
Reproduction, 41, 192
Resh, 182
Respiration, 183, 184
Roof, 176
Rosicrucians, 5, 10, 298
Rota, 9

Samech, 164
Saturn, 184
Savants, 107
Sceptres, 36, 311
Sepher Bereschit, 7
Septenaries, 54—58, 61—65, 75, 99, 132, 133
Shin, 185
Signs, primitive, 91
Siva, 75, 146, 195, 203
Societies, secret, 4
Son, 75
Soul of the Universe, 122
Spades, 36
Speech, 112, 171
Star, seventeenth card, 171
Stars of Solomon, 162
Sun, 179
Swords, 36, 44, 107, 313

Symbols, 11
Synthesis, 3

Table of the twelve hours of the Initiation, by Barlet, 273
Table indicating the meaning of the twenty-two major arcana, 76, 220, 221
Tarot of Florence, 85
Tau, 188
Temperance, 162, 163
Templars, 5
Ten, 38
Ternaries, 53
Teth, 142
Tetractys of Pythagoras, 33
Theogony, 194
Theosophite Society, 5
Thoth, book of, 9, 292
Three, 30, 38
Throat,
Thummim, 136
Thursday, 122
Tipheroth, 131
Transformer, 72
Tuesday, 150
Two, 30, 38
Tzaddi, 174

Universe, 102, 111, 177
Urim, 136

Vau, 21, 66, 127
Vegetable kingdom, 184
Venetian Tarot, 85
Venus Urania, 116, 175
Virgin, 146
Vishnu, 75, 146, 195, 204
Vital force, 41
Vulcan, 195

Watillaux, 89
Wednesday, 173
Will, 102
Wirth, 89, 90, 242—251, 299
Womb, 119, 188
Word, 32
World, visible, 103, 169, 170
Worlds, 43, 48

Zain, 135, 168

ALPHABETIC TABLE

OF THE

AUTHORS AND PRINCIPAL WORKS QUOTED.

PAGE

AGRIPPA.—*La Philosophie Occulte*, La Haye, 1727. 2 vols. 8vo. (Bib. Nat., Z. 1983, A.²)
APOCALYPSE 7
AMARAVELLA.—A theosophic writer known by his fine works in *Le Lotus*, and in the *Revue Théosophique*.
APOLLONIUS OF TYANA.—A great initiate and thaumaturge, contemporary with Christ ... ... 265, *sqq.*
ARNOULD (Arthur).—President of the Theosophite Society Hermes, the French branch of the Theosophite Society of Adyar (Madras).
ABBEMA (Louise).
ADAM (Mme. Juliette).
ADHÉMAR, D' (Countess Gaston).
BARROIS.—*Dactylologie ou Langage Primitif*, Paris, 1850, 4to. (Bib. Nat., X. 4,679.)
— *Eléments Carlovingiens*, Paris, 1854, 4to. (Bib. Nat., Z:)
BLAVATSKY (H. P.)—*Isis Unveiled*, New York, 1884 300
BOITEAU.—*Les Cartes à jouer et la Cartomancie*, Paris, 1854, 4to.
BOEHME (Jacob).—*Les Trois Principes*, translated by Claude de Saint-Martin.
BERTRAND (le F.·.).—Venerable de la L.·. *La Renaissance*, a conference in defence of occult symbolism in the F.·. M.·.
BARLET (Ch.).—Editor of the *Initiation*. The author of the most learned works that France possesses upon *Occult Science* 15, 299
COURT DE GÉBÉLIN.—*Le Monde Primitif*, 9 vols., 4to., 1773—1783.
CAILLIÉ (René).—*Dieu et la Création*, Paris (Carré), 3 vols., 8vo., 1886.
CHATTO.—*Facts and Speculations upon the Origin and History of Playing Cards in Europe*, London, 1848, 8vo.
DÉE (Jean).—*Monas Hieroglyphica* (in *Theatrum Chemimum*), 1560.
ELY STAR (*Les Mystères de l'Horoscope*, 18mo., Dentu, 1884 ... 300
ETTEILA.—Works by.
FRANCK (A.)—*La Kabbalah*, Paris, Hachette, 1889, 8vo.
FABRE D'OLIVET.—*Les Vers dorés de Pythagore*, Paris, 8vo., 1816 ; *La Langue Hébraïque restituée*, 1825, 4to., Paris. (Fundamental works of one of the greatest contemporary masters of occult science.)
GUAITA (Stanilas de).—*Au seuil du Mystère*, Paris, 1886, 8vo., 2nd enlarged edition, 1889 294

354 AUTHORS AND PRINCIPAL WORKS QUOTED.

PAGE

GARY (See Polti).
GOYARD (Dr.).—Former President of the Vegetarian Society, author of several works upon occultism.
GOUDEAU (Emile).
HARTMANN.—Works by.
HERMES TRISMEGISTUS 9
HOLMES (Augusta).
HOMER.—*The Odyssey* 7
HESIOD.—*Op. et Dies* 104
KIRCHER (the R. F. Jesuit).—*Œdipus Ægyptiacus*, 3 vols., fol., Rome, 1622.
KABBALA DENUDATA.—Frankfort, 1764, 2 vols., 4to., (Bib. Nat., A. 969).
KORAN, the.
LEVI (Eliphas, pseudonym of the Abbé Constant).—*Dogme et Rituel de la Haute Magie*, Paris, 2 vols., 8vo. ; *Histoire de la Magie*, 8vo., Paris ; *La Clef des grands Mystères*, 8vo., Paris (Fundamental works) 299
LENAIN.—*La Science Kabbalistique*, Amiens, 1823, 8vo. (A good summary.)
LACURIA (P. F. G.).—*Harmonies de l'Être exprimées par les nombres*, Paris, 1847, 8vo., 2 vols. (Fundamental work.)
LEJAY (Julien).—Editor of the *Initiation*. Has made an application of occult synthesis to Sociology.
LACOUR.—*Les Œloïm ou dieux de Moise*, Paris, 1825, 8vo., 2 vols.
LOUIS LUCAS.—*La Chimie Nouvelle*, 1854, 8vo. ; *La Médecine Nouvelle*, 1863, 2 vols., 8vo.; *Le Roman Alchimique*, 1853, 8vo. (Fundamental works) 226
MONTIÈRE (George).—Chief Editor of the Revue *l'Initiation*.
MOSES.—*Le Sepher Bereschit* (Genesis).
MERLIN.—*Origine des cartes a jouer, recherches nouvelles sur les naïbis, les tarots et sur les autres espèces de cartes*, Paris, 4to., 1869.
MANOEL DE GRANDFORT.
MORSIER (Emilie de).
NUS (Eugène).—Philosopher, the author of several works upon Spiritualism. *Les Grands Mystères*, Paris, librarie des Sciences, psychologiques, 8vo.
OLCOTT (Colonel).—President of the Theosophite Society of Adyar, which now includes more than 175 branches in different parts of the world.
PAPUS.—*Traité Élémentaire de Science Occulte*, Paris, 1887, 18mo. (4th edit.).
PARACELSUS.—Works by.
POSTEL (Guillaume).—*La Clef des Choses Cachées* (Latin), 12mo. ... 297
POLTI and GARY.—*La Théorie des Tempéraments*, 1889, 18mo. (Carré, publisher.)
PÉLADAN (Joséphin).—*La décadence Latine*, Ethopœia, in 7 vols. (Edinger, Paris) 299
POIREL, E.—Occultist, editor of the *Tarot de Wirth*, and of several other reproductions deduced from occult science 300
RABELAIS (epigraph) 3

AUTHORS AND PRINCIPAL WORKS QUOTED.

PAGE

RAGON.—*Orthodoxie Maçonnique*, followed by *Maçonnerie Occulte* and the *Initiation Hermitique*.
— *Maçonnerie Occulte*, with a Treatise on the Planets, 8vo.
— *La Messe et ses Mystères*, 18mo., Paris, 1863.
ROCA (Abbé).—*Le Monde Nouveau*, 1889, 8vo., Paris.
ROUXEL.—The author of important works upon *Magnetism*, published in the *Initiation*.
SAINT MARTIN (Louis Claude de).—*Tableau naturel des Rapports qui existent entre Dieu, l'Homme et l'Univers*, 2 vols., 8vo., Edinburgh, 1782 298
SEPHER YETZIRAH, the (translation by Papus), Paris, 1888, 8vo. (Carré).
SCHOPENHAUER.—First principles.
SCHURÉ.—Editor of the *Revue des Deux Mondes*. Has just published a fine study upon esoterism, *Les grands Initiés* (Perrin, editor).
SIMON.—*La Cité Chinoise*, 18mo., 1884.
SIVRY (Ch. de) 300
SINNET.—*Esoteric Buddhism*, 1884, 18mo.
TRITHEMUS (1462—1516).—A remarkably learned man, the master of Cornelius Agrippa.
VAILLANT (J. A.)—*Les Rômes, histoire vraie des vrais Bohemiens*, Paris, 1850, 8vo. 298
VIRGIL.—The *Æneid* 7
VEDAS, the.
VAN HELMONT (Mercure).—*Principia Philosophiæ antiquissimæ et recentissimæ*, Amsterdam, 1690. Mercury Van Helmont is reputed to have initiated Leibnitz.
WEBER (Louis Zénon).—Author of important philosophical works published in the *Initiation* 178
WIRTH (Oswald).—The Astronomical Tarot (in the course of work). See Index.
WRONSKI (Hoené).—*Le Messianism ou Réforme Absolue du Savoir Humain*, Paris, 1825, 3 vols., small folio. See the complementary list of his numerous works in *Occultism Contemporain by Papus*.
WOLSKA (A. de).
YVES D'ALVEYDRE (Saint).—*La Mission des Juifs*, Paris, 1884, large 8vo. of more than 1000 pp. Alcan Levy, publisher. (Fundamental work.)

Lightning Source UK Ltd.
Milton Keynes UK
UKHW010637260820
368857UK00001B/226